AVID

READER

PRESS

What It Takes

LESSONS IN THE PURSUIT
OF EXCELLENCE

Stephen A. Schwarzman

Avid Reader Press

New York   London   Toronto   Sydney   New Delhi

AVID READER PRESS
An Imprint of Simon & Schuster, Inc.
1230 Avenue of the Americas
New York, NY 10020

First Avid Reader Press hardcover edition September 2019

AVID READER PRESS and colophon are trademarks of Simon & Schuster, Inc.

For information about special discounts for bulk purchases,
please contact Simon & Schuster Special Sales at 1-866-506-1949
or business@simonandschuster.com.

The Simon & Schuster Speakers Bureau can bring authors to your live event.
For more information or to book an event, contact the Simon & Schuster Speakers
Bureau at 1-866-248-3049 or visit our website at www.simonspeakers.com.

Manufactured in the United States of America

1   3   5   7   9   10   8   6   4   2

Library of Congress Cataloging-in-Publication Data has been applied for.

ISBN 978-1-5011-5814-8
ISBN 978-1-5011-5825-4 (ebook)

CONTENTS

CONTENTS

SEEING AROUND CORNERS

SPRINTING DOWNFIELD

MADE, NOT BORN

In spring 1987, I flew to Boston to meet with the endowment team at the Massachusetts Institute of Technology. I was trying to raise money for Blackstone's first investment fund and had set a target of $1 billion. This would make us the biggest first fund of our kind and the third biggest in the world. It was an ambitious goal. Most people said it was impossible. But I've always believed that it's just as hard to achieve big goals as it is small ones. The only difference is that bigger goals have much more significant consequences. Since you can tackle only one personally defining effort at a time, it's important to pursue a goal that is truly worthy of the focus it will require to ensure its success.

Countless rejections later, though, I was starting to panic.

Pete Peterson and I had started Blackstone in 1985 with high hopes and a carefully conceived strategy. But business hadn't been coming in at anything like the rate we had planned. We had gone from the pinnacle of Wall Street at Lehman Brothers, a famous investment bank where Pete was chief executive and I had run the world's busiest mergers and acquisitions department, to objects of potential ridicule. If we couldn't raise this money, it would call our entire business model into question. Our former rivals were hoping we would fail, and I was worried they might be right.

I confirmed our appointment at MIT the day before and arrived on Massachusetts Avenue with Pete, ready to talk about our plans and get a commitment. We found a door with a frosted window, marked MIT Endowment, and knocked. No answer. We knocked again, then a third and fourth time. I checked my schedule to make sure we were in the right place. Pete, who at sixty-one was twenty-one years older than me and had been commerce secretary under President Nixon before joining Lehman, stood behind me looking unamused.

Finally, a passing janitor saw us and stopped. We told him we were there to see the people at the endowment fund.

"Oh. It's Friday. They left a while ago," he said.

"But we have a 3:00 p.m. appointment," I said.

"I saw them leave. They'll be back on Monday morning."

As Pete and I left with our heads down and shoulders slumped, it began to rain. We were unprepared for the weather, without a raincoat or umbrella, so we stood at the exit to MIT's administration building, hoping to wait it out. Twenty minutes later, it was pouring harder.

I had to do something. I left Pete and ran into the street to try to hail a taxi. In no time, the rain soaked through my jacket and shirt straight to my skin. My clothes were hanging off me like rags, the water streaming into my eyes and down my face. Every time I thought I finally had a taxi, someone else grabbed it before me. Desperate and drenched, I spotted a cab sitting at a red light and ran over to it. I banged on the back window and held up a limp twenty-dollar bill, hoping the bribe would be enough for the passenger to let us get in with him. He stared at me through the glass. I must have looked bizarre, hammering on the window in my sopping wet suit. He refused. Two more people did the same. I raised my offer to thirty dollars and finally someone accepted.

It was the closest to a deal I had gotten in weeks.

I waved Pete over and he began slowly walking toward me,

wetter and grumpier with every step. His full head of hair was pasted to his head as if he were standing in the shower. Pete was used to having cars waiting for him, drivers holding umbrellas as he got in and out. But a year and a half before, he and I had decided to start a business together. And from the look on his face as he walked through the puddles, I could tell he regretted it.

It hadn't been that long ago that Pete and I could call anyone in Corporate America or in governments around the world and find a receptive audience. Neither of us imagined starting a business would be easy. Nor did we envision being slumped in our seats at Logan Airport on a Friday night, soaked to our skins, without a dollar to show for our efforts.

Every entrepreneur knows the feeling: that moment of despair when the only thing you are aware of is the giant gap between where you find yourself and the life and business you imagine. Once you succeed, people see only the success. If you fail, they see only the failure. Rarely do they see the turning points that could have taken you in a completely different direction. But it's at these inflection points that the most important lessons in business and life are learned.

In 2010, Drew Faust, then president of Harvard, came to see me in New York. We spoke about a lot of things, but spent most of our time talking about running large organizations. When she retired from Harvard in 2018, she found the lengthy notes she had taken at our meeting and sent them to me. Among the many things she jotted down, one stood out: "The best executives are made, not born. They absorb information, study their own experiences, learn from their mistakes, and evolve."

I certainly did.

Not long after I saw Drew, I had a conversation with Hank

Paulson, the former US treasury secretary and chief executive of Goldman Sachs, who suggested I go over my old calendars, record my thoughts on building and managing an organization, and have them transcribed in case I might someday want to publish them. He thought my experiences and lessons would be of interest to a much wider audience. I took him up on his suggestion.

I regularly speak to audiences of students, executives, investors, politicians, and people at nonprofit organizations. The most frequent questions I get are about how we built, and now manage, Blackstone. People are fascinated by the process of imagining, starting, and growing an organization and creating a culture that attracts highly talented people. They also want to know what kind of person takes on such a challenge—what traits, values, and habits this person must have.

I never wanted to write a memoir chronicling every moment of my life. I never considered myself worthy enough. Instead I decided to pick events and episodes where I learned something important about the world and my work in it. This book is a collection of some of the inflection points that led to who I am today and the lessons they taught me, which I hope will be useful to you.

I grew up in the middle-class suburbs of Philadelphia, absorbing the values of 1950s America: integrity, straightforwardness, and hard work. My parents had never given me any money beyond my allowance, so my brothers and I had to earn our own. I worked in my family's linens store, sold candy bars and lightbulbs door-to-door, delivered telephone books, and started a lawn-mowing service with two part-time employees—my younger twin brothers. They got half the revenue for doing the work, and I kept the other half for securing clients. The business lasted three full years before we had an employee strike.

Today my calendar is filled with opportunities that I could never have imagined: meetings with heads of state, the most senior business executives, media personalities, financiers, legislators, journalists, university presidents, and leaders of illustrious cultural institutions.

How did I get here?

I had incredible teachers. My parents taught me the values of honesty, common decency, and achievement, and the importance of generosity toward others. My high school track coach, Jack Armstrong, helped me develop a high tolerance for pain and to understand the power of preparation, essential lessons for any entrepreneur. Running track with Bobby Bryant, my high school best friend, I learned about loyalty and what it means to be part of a team.

In college, I studied hard, pursued adventure, and initiated projects to improve our community. I learned to listen to people, pay attention to what they want and need even when they don't say it, and be fearless when it comes to tackling difficult problems. I never imagined myself in business, though; I never took an economics course—and still haven't. When I started on Wall Street at the securities firm Donaldson Lufkin Jenrette, I didn't even know what a security was, and my math skills were modest at best. My brothers never missed a chance to express their amazement. "You, Steve? In finance?"

But what I lacked in basic economics, I made up for with my ability to see patterns and develop new solutions and paradigms, and with the sheer will to turn my ideas into reality. Finance proved to be the means for me to learn about the world, form relationships, tackle significant challenges, and channel my ambition. It also allowed me to refine my ability to simplify complex problems by focusing on only the two or three issues that will determine the outcome.

———

Building Blackstone has been the most consequential personal challenge of my lifetime. The firm has come a long way since Pete and I stood in the rain outside MIT. Today it is the world's largest manager of alternative assets. Conventional assets are cash, stocks, and bonds. The broad category of "alternatives" includes pretty much everything else. We build, buy, fix, and sell companies and real estate. The companies we invest in employ more than 500,000 people, making Blackstone and its port-folio companies one of the largest US–based employers and one of the largest employers anywhere in the world. We find the best hedge fund managers and give them money to invest. We also lend money to companies and invest in fixed-income securities.

Our clients are large institutional investors, pension funds, government-run investment funds, university endowments, insurance companies, and individual investors. Our duty is to create long-term value for our investors, the companies and assets we invest in, and the communities in which we work.

Blackstone is a remarkable success because of our culture. We believe in meritocracy and excellence, openness and integrity. And we work hard to hire only people who share those beliefs. We are fixated on managing risk and never losing money. We are strong believers in innovation and growth—constantly asking questions in order to anticipate events so that we can evolve and change before we are forced to. There are no patents in finance. A good business with high profits today can be a poor business with low profits tomorrow. Because of competition and disrup-tion, if all you rely on is a single line of business, your organization may not survive. We have assembled an extraordinary team at Blackstone, driven by a common mission to be the best in the world at whatever we choose to do. With a benchmark like that, it's always easy to measure where we stand.

As Blackstone's breadth and reach have grown, so have the opportunities available to me outside business. I would never have thought that the lessons I learned as an entrepreneur and deal maker, coupled with the relationships I built across industry, government, education, and the nonprofit world, would someday enable me to serve as chairman of the John F. Kennedy Center for the Performing Arts in Washington, DC, or establish a prestigious graduate fellowship program in China: the Schwarzman Scholars. I am lucky to have been able to approach my philanthropy with the same principles I apply in business: identifying and addressing complex challenges by developing creative, thoughtful solutions. Whether it's building a first-of-its-kind student and cultural center on Yale's campus, or establishing a college to make MIT the first artificial intelligence–enabled university in the world, or designing an initiative at Oxford to redefine the study of the humanities for the twenty-first century, the projects I work on these days focus on applying resources to change paradigms in a way that will have an impact on lives, not just the bottom line. It has been my privilege to give more than $1 billion to support transformational projects whose impact will far exceed their financial value and long outlive me.

I also spend significant time answering calls or meeting with senior government officials around the world who are facing major challenges and need solutions. I am still astonished every time I hear from a world leader who wants my advice or point of view on a domestic or international issue of importance. In every instance, I do my best to help if I can.

I hope the lessons in this book are of use to you, whether

you are a student, an entrepreneur, a manager, a member of a team trying to make your organization better, or simply someone searching for ways to maximize your potential.

For me, the greatest rewards in life have come from creating something new, unexpected, and impactful. I am constantly in pursuit of excellence. When people ask me how I succeed, my basic answer is always the same: I see a unique opportunity, and I go for it with everything I have.

And I never give up.

REMOVE THE OBSTACLES

GO BIG

Schwarzman's Curtains and Linens sat beneath the elevated train in the middle-class Frankford section of Philadelphia, selling draperies, bedding, towels, and other household goods. The store was busy, the products good, the prices fair, and the customers loyal. My father, who had inherited the business from my grandfather, was knowledgeable and friendly. He was happy running the business just as it was. For all his intelligence and hard work, he had no ambition to move beyond his comfort zone.

I started working at the store when I was ten years old for ten cents an hour. I soon asked my grandfather for a raise to twenty-five cents an hour. He refused. "What makes you think you're worth twenty-five cents an hour?" I wasn't actually. When a customer came in with window measurements and wanted to know how much fabric she needed for drapes, I wouldn't have the foggiest idea how to figure it out or what to tell her, or even the desire to learn. During the Christmas season I was put in charge of selling linen handkerchiefs to elderly ladies on Friday nights and Saturdays. I'd spend hours opening box after box of nearly identical handkerchiefs, none costing more than a dollar, and then pack them all away again once the customer had made her choice or rejected everything after five or ten minutes. It felt like a waste of time. In my four years as an employee, I evolved from a grumpy child to an argumentative teenager. I was particularly upset about the toll this job was taking on my social life. Instead of attending football games and high school dances, I was stuck at the store, cut off from the world I wanted to be a part of.

But while I could never master gift wrapping, I could see the potential for Schwarzman's to grow. The Greatest Generation had returned from World War II. We were in an era of extraordinary peace and affluence. Homes were being built, suburbs were expanding, and the birthrate was spiking. That meant more bedrooms, more bathrooms, and more demand for linens. What were we doing with one store in Philadelphia? When America thought linens, it should be thinking Schwarzman's Curtains and Linens. I could imagine our stores from coast to coast like today's Bed Bath & Beyond. That was a vision I could fold hankies for. My father disagreed.

"Okay," I said. "We could just expand all over Pennsylvania."

"No," he said. "I don't think I want to do that."

"How about Philadelphia? That couldn't be too difficult."

"I'm not really interested."

"How can you not be interested?" I said. "We have all these people who come into the store. We could be like Sears."—which was prosperous and ubiquitous at that point—"Why don't you want to do this?"

"People will steal from the cash register."

"Dad, they're not going to steal from the cash register. Sears has stores all over the country. I'm sure they've figured it out. Why don't you want to expand? We could be huge."

"Steve," he said, "I'm a very happy man. We have a nice house. We have two cars. I have enough money to send you and your brothers to college. What more do I need?"

"It isn't about what you need. It's about wants."

"I don't want it. I don't need it. That will not make me happy."

I shook my head. "I don't understand. This is a sure thing."

Today, I understand. You can learn to be a manager. You can even learn to be a leader. But you can't learn to be an entrepreneur.

My mother, Arline, was restless and ambitious, a great complement to my father. She saw our family coming up in the world. She once decided to learn to sail—I suppose she imagined us like the Kennedys, hair blowing in the salt breeze off Hyannis Port—so she bought a twenty-foot sailboat, learned to sail it, and entered us in races—Mom at the helm, Dad doing as he was told. She won lots of trophies. My twin brothers and I always admired her competitiveness and will to win. In a different era, she would have been CEO of a major corporation.

We lived in a semidetached stone and brick house in Oxford Circle, an almost entirely Jewish neighborhood of Philadelphia, and I grew up playing on playgrounds littered with broken glass bottles, surrounded by kids smoking. The father of one of my best friends, who lived across the street, was killed by the mafia. My mother didn't like seeing me with the guys in black leather jackets who hung out at the bowling lanes along Castor Avenue. She wanted better schools for us. So not long after I started junior high, she decided to move us out to the more affluent suburbs.

In Huntingdon Valley, Jews were a rarity, about 1 percent of the population. Most people were white, Episcopalian or Catholic, happy with their place in the world. I found everything there incredibly easy. No one was trying to hurt or threaten me. I did well academically and led the state championship track team.

In the 1960s, the United States felt like the economic and social center of the world. Everything, from civil rights to sex to attitudes toward war was changing, as the United States escalated its involvement in Vietnam. I was part of the first generation to grow up seeing the president on television all the time. Our leaders were not mythical figures; they were accessible to people like us.

Even Abington High School became part of this change during my sophomore year. Every morning at school, in accordance with Pennsylvania state law, we listened to verses from the Bible and said the Lord's Prayer. I didn't mind, but Ellery Schempp's family did. They were Unitarians and felt that the school's Christian emphasis violated their rights under the First and Fourteenth Amendments to the Constitution. The *Schempp* case reached the US Supreme Court, which ruled 8–1 that the Pennsylvania prayer statute was unconstitutional. The case put Abington High School at the center of a national debate, with many Christians arguing that this case was the beginning of the end for their religion in public schools.

At the end of my junior year, I was elected president of the student council. In that position, I first experienced what it means to be an innovator.

My father may have vetoed my idea to turn Schwarzman's Linens into the first Bed Bath & Beyond, but now I was in charge of something of my own. The summer between my junior and senior years, we took a family car trip to California. I sat in the back seat with my mother driving, the warm air blowing in my face, imagining what I could create with my new position. I didn't want to be just another name on a long list of student leaders. I wanted to do something that no else had done, or even thought to do. I wanted to develop a vision that was so exciting that the whole school would rally to help make it happen. As we drove from coast to coast and back, I scribbled notes on postcards to my fellow officers of the student council, random ideas, which I would mail every time we stopped. They were all at home, lounging around, getting this blizzard of cards, while I was in search of a great idea.

It finally came to me as we were driving. Philadelphia was the home of *American Bandstand*, a television show for teenagers hosted by Dick Clark. The city also had really wonderful radio stations, like WDAS, one of the leading African American radio stations in the country. I listened to music obsessively, from James Brown to Motown, the great doo-wop groups of the 1950s, then the Beatles and the Rolling Stones. At school, I could barely walk the halls without hearing the student rock groups practicing the songs they heard in the bathrooms and stairwells, wherever the acoustics were good. One of their favorites was "Tears on My Pillow" by Little Anthony and the Imperials. That was the sound and emotion of high school. *Tears on my pillow, pain in my heart.*

How great would it be, I asked myself, if we could get Little Anthony and the Imperials to come to school and perform in our gym? Sure, they lived in Brooklyn and were one of the most popular groups in the country at the time and we had no money. But why not? It would be unique. Everyone would love it. There had to be a way, and I made it my job to figure out how.

Fifty years on, the details are hazy. But there were a lot of phone calls, a lot of whose dad knows whom. And at the end of it, Little Anthony and the Imperials came to Abington High School. I can still hear the music, see the band onstage, and feel everyone having a great time. If you want something badly enough, you can find a way. You can create it out of nothing. And before you know it, there it is.

But wanting something isn't enough. If you're going to pursue difficult goals, you're inevitably going to fall short sometimes. It's one of the costs of ambition.

Jack Armstrong, my track coach at Abington, was medium height, medium build, with gray hair swept back behind his ears. Every day, he wore the same maroon sweatshirt and windbreaker, the same stopwatch on a lanyard around his neck. And every day, he brought the same positive, cheerful demeanor to work. He never shouted or got angry, just raised or lowered his voice within a narrow range, the slightest change in cadence to get his point across. "Look at what those guys have just done. And you're making pretend you're working out!" There wasn't a day I didn't throw up after practice, sick from the effort.

One day, he'd make the sprinters run a mile, far more than we liked. We'd tell him what we thought, but we knew we were in the hands of a genius. We wanted to please him. Even during winter, he didn't let up. He'd make us run lap after lap around the school parking lot, set on a hill and whipped by the wind. We kept our heads down to make sure we didn't slip on the ice. He stood against the wall, bundled up in his coat, hat, and gloves, smiling and clapping us on. Our high school had no special facilities, but while our rival teams were doing nothing during the winter, we were training in harsh conditions. When spring came, we were ready. We never lost a meet.

Whether he was coaching future Olympians or boys joining in from the bench, Coach Armstrong treated all of us the same, communicating a simple and consistent message, "Run as well as you can," to satisfy the demands of the training schedule he designed. He didn't terrorize or cheerlead. He let us figure out what we wanted. In his entire career, his teams lost just four times: 186–4.

In 1963, we were the Pennsylvania state champions in the mile relay and invited to compete in a special event in New York City at the 168th Street Armory. On the bus ride there, I sat, as usual, next to my best friend, Bobby Bryant, a six-foot African American superstar. Bobby was so warm and kind that it would take him forever to get through the school cafeteria because he had to stop and joke with every table. School was a struggle for him academically, but on the track, he was magic. His family never had much money, so I bought him a pair of Adidas spikes with the money I made working. It was a gesture of friendship, but also more than that: Bobby running in a great pair of spikes made all of us look good.

Six teams lined up in the final. I always ran the first leg, and I never passed the baton in second place. When the gun went off, I broke out in front. But coming around the first curve, I felt my right hamstring rip. The pain was sudden and excruciating. I had a choice: I could pull over and stop, the sensible choice for my body. Or I could continue and find a way to keep us as close as I could and give us a chance to win.

I drifted to the middle of the track, forcing the runners behind me to find a way around. I gritted through the remaining distance, choking down the pain and watching my competitors sprint ahead. I passed the baton to our second leg runner twenty yards behind the leader. I limped to the infield, bent over, and vomited. I had done all I could, but there was no way we could make up the distance. I had imagined victory and worked ferociously to ensure it. I had put in those hard and lonely laps through the winter. Now I was certain we would lose.

But as I stood there, my hands on my knees, I heard the crowd stirring, shouts bouncing off the brick walls. My teammate running the second leg was starting to gain. Then our third runner closed the gap further. The spectators in the balcony took off their shoes and started banging them on the metal panels lining the track. After the third leg, the gap was down to twelve yards, still a huge distance to make up. Brooklyn Boys High School had their best runner, the best runner in the city, waiting to grab the baton. Oli Hunter was six feet three inches tall with a shaved head, wide shoulders, a tapered waist, and extremely long legs, perfectly engineered to run. He had never been beaten in any competition. Our final leg runner was Bobby.

I watched Bobby take off on the flat, wooden armory floor, his eyes wild with intensity, focused on Hunter's back. Stride by stride, he reeled him in. I knew Bobby better than anyone else, but even I couldn't tell where he got that combination of spirit and strength from. Right at the tape, he lunged forward to win. He did it! The crowd went wild! How could that possibly have happened? It had been a superhuman effort. Afterward he came over to me in the infield. He put his big arms around me and hugged me. "I did it for you, Steve. I couldn't let you down." Training and competing together, we made each other better.

———————

During my senior year, I realized that Harvard was the best-known Ivy League university in America. I believed that my record merited my admission. As it turned out, Harvard didn't agree. They put me on the wait list. Coach Armstrong suggested I go to Princeton to run track and even arranged for it. Like a petulant teenager, I said no because I thought Princeton wanted me just for my athletic ability. I won a place at Yale, but Harvard was a fixation, part of the vision I had for myself. So I decided to call the head of admissions at Harvard and convince him to admit me. I found his name and the central phone number for the admissions department. I brought a pile of quarters with me to school to use in the pay phone. I didn't want my parents to hear me make the call; it was something I needed to do on my own. I was practically shaking with fear as I dropped the coins into the phone, one by one.

"Hello, I'm Stephen Schwarzman from Abington High School in Abington, Pennsylvania. I've been accepted by Yale, but I'm on your waiting list, and I'd really like to go to Harvard."

"How did you get to me?" asked the dean. "I never talk with students or parents."

"I asked for you, and they put me through."

"I'm sorry to say we're not taking anyone from the waiting list this year. The freshman class is full."

"That's really a mistake," I said. "I'm going to be very successful, and you'll be very happy that you accepted me at Harvard."

"I'm sure you'll be successful, but Yale is a lovely place and you'll enjoy it and have a good experience there."

"I'm sure I will," I said, persisting. "But I'm calling because I want to go to Harvard."

"I understand that, but I won't be able to help you."

I hung up the phone and practically collapsed. I had overestimated my ability to sell myself. I accepted my rejection and resigned myself to my second choice: Yale.

In the final speech I made as student council president, I laid out a philosophy on education that has remained remarkably consistent throughout my life:

> I believe that education is a discipline. The object of this discipline is to learn how to think. Once we have mastered this we can use it to learn a vocation, appreciate art, or read a book. Education simply enables us to appreciate the ever-changing drama fashioned of God's own hand, life itself. Education continues when we leave the classroom. Our associations with friends, our participation in clubs all increase our store of knowledge. In fact, we never stop learning until we die. My fellow officers and I just hope that you will become aware of the purpose of education and follow its basic tenets, questioning and thinking, for the rest of your life.

That summer, as my father drove me back from summer camp where I had been a counselor, he told me that I was entering a world he knew nothing about. He knew no one at Yale or anyone who had been to Yale. The only help he could give me in this new world was to love me and let me know I could always come home. Other than that, I was on my own.

––––––––––

Freshman year at Yale, I shared two bedrooms and a study with two roommates. Luckily, I got the single bedroom. One of my roommates was a private school boy from Baltimore who pinned a Nazi flag to our living room wall. He had a glass case where he kept Nazi medals and other paraphernalia from the Third Reich. Every night we went to sleep to the sound of an album called *Hitler's Marching Army*. My other roommate didn't change his underwear for practically the entire first semester. College was a real adjustment for me.

Commons at Yale is a soaring brick building in the middle of campus. It was constructed in 1901 for Yale's two-hundredth anniversary. It seemed like a train station full of hundreds of people eating. Plates, cutlery, and trays clattering on the tables, chairs scraping backward on the floor. The moment I walked in on my first day, I stopped and thought, *Something's terribly wrong.* It didn't sound anything like the cafeteria at Abington. It took me a moment to figure it out. There were no women. At Abington, I had known everyone. At Yale in fall 1965, there were ten thousand students, of whom four thousand were undergraduates. I didn't know a single one. Two crazy roommates, no girls, and nobody I knew. The loneliness was crushing. Everything and everyone intimidated me.

Although I had told Coach Armstrong I didn't want to go to Princeton to run, the irony was that I'd gotten into Yale because of my sprinting. I had one of the fastest 100-yard times in Pennsylvania and ran leadoff for Abington's state champion 440- and

880-yard relay teams, which were fourth in the United States. I had the good grades and SAT scores. But I was admitted to run.

Yale had a famous coach at the time, Bob Giegengack, who had coached the US Olympic team the year before. New runners went to practice, took a card detailing their routine, and then ran alone. There was no Coach Armstrong to bring out your best. There were no teammates to laugh and joke with, and no one for whom you'd ever run until you vomited. I figured the best I could do was win an Ivy League sprint title. To do that, though, I'd have to train for a lackluster coach and a team that didn't seem to care about me. So, uncharacteristically, I quit. I wasn't sure what I wanted yet, but track, which had been such a formative part of my life, no longer seemed the way to get there.

Academically, I discovered, I was underprepared. I chose an unusual major, culture and behavior, an academic creation of the 1960s that combined psychology, sociology, biology, and anthropology. I chose it because it sounded fascinating, a comprehensive study of the human being, which would help me understand people's objectives and motivations. But I still had a way to go on the basics. There were only eight of us in the class and four professors assigned to teach us. Many of my peers came from the best prep schools in the country. Not only did they all seem to know each other, they also knew the work. My first English paper was on Melville's *Bartleby the Scrivener*. I got a 68. I then got a 66 on my second. I was failing. My instructor, Alistair Wood, asked me to his garret office for a meeting. He was a young man dressed like an elderly professor, wearing a tweed sweater and a J.Press sport jacket with patches at the elbows, a tattersall shirt, and a green knit tie.

"Mr. Schwarzman, I want to talk to you about your papers."

"There's really nothing to talk about," I said.

"Why is that?"

"I had nothing to say, and I said it poorly."

"My God, you're not stupid. I couldn't have put it any better myself. So I have to teach you how to write, and after that, I'll teach you how to think. Because you can't learn both at the same time, I'll give you the answers to the next several essays and we'll concentrate on the writing. Then we'll concentrate on thinking."

He saw I had potential and systematically set about equipping me with what I needed. I'll never forget his patience and kindness. Teaching, I came to believe, is about more than sharing knowledge. You have to remove the obstacles in people's way. In my case, the obstacle was the gap between my education up to that point and the education of my peers. That year, I went from failing to the dean's list, at the top of my class.

———

After my freshman year, I needed an adventure, something different from the typical summer job. A summer at sea, I thought, stopping in exotic ports might prove a useful cure to the all-male campus at Yale. I started by trying to get a job at the docks in New York City, but the longshoremen's union, then controlled by the mob, wouldn't take an unconnected college kid. They recommended I go to the Scandinavian seamen's union in Brooklyn. The money wouldn't be as good, they warned me, but at least there might be work. I got there shortly before the union building closed for the day and found a wall covered in 3- by 5-inch notecards advertising jobs. I was qualified for none of them. But the receptionist said that if I joined the union, I could have a place to sleep and see if there was anything tomorrow. I took him up on his offer, but my night was interrupted by a giant Scandinavian sailor who tried to get into bed with me. I freaked out, fled, and slept on the street. When the sun rose, I went to a Baptist church across the street for the morning service and waited until the union hall reopened.

The notice board had been rearranged, and I spotted a card that said simply "Destination Unknown." I asked the receptionist what that could mean. He told me that it all depended on the cargo. You found out where you were going as you sailed under the Verrazzano-Narrows Bridge. If you turned left, you were going to Canada; right for the Caribbean or Latin America; and straight ahead for Europe. All that was available was a job as an engine room wiper, the lowest rank aboard a Norwegian tanker. I took it. My job was to keep the engine room clean from grease. As we went under the Verrazzano-Narrows Bridge, we turned right, headed for Trinidad and Tobago.

All we had to eat and drink was smoked fish, awful cheese, and Ringnes beer. It was so hot in the engine room that I could drink a beer and watch it seep out of my body on my skin. When I wasn't working, I read the works of Sigmund Freud, which I had brought with me in a wooden crate. Every last one of his books. The Norwegian crew and I didn't have much to say to each other. But they were there for me when it counted. In a bar in Trinidad, I spoke to the wrong girl and soon punches and chairs were flying, like an old Western saloon fight, as my crewmates rallied to my defense.

After we sailed north to Providence, Rhode Island, I took a bus back to Brooklyn in search of another job. I was hired onto a much more pleasant ship, a freighter, the Danish *Kirsten Skou*, smartly painted in white with blue trim. My job there was second cook. I would wake up at 4:00 a.m., bake the bread, and cook breakfast. I loved it. We turned left toward Canada, picked up liquor and lumber, and sailed to Colombia for bananas. Every time we stopped in a port, the ship had to be loaded and unloaded using nets. There were no containers then, and the whole process would take three or four days, giving me time to explore. In Santa Marta, I spent an evening in a bar on the beach that was lit with Christmas lights. For the only—first and last—time in my life, I got so drunk I passed out. Later, someone drove me to the docks and dropped me there. After two days, I awoke back on the boat, covered in bruises. I must have been robbed and beaten. My crewmates had found me and had taken turns watching over me until I woke up. By the time I regained consciousness, we were out at sea and I could barely walk. We kept on to Cartagena, through the Panama Canal to Buenaventura. And then I had to get back to Yale.

It was a jolt to be back in drab New Haven after three months at sea. On the front page of the *Yale Daily News*, I saw an advertisement saying that if you were feeling depressed, you should see the psychiatrist at DUH, the Department of University Health. I decided to give it a go. The psychiatrist looked the part, with a pipe and a bow tie. I told him about my summer, about the ships, the girls, the ports, and how I didn't want to be back at school.

"Of course you don't," he said. "Why would you? You don't need therapy. You're just suffering from withdrawal. Hang in there. In a few months, you'll be fine."

He turned out to be right. Maybe it was the Freud, or the bars, or the girls I had met along the way. Maybe it was having taken on a challenge and survived. While my classmates were spending the summer hitting tennis balls and working in offices, I had been sweating in an engine room and dodging blows in Colombian bars. But now, I was ready to approach Yale on my own terms.

———

I moved to Davenport College, one of Yale's residential colleges, where a future president, George W. Bush, was a year ahead of me. The dining room was much smaller than Commons, so instead of going back to my room or the library straight after lunch or dinner to study, I would pour myself a cup of coffee and sit down with any students there and join in the conversation.

To make spending money, I took over the Yale stationery concession and walked every stairway in the entire university trying to get students to buy writing paper with personalized letterhead. With the money I made, I bought myself a stereo. I loved listening to music.

I set my sights on the "senior societies," secretive clubs whose members included the most prominent students on campus, the captains of the sports teams, the editors of student publications, the leaders of the Whiffenpoofs, an a cappella group. The clubs had mysterious names, like Skull and Bones, Scroll and Key, Wolf's Head, Book and Snake. Tapped to join, you swore never to mention it or speak about what went on behind the club's closed doors. Skull and Bones was the most exclusive. I had two years before my senior year to get its members' attention.

I'd often go and sit on a bench in the courtyard of Branford College, the prettiest college at Yale, where I could listen to the carillon of Harkness Tower, and think, *What could I do that would get the whole undergraduate body excited? Something inventive?* One of my more unusual achievements had been to set the university's vertical jump record, forty-two inches, during the physical exam we took when we arrived. But I knew there was more I could do, and my experience at Abington with Little Anthony had taught me a lesson I have replicated throughout my life: if you're going to commit yourself to something, it's as easy to do something big as it is to do something small. Both will consume your time and energy, so make sure your fantasy is worthy of your pursuit, with rewards commensurate to your effort.

The most glaring need I sensed among Yale's undergraduates was the companionship of women. There were thousands of men in neo-Gothic buildings starved of even the sight of women, let alone their company. It was an obvious problem to solve, but nobody was trying. I decided to change things.

When I was sixteen, my parents had taken me to the ballet to see Rudolf Nureyev dance with Margot Fonteyn. Their grace and movement captivated me. Later, still a teenager, I was immobilized for a month with a badly separated shoulder. I listened to record after record of classical music, ten hours a day, starting with Gregorian chants and ending with the great ballet scores of Tchaikovsky. When I arrived at Yale, Mary Jane Bancroft, the wife of my college dean, Horace Taft, the grandson of President Taft, discovered my interest in ballet. She shared books with me and taught me a lot. *So what,* I asked myself, *if I took my interest in ballet, bolted it to my social ambitions, and brought a troupe of ballerinas to perform for Yale's men? That would get me noticed.*

I needed an organization, so I invented the Davenport Ballet Society. Then I started calling the heads of the dance departments at the all-women Seven Sisters colleges, inviting their dancers to perform at the Davenport Ballet Society Dance Festival. Five of them agreed. Finally, I called Walter Terry, an eminent newspaper dance critic, and persuaded him to travel from New York to review the festival. Out of nothing, I brought together dancers, critics, and an audience. My hunch about the Yale men proved right: we packed them in, and I had the beginnings of a profile on campus.

If we could get the best dancers from other colleges, why not shoot for the professionals? The greatest ballet company in the world at the time was the New York City Ballet, where George Balanchine was artistic director. I took the train to New York and hung around the stage door waiting for the security guard to take a break. When he did, I ducked into the offices backstage and asked until I found the manager.

"What the hell are you doing back here?" he demanded.

"I'm from the Yale University Ballet Society, and we want to invite the New York City Ballet to come to New Haven to perform." I had given some thought to what was in this proposal for him. "The students don't have money, but they love ballet and they're your future audience and patrons." I kept talking until the manager caved.

"Look," he said, "we can't bring the whole company up. Would it be okay if we just bring a small group?" Absolutely fine, I told him. So a New York City Ballet group came to New Haven to perform. Another big hit. Now that I had a relationship with the New York City Ballet, I upped the stakes again and went back to the manager. "We're just a bunch of poor college students, hundreds and hundreds of college kids who love ballet. Why don't you let us come to a performance for free? Because we can't afford tickets."

"We can't do that," he told me. "We depend on selling tickets. But we do dress rehearsals, so if you want to bring down as many students as you want to a dress rehearsal of *The Nutcracker*, we can arrange that." So they arranged it on their end, and I took care of it on ours, inviting all the women's colleges. We filled the house for a dress rehearsal of *The Nutcracker*, men from Yale, women from the women's colleges. By the time it was over, I had become a student ballet impresario, sort of the Sol Hurok of Yale. I was developing a reputation as someone who made the improbable happen.

———

Around the same time, I learned that Yale's efforts to recruit more students from the inner cities were floundering, just as they were at most of the other Ivy League universities at that time. I went to the admissions dean with an idea. Despite its best intentions,

Yale did not have enough people on the admissions staff to reach all the parts of America where they might find good candidates. If they couldn't get out to the cities, towns, and rural areas far beyond New Haven, they could not describe a Yale education or what it offered. Many potential candidates didn't apply because they never imagined they could fit in, let alone afford it. My idea was to send out small groups of students and invite candidates to visit, at Yale's expense. Instead of the college going to them, they would come to us. While we had them on campus, we could explain Yale's generous financial aid program. No one was ever turned down for lack of money.

The dean liked my idea. We decided to start in my hometown, Philadelphia. It would be a pilot project, the first of its kind attempted by a major university. On my first visit to South Philadelphia High School, I met a boy who had been born in Cairo and forced to leave because he was Jewish. He had moved to France, then Italy, and finally to the United States, five years earlier. He had high standardized test scores; spoke Arabic, French, Italian, and English; and read Hebrew. And there he was living in the inner city, a great candidate, and he had never heard of Yale.

I worried that when these students, mostly second-generation immigrants from Europe or African Americans, visited Yale, they might be turned off by a bunch of self-involved Yale preppies, so we designed the day to be as practical as possible. The eighty students who came on the first visit would be broken into groups of two or three, depending on their interests, and assigned to an undergraduate. They would visit labs or use the college broadcast studio. They would then discuss how to pay for their education at the admissions office.

High schools were wary of having their students treated as tokens. We made sure these students knew that this path was not easy. They would have to compete for spots and apply to other schools as well. What mattered was they knew Yale was available to them. The boy from Cairo was eventually accepted and enrolled at Yale, and the program thrived long after I graduated.

————

In my final year, I decided to take on the biggest issue of all for Yale's men: the 268-year-old parietal rules that forbade women staying overnight in a dorm room. I was dating a woman at a local college, so for me, it was as much a personal as a community issue.

The conventional approach would have been to set up a meeting with a university administrator to try to change the situation. But I knew what would happen. He'd sit there in his blazer and bow tie and tell me women would be a distraction. They would stop the young men from studying. They would change the atmosphere in the college dorms. There was a long list of reasons that a young man like me wouldn't understand. He would smile and nothing would change, as it hadn't for almost 270 years. I needed a different approach, so I started with the students. I made a list of the university's likely objections and turned them into a long questionnaire. Do you think changing parietal rules will stop you from studying? Would having more women around be a distraction? And so on.

I recruited eleven students to stand outside each of the eleven college dining halls during mealtimes and hand out the questionnaire to the entire undergraduate body. We had a response rate of close to 100 percent. Then I went to a friend, Reed Hundt, who was deputy editor of the *Yale Daily News*. (He became head of the Federal Communications Commission under President Clinton.) "Reed, I've got this survey about getting rid of parietal rules," I told him. "It's dynamite."

Three days later, the parietal rules were history, and I made the front page of the school newspaper: "Schwarzman's Initiative: Poll Votes Down Parietals." The university didn't want to fight. It was my first lesson in the power of the media. Skull and Bones later tapped me to be a member, and I was put in charge of Class Day the following June. I would be the public face of Yale College's graduation ceremony.

It had been some journey since my first, lonely meal at Commons.

EVERYTHING IS
INTERCONNECTED

S hortly before I graduated, I was asked in a job interview what I wanted to be. I didn't have a conventional answer.

"I want to be a telephone switchboard," I told my interviewer, "taking in information from countless feeds, sorting it, and sending it back out into the world."

He looked at me as if I were a lunatic. But I was sure of it, and even more so after a meeting I had near the end of my senior year. I was looking for ideas about what to do next. I wrote a letter asking for advice from Averell Harriman, a member of Skull and Bones, class of 1913, one of the "Wise Men" of American diplomacy and former governor of New York.

He wrote back, inviting me to his home for a meeting at 3:00 p.m., which he later changed to lunch.

I rushed out and bought my first suit, gray with a white pinstripe, at J.Press. Harriman's house was at 16 East Eighty-First Street, half a block from the Metropolitan Museum in New York. A houseman in a white jacket and black tie opened the door and led me to a sitting room lined with Impressionist paintings. In the room next door, I could hear the voice of Robert Wagner, the former mayor of New York. Finally, it was my turn. Harriman was sitting in an armchair. He was almost eighty, but he rose to greet me and asked me to sit on his right because he couldn't hear well in his left ear. On the mantel was a bust of the brother of slain President John F. Kennedy, Robert Kennedy, a friend of his who had been assassinated the previous year. After we had spoken for a few minutes about the possibility of my going into politics, Harriman said, "Young man, are you independently wealthy?"

"No, sir. I'm not."

"Well," he said, "that will make a great difference in your life. I advise you, if you have any interest in politics whatsoever, to go out and make as much money as you can. That will give you independence if you ever decide you want to go into politics. If my father wasn't E. H. Harriman of the Union Pacific Railroad, you wouldn't be sitting here talking to me today."

He told me the story of his life, a nonstop series of adventures. He attended boarding school at Groton, then college at Yale, where he put his inherited wealth to use drinking and playing polo. After graduating, he built a career in business. With his father's support and connections, he traveled to Russia after the Revolution of 1917 and led a wave of US investment in the new Soviet Union. He got to know Lenin, Trotsky, and Stalin. Back in the United States after the Bolsheviks had seized most of the US funded assets, he came up with the idea for a ski resort in Idaho modeled on St. Moritz in Switzerland. He called it Sun Valley. During World War II, his father's friend, President Franklin Roosevelt, sent him back to Moscow as US ambassador. In 1955, he became governor of New York State and later returned to the State Department under President Kennedy, another family friend. By the time I met him in early 1969, he was America's lead negotiator in the Paris Peace Talks seeking to end the war in Vietnam. While Harriman was talking, the phone kept ringing, the negotiators in Paris asking for his advice.

I was enthralled and lost track of time until Harriman said, "Let's have lunch. Do you mind eating on a tray?" I had never before been in an exquisite house such as his. But I did know about eating on a tray.

After I left, I ran to a public telephone to tell my mom and dad all about it. I had gone to see Harriman for advice on what to do with my life. He had told me I could do anything to which I set my mind. At some point in life, we have to figure out who we are, he said. The sooner we do it the better, so we can pursue the opportunities that are right for us, not some false dream created by others. But if I was going to turn my worthy fantasies into reality, to become a telephone switchboard filled with inputs, I'd need money.

———————

I arrived for my first interview on Wall Street an hour early, because I didn't want to be late. I sat in a Chock Full o'Nuts coffee shop nursing a cup of coffee, the one cup I could afford, checking my watch every couple of minutes. When 9:00 a.m. arrived, I went into the headquarters of Donaldson Lufkin Jenrette at 140 Broadway, up to the thirty-sixth floor. I took a seat in reception and watched as sophisticated young women with black headbands and fancy shoes and young men in ties and shirtsleeves, only slightly older than me, ran around the office alert and purposeful. The energy of the place was electric.

After half an hour, an assistant ushered me in to see Bill Donaldson, the D in DLJ. It was surprising to see a man so young sitting in a rocking chair, but this was fashionable post-JFK. Our meeting had been arranged by Larry Noble, Bill's Yale classmate, who was now working in the Yale admissions office. I had met Larry when I had seen him with his young family at a Yale fifteenth reunion and felt compelled to buy a copy of *Babar the Elephant* for his son. I had no idea who Larry was, but my random act of generosity led to a friendship and now this interview.

"Tell me," said Bill, "why do you want to work at DLJ?"

"Frankly, I don't know much about what DLJ does," I said. "But it seems you've got all these amazing young people working here. So I want to do whatever they're doing."

Bill smiled and said, "That's as good a reason as any."

After we talked a bit, he said, "Why don't you go around and see some of my partners?" I did, but when I got back to Bill's office at the end of the day, I told him they seemed uninterested in me. "Listen," he said laughing, "I'll give you a call in two or three days." He came through with an offer of a job. The starting salary was $10,000 a year.

"That is absolutely terrific," I said. "But there's only one problem."

"What's that?"

"I need $10,500."

"I'm sorry," he said. "What do you mean?"

"I need $10,500 because I heard there's another person graduating from Yale who's making $10,000, and I want to be the highest-paid person in my class."

"I don't care," said Bill. "I shouldn't be paying you anything at all. It's $10,000!"

"Then I won't take the job."

"You won't take the job?"

"No. I need $10,500. It's not a big deal to you, but it's a really big deal to me."

Donaldson started laughing. "You've got to be kidding."

"No," I said, "I'm not kidding."

"Let me think about it." Two days later he called back. "Okay. $10,500." And with that I entered the securities business.

———

When I showed up for my first day on the job, I had an office with a majestic view uptown and a secretary. After a while, someone dropped an annual report on my desk for Genesco, a footwear and apparel business. My job was to analyze it. It was the first time I had even seen such a report. As I turned the pages, I saw that Genesco had a balance sheet and an income statement. The balance sheet had footnotes referring to preferred stock and convertible preferred stock, subordinated and convertible subordinated debt, senior debt and bank debt. Reading it today, I could have seen in an instant that it was a company in financial disarray. But at the time, I may as well have been reading Swahili. And there was no Internet or anyone around offering to help me translate. Even today, say the word *Genesco* and I can feel moisture trickle down my back, the fear that at any point someone will walk in, ask me a question, and expose me as a fraud. Here was a world in which huge amounts of money were at stake, yet no one even bothered to train new people. They assumed we were smart enough to figure it out. That seemed like a crazy approach to me.

My next assignment was to investigate a new chain of German-style sausage restaurants being launched by Restaurant Associates, the owner of various high-end restaurants in New York. Zum Zums promised knockwurst for New Yorkers. I arrived at Restaurant Associates' headquarters, the first company I had ever visited, and began asking questions of the chief executive and other corporate officers. They didn't seem too friendly, and I didn't learn much. I took the subway back to my office. My secretary, who usually had little to do owing to my own incompetence, awaited me with a message: "Mr. Jenrette needs to see you immediately." Dick Jenrette, one of the most charming and intelligent men in finance, would become a close friend and confidant. But that afternoon, he was president of DLJ, and I barely knew him.

"What did you do to these people at Restaurant Associates?" he said. "They're furious at us."

"Why would they be furious?" I said, startled.

"They said you were looking for inside information."

"All I asked for was what I thought I needed to know to predict what was going to happen with their company. How many units do they have, what's their profit per unit, what's the overhead. Stuff like that so I could figure something out."

"Steve, they're not allowed to tell you that kind of information."

"Then how can I know what's going to happen? Why can't I get it?"

"Because the SEC has rules about what you can and can't get, and that qualifies as inside information. If they tell you, they'd have to tell everybody. Don't do it again."

No one had bothered explaining this rule to me.

After my Zum Zums debacle, I began researching National Student Marketing, a company trying to sell anything they could to college students. They were selling a life insurance product, which no twenty-year-old I had ever met would think of buying, and leasing refrigerators to students to keep in their dorm rooms. I had just graduated from college and knew how students treated appliances. It wasn't pretty. This company accounted for its refrigerators as if they lasted six years. Every undergraduate I knew destroyed them in two. When I visited the company's offices, the first executive I met couldn't tell me the name of the person in the next office. He seemed disengaged. I didn't need any inside information to tell me this company was heading straight for bankruptcy. I wrote up my opinion and filed it, not knowing that DLJ was at the same time arranging a private placement of equity for National Student Marketing.

A few years later, as I predicted, the company collapsed. DLJ was sued for selling stock in a company it knew was rotten, and I had to defend my opinion before a roomful of lawyers. DLJ depicted me as an idiot who had no idea what he was doing, which explained why no one listened to me. The plaintiffs portrayed me as a genius savant, who saw what all of DLJ's higher-paid professionals had missed. The plaintiffs won.

―――――――

While I was working at DLJ, I moved from sublet to sublet, a succession of cockroach-infested walk-ups. For a while, I lived in one on Second Avenue between Forty-Ninth and Fiftieth Streets above the Midtown Shade Company. This stretch of the road went slightly uphill, so all night long, I heard trucks changing gear. Most nights, I got home and made myself spaghetti with tomato sauce in a single pot on my hot plate. I had no kitchen. The bathroom was down the hall. One evening, I invited a woman out for a date. When I picked her up, she was wearing a mink coat. At dinner, I kept staring at the menu while she ordered, hoping she didn't realize that I could afford an appetizer and dessert only for her, not both of us. I had just enough money afterward to drop her off in a cab. After we said good-bye, I walked home fifty blocks wondering when my life would change.

The other people my age at DLJ were the sons and daughters of famous people in New York. I didn't know any of them. And that wasn't going to change with me living in a hovel, working on the bottom rung of a securities firm. If they weren't all so well bred at DLJ, I was convinced they would have had me emptying the trash. But I at least got a glimpse of what else New York might offer. Laura Eastman, a DLJ colleague a few years older, took pity on me and invited me to her family's apartment for dinner a few times and to play squash in the basement of their building on Seventy-Ninth and Park. Laura's sister, Linda, would soon marry Paul McCartney, and her father, Lee, became his attorney. Theirs was the first Park Avenue apartment I had ever visited, and I'd never before seen anything like it. It had been decorated by Billy Baldwin, the top decorator in the country at the time. At the entrance, there was a small library, its walls covered in beige grass cloth and hung with Willem de Kooning paintings. When I asked Laura about them, she told me that the artist lived and worked in East Hampton close to her dad's beach house. De Kooning had come to him for some legal advice and paid with paintings instead of cash. He had needed a lot of advice, so the Eastmans now had a lot of paintings. This had never happened to the Schwarzmans of Abington. Lee made a great impression on me during those family dinners. He was positive, dramatic, engaged, and insightful. He was living the New York life I aspired to have if I could become successful.

The Vietnam War interrupted my efforts. I had signed up for the Army Reserves instead of waiting for the results of the draft lottery, which would almost certainly have sent me into combat. The Reserves required six months of active-duty training and sixteen hours a month at a local unit for five more years. Six months after I joined DLJ, I was summoned for training. Bill Donaldson was nice enough to invite me for an exit interview. I was candid with him and said I felt bad about my time at DLJ. I had been more or less useless. No one had bothered to train me, and I had drifted around. Unlike at Yale, I hadn't found a way to accomplish much of anything.

"Why in the world did you ever hire me?" I asked. We were sitting in the small employee cafeteria, eating off plastic trays. "You wasted your money. I haven't accomplished a thing."

"I had a hunch."

"Really? What kind of hunch?"

"That one day you'd be the head of my firm."

I sat there, astounded. "What?"

"Yeah," he said. "I have a sixth sense about these things."

I left for the Reserves thinking Wall Street was crazy.

———————

In January 1970, Fort Polk, Louisiana, was a major combat training center for those getting ready to be shipped to Vietnam. It was damp and cold in the barracks and freezing when we had to sleep on the ground during maneuvers. My company trainees were from tiny West Virginia and Kentucky towns, some almost illiterate, most drafted and bound for combat. It was a sharp jolt after Yale and DLJ. Our drill sergeant had been a tunnel rat in Vietnam. His specialty was going down tunnels dug by the Vietcong and North Vietnamese to plant explosives. Armed with just a flashlight and a .45 caliber pistol, he never knew who was waiting for him around a dark corner or what traps might have been set. He was the bravest person I had ever met. He was an instructor now because he had a metal plate in his head and couldn't fight anymore. He had nothing but contempt for the war.

"There's no sense to it," he told us. "None. Zero. You spend your time trying to take a hill. You take it. And five days later, you abandon it and the bad guys go right back up the hill. It's the stupidest fucking thing I've ever been involved with in my life. We don't know who the good guys are or the bad guys are. Nobody can speak their language. They're friends by day, and try to kill us at night. Our officers are mostly idiots." He even told us that if we had to kill one of our officers to save ourselves from a pointless death, we should consider it.

He was a good, brave man whose life had been changed by decisions made at the highest levels of government. His anger and frustration cast a shadow over our experience. Vietnam, I quickly realized, was more than a strategic game for politicians, diplomats, and generals or an ideological piñata for student radicals. It had a personal impact on thousands of Americans. Later in my life, when I found myself in positions to influence decisions of national and global significance, I tried to remember the effects on individual people who would bear the consequences.

I was no longer in the physical shape I'd been at high school, but I hadn't lost the taste for hard effort. I enjoyed toughening up with long runs in combat gear at five in the morning. I liked learning how to use weapons. I didn't enjoy the stupidity. One morning we stood in formation in the pouring rain for an hour and a half waiting to go in for breakfast. Our sergeant had forgotten we were out there and no one had the guts to break formation to tell him. On the days we did get breakfast, we often ran out of food. We were in Louisiana, not Vietnam. There should have been enough to eat, so I took it upon myself to investigate.

When we had arrived at Fort Polk, a colonel had told us that if we saw anything wrong, we should talk to him. I decided to take him up on his offer. I walked into the colonel's office, covered in dust from training. His clerk asked me what I was doing there. I gave him my name and number. "Get the fuck out of here," said the clerk. I refused to move. He summoned a lieutenant. I said I only wanted to talk to the colonel.

"Who the fuck do you think you are?" said the lieutenant. "This is the army. You do what you're told and get your ass back to your company." A captain came in, and we went through the same routine. I thought my own company captain would burst through the door at any moment, grab me by the neck, and dump me in a swamp. But eventually I was sitting in front of the colonel, lean with cropped gray hair.

I explained the food situation. I told him what we got for

breakfast, lunch, and dinner, and he looked stunned. He fished out a sheet of paper detailing our company's proficiency scores. We were the worst company in the whole brigade. He told me to go back to my company and not say a word. Two days later, all of our officers were gone. It turned out they were stealing our food and selling it. The colonel called me back in and thanked me for breaking through the structure of the military to make my point. It was the reason he gave that speech to all the incoming trainees, but no one had ever come to see him.

The Reserves reinforced my suspicion of hierarchy and my confidence in going against it if I saw something wrong. The different fates of all of us at Fort Polk also reminded me of the importance of luck. No matter how successful, smart, or brave you are, you can always end up in a tough place. People often think theirs is the only reality, but there are as many realities as there are individuals. The more you see of them, the more likely you are to make sense of them.

Another life lesson I took from my time in the army is that the commitment and sacrifice of our service members must always be honored. This belief is what drove my involvement with the Navy SEAL Foundation many years later in 2016, when I led a Blackstone effort to raise funds in support of the families of SEALs who were killed in the line of duty. I made it a personal mission to visit with every business group to ensure they understood the importance of giving back to the people who were responsible for securing their everyday freedoms. In the end, every single US Blackstone employee contributed and the Navy SEAL Foundation raised a record $9.3 million.

———

I left Louisiana in July, and by late August, I was sitting in a classroom in Boston. Before I'd left Yale, I had applied to graduate school. My top choice was law school, preferably Harvard, Yale, or Stanford. But the only law school to accept me was the University of Pennsylvania, and I wasn't ready to go back to Philadelphia. Almost as an afterthought, I applied to Harvard Business School. Business schools weren't the smart kids' choice then. They were seen as funnels for middle managers at big corporations, not entrepreneurs or intellectuals. In 1970, getting an MBA meant going to work at military-industrial giants like Dow, the makers of napalm, and Monsanto, which made Agent Orange, both used to kill or maim people in Vietnam. But when HBS offered me a place, I decided to go. Maybe, I thought, this was the way to the fortune Averell Harriman had recommended.

I arrived at Harvard feeling the same way I had when I arrived at Yale: socially isolated and suspecting the brilliant people were elsewhere. The same year I arrived at HBS, Bill and Hillary Clinton started at Yale Law School. The leaders of the future were fighting intellectual duels in moot court, not studying widget companies.

My first class was in a course called Managerial Economics. The core of it was drawing decision trees, chains of logic in which you apply probabilities to different courses of action and try to calculate the best one based on your predicted outcomes. After all I'd seen and done in infantry training, it seemed beyond abstract. Our first case study involved a scavenger company hunting for sunken treasure. The question before us was how much money to spend diving for gold given the expected value of the gold that might lie buried in a galleon at the bottom of the sea. Our professor, Jay Light, was just a little older than we were and in his first year of teaching. At the start of the class, I raised my hand, and Jay pointed to me.

"Mr. Schwarzman, would you like to open the case?"

"Actually," I said, "I have a question."

"Okay, what is it?"

"I read the case," I said. "But it seems to be nonsense. If this is what the class is going to be, it's basically got no practical application to someone like myself."

Jay stared at me. "Tell me, Mr. Schwarzman, why would that be?"

"Because this case about expected value is premised on having an infinite number of dives to find the gold. I don't have an infinite number of dives in my life. When I dive, I have to have a 100 percent probability of finding the gold, because otherwise this whole enterprise can bankrupt me. This case applies to giant corporations that have no practical limit on how many dives they can make. But most people aren't Exxon. They have limited resources. Personally, I have no resources."

"Hmmm," said Jay. "I never thought of it that way. Let me think some more, and we'll go on."*

After a few weeks, I concluded that Harvard Business School was teaching only one idea, disguised as different courses. The lesson was that everything in business relates to everything else. For a business to succeed, each part has to work on its own and with all the other parts. It's a closed, integrated system, organized by managers. If you are making cars, you have to have good research so you'll know what people want to buy; good design, engineering, and manufacturing so you can produce a good product; effective programs to recruit and train your labor force; good marketing so you can create desire for what you are making; and good salespeople who know how to close deals. If any parts in the system break and you can't fix them quickly, you risk

---

* Jay Light continues to put up with my questions. Despite my best efforts to disrupt his career, he went on to be dean of Harvard Business School and has been a longtime member of Blackstone's board of directors. Whatever I thought of his sunken treasure case study, I've been lucky to have his advice ever since.

losing money and going out of business. I got that. What's next? Three more cases tomorrow that teach the same thing. And after that? Three more cases that teach it some more.

By the time I got to the December holiday, I was ready to drop out. I was bored. Boston was cold. The teaching was mediocre, done mostly by young assistant professors still finding their way in the classroom. Why was I wasting my life here? I was ready to go back to work.

Bill Donaldson, who had hired me at DLJ, had left the firm for a job in Washington as deputy secretary of state. Dick Jenrette had succeeded him as president. The last time I'd seen Dick was when he'd reprimanded me for accidentally asking for inside information at Restaurant Associates. But he had gone to HBS, so I decided to ask his advice.

"Dear Dick," I wrote. "I hate it here. I've gotten their message, and I'm thinking of dropping out. Maybe I could come back to DLJ or go somewhere else. Please tell me what you think."

To my astonishment, Dick took the time to write a six-page, handwritten reply that changed my life. It said something to the effect of "Dear Steve, I know exactly what you're thinking. I too was prepared to drop out of Harvard Business School in December of my first year. I found it very unsatisfying intellectually, and I was going to transfer to the economics department to get a PhD. But I stayed. It was the best decision of my life, and it's exactly what you should do. Don't leave. Stay."

I took his advice, and I'm still grateful. Whenever young people write or call me asking for advice, I think back to Dick's thoughtful, considerate letter. Like Jay Light, Dick Jenrette became a longtime member of Blackstone's board of directors. I decided to stay at HBS, and all that I hadn't learned at DLJ I began learning, from the basics of corporate finance to accounting, operations, and management. I completed my first year with honors and was selected by the faculty to be a member of the Century Club, an organization comprising the top three students of each section of seventy-two. I was elected president by other members of the club, and just as I had in high school and at Yale, I set out to make the experience unique and better for everyone. I started a program of inviting successful young men, just a few years older than us, to talk to the club. My first two guests were John Kerry, a Vietnam veteran who opposed the war and would eventually become a senator, secretary of state, and the Democratic nominee for president; and Michael Tilson Thomas, then assistant conductor of the Boston Symphony Orchestra, who would later lead the London and San Francisco Symphony orchestras. During my second year, I also met and married Ellen Philips, who was working as a course assistant at HBS.

I also decided to try to help improve the HBS experience. Fortified by my success changing the parietal rules at Yale and fixing the food mess at Fort Polk, I set up a meeting with the dean of Harvard Business School, Larry Fouraker, to suggest how the school could be better. Fouraker had been a compromise choice for the position, a mechanical, unspectacular administrator who spent most of his time away from the school serving on corporate boards. Despite its still-vaunted reputation, the school was showing signs of major problems. It took five months to get an appointment with Fouraker.

"You've got teachers who can't teach, students who can't learn, and an outmoded curriculum. And the administration is extremely ineffective." I gave him examples of each and proposed solutions.

"Mr. Schwarzman," he replied, "have you always been a misfit?"

I told him I had been president of my junior high school, president of my high school, presided during Class Day ceremonies at Yale graduation, and was now president of the Harvard

Business School Century Club. So, no, hardly a misfit. But he might be. At Yale, a university many times the size of HBS, the president, Kingman Brewster, made a point to see anyone who had asked for an appointment within four days. It was obvious to me, I told him, why HBS was going downhill. "I told you what's going on. I even suggested how you might solve it. And you have no interest whatsoever," I said. "I'm really sorry I stopped in to try to help you."

"I think that'll be enough," said Fouraker.

He took my argument as an affront. I didn't think I was smarter than the dean, but I did have a different perspective from down in the trenches of student life. Despite the school's shortcomings, I had come to care about Harvard Business School. Through her job, Ellen had formed a similarly dim view of the teaching and the caliber of the students, which also informed my suggestions for the dean. My only mistake was to think he might value my honesty. But he didn't even want a conversation.

If ever I ran an organization, I promised myself I would make it as easy as possible for people to see me and I'd always tell the truth, no matter how difficult the situation. As long as you can be honest and rational and are able to explain yourself, there is no reason to feel uncomfortable. No one person, however smart, can solve every problem. But an army of smart people talking candidly with one another will. It was the only lesson I learned from Larry Fouraker.

My time at HBS convinced me that despite my false start at DLJ, finance might be for me. In the cases we studied, I could spot patterns, sense the problems, and suggest potential solutions without getting lost in the numbers. And my extracurricular activities had taught me I enjoyed working with people to take on difficult, even improbable challenges. As graduation approached, I decided that I would like another try at Wall

Street, despite my poor start at DLJ and despite my math skills, which were then, and are still now, average at best.

At the time, investment banks did two things. First, sales and trading, which meant buying and selling securities such as bonds, stocks, options, Treasury bills, financial futures, commercial paper, and certificates of deposit. Second, they advised corporations on financial alternatives, capital structures, or mergers and acquisitions. These activities attracted different kinds of people. In the early 1970s, before computers revolutionized the way markets function, trading floors were frenzied and noisy, full of volatile characters. Advisory work tended to be more cerebral, involving long negotiations and patient relationship building. I'd be trying to get senior executives at major companies to trust what I had to say and act on it. I'd have to innovate, persuade, close, and compete. That seemed like work I might be good at.

I applied to six firms. As I went around their offices, I thought back to my culture and behavior studies at Yale, and an idea struck me for my senior paper in my most important course at HBS: What did these banks' offices suggest about their culture? At Kuhn, Loeb, the firm's history was overwhelming. Just inside the front door was a huge portrait of Jacob Schiff, its founder, and smaller ones of every partner in the firm's history. The partners sat behind closed doors, cut off from the activity in the bullpen where the associates sat. It was dark and inward looking. Unlikely to adapt and survive.

Morgan Stanley was in the same building as DLJ, but right at the top and flooded with light. Gold carpets and antique roll-top desks in the partners' area were reminders of the past, but otherwise it was modern and open to change. Then there was Lehman Brothers at 1 William Street, a massive, ornate stone building like an Italian palazzo with a Romanesque tower on top. Every floor was divided into a warren of small offices. It felt to me like a feudal castle with lots of intrigue and nothing transparent. Anyone who worked there would have to fight to succeed. Lehman, I thought, would do well until the infighting destroyed it.

The paper was easy to write. It had no numbers in it, no research. My professor thought it was creative and gave me a great grade.

My interviews didn't go nearly as well. First Boston didn't have a single Jewish professional in 1972, and apparently I wasn't going to be the first. Goldman Sachs said they liked me but worried I was a little too much my own person, and I never got an offer.

Morgan Stanley was the most prestigious investment bank in the world at the time. It served the most important companies, the definition of the establishment. It had one Jewish professional, Lewis Bernard, who was a partner. Otherwise, it was straight white Anglo-Saxon Protestant. They invited me back for a second-round interview and assigned me a shepherd, an older employee who took me around to meet the partners. My shepherd talked a lot about the importance of precision in the drafting of prospectuses. Precision was clearly important to the culture at Morgan Stanley, but it wasn't exactly thrilling.

Finally, I was invited in to see Robert Baldwin, the president of the firm. Bob had been under secretary of the navy. A navy flag and the flag of the United States stood behind the desk in his office. Morgan Stanley would be hiring just seven associates that year, and Bob offered me the chance to be one of them. It was an enormous honor, but it came with a significant condition: I would have to change my personality. Morgan Stanley was a buttoned-down, hierarchical culture. I couldn't be my opinionated, proactive self. Bob said I had the talent to work there; I just had to adapt.

I thanked him for the offer but said I couldn't take it. I would rather work somewhere where my personality was a natural fit. He should rescind my offer and give it to someone more suitable. But Bob refused. If Morgan Stanley makes you an offer, he said, it's yours to do with what you will. His firm would always keep its word. I was impressed. Over the next decade, Bob would transform the culture at Morgan Stanley, modernizing it and shedding many of its old traditions. But he had to do so with guardrails and under certain conditions, respecting the culture he inherited. He saw he would struggle to domesticate me, but had a sense I might help take the firm in the direction he wanted.

Lehman was much more attractive to me. It wasn't an MBA factory. It was full of interesting characters—ex-CIA agents and military, strays from the oil industry, family, friends, randoms. No two floors were designed the same, and there were no layers between the thirty partners and the thirty associates. It seemed an exciting and complex place to be.

On the day of our interviews, the interviewees began sitting around a table in the partners' dining room, with the partners sitting in back. The chairman, Frederick Ehrman, was wearing a very un–Wall Street cowboy belt with a big silver buckle and told us we would be interviewed in pairs: two interviewees rotating through pairs of partners in forty-five-minute sessions through the day. This pairing strategy, I thought, could end in disaster, with two interviewees dueling to outshine each other. If I were my most supercompetitive self through nine interviews, we'd end the day with blood on the carpet, so I figured the best approach was to be generous and friendly with my partner, a woman my own age. It turned out I was right: the firm rejected the people who fought and competed during their interviews. Those who cooperated received offers.

There was an even longer-term benefit to my decision. My fellow interviewee, Betty Eveillard, had a long, successful career

in investment banking. We often ran into each other professionally. Decades after we navigated that treacherous day of interviews, we serve together on the board of the Frick Collection,
an art museum on the Upper East Side of Manhattan, where
she became chairperson. Those early encounters and friendships
have a way of reappearing throughout your life.

At DLJ, I had been left to myself to grope through the fog
of Wall Street. As soon as I was offered a job at Lehman, I was
assigned a partner, Steve DuBrul, a product of both HBS and the
CIA, to guide me. Steve was a corporate financier from central
casting: tall, slim, handsome, his dark hair parted to one side. He
had been a protégé of the previous chairman, Robert Lehman.
He took me to dinner and explained how the firm worked.

But just a week after I accepted Lehman's offer, Steve called
me at home. "I don't want you to find this the least bit upset-
ting," he said, "but I'm leaving Lehman. I'm joining Lazard."

"Hold it," I said. "You're the guy wining and dining me. And
you're disappearing? Why shouldn't that affect me?"

"It doesn't have anything to do with the quality of Lehman
Brothers, and you'll fit in great there. You'll be enormously successful. But I've spent my entire career here. It's time for me to
move on. I wanted to tell you personally, so that you understand
that this is personal for me. It's not about the firm. You should
feel good about being at Lehman."

"If you're going to Lazard," I said, "maybe I should go with
you."

"Your loyalty shouldn't be to me. It should be to the firm. But
if you want, I can set you up for an interview." I took him up on
the offer and flew to New York to meet with Felix Rohatyn, the
famous mergers and corporate finance adviser at Lazard Frères.
Rohatyn, a slight man in a rumpled suit, was a commanding force
in the financial world. He had come to New York as a boy at the

start of World War II, escaping Europe with his mother. He had joined Lazard straight out of college and become New York's preeminent investment banker. His greatest act would come in 1975, when he helped save New York City from bankruptcy. We talked in his office for an hour or so. At the end, he said, "Steve, you're an interesting guy. If you want to work at Lazard, I'll make you a job offer right here on the spot. But I advise you not to take it."

"Why?"

"Because at Lazard, there are two types of people: masters like me and slaves like you would be. I don't think you'd be happy being a slave. You should go work at Lehman Brothers, let them train you, and then come here to Lazard as a master."

When I flew back to Boston, Ellen asked me how it had gone. "Rohatyn made me a job offer. Then he told me not to take it. It's crazy down there."

So I went to Lehman to be trained, to sit in the middle of Wall Street with feeds running in from around the world, to be a telephone switchboard.

HOLD THE TABLE:
ADVICE ON INTERVIEWS

———————

Being a strong and accurate assessor of talent is perhaps one of the most critical skills required of any entrepreneur. I've been thinking about how to do this well since those early interviews on Wall Street.

Finance is a field that is filled with capable, ambitious individuals looking to leave their mark. But being capable isn't always sufficient. When I interview people for Blackstone, I'm looking to understand whether an individual will fit our culture. At a minimum, this includes the airport test: Would I want to be stuck waiting at the airport with you if our flight were delayed?

After thousands of interviews, I have developed my own style of interviewing. I rely on a combination of verbal and nonverbal cues, looking to see how a candidate reacts to my attempts to engage. I don't have a set formula, but in every case, my goal is to get into candidates' heads to assess how they think, who they are, and whether they are right for Blackstone.

I prepare for an interview like most others do, by reading a candidate's résumé. I look for consistency in terms of a narrative and make special note of any anomalies or standout pieces of information. Sometimes candidates are surprised that I have read their résumé so closely, but mostly they are relieved when I can ask them about a familiar topic or interest.

My goal is to start the conversation with something that both the candidate and I will find interesting, but I won't know how I'm going to start until we are in the same room. I choose my course by intuition.

Sometimes I go straight to one of the anomalies on the résumé. Other times I'll take a lead from what their body language tells me before they even say a word. Do they look happy or sad, alert or tired, excited or nervous? The more I can get candidates out of interview mode and into a natural conversation, the easier it becomes for me to evaluate how they think, react, and might adapt to change.

In some cases, I ask candidates if they had fun meeting people at the firm, if our people met their expectations, and how Blackstone is different from the other organizations they have worked or interviewed with.

Other times I will have just finished doing something exciting and will tell them about it to see how they react. Most candidates don't expect to be drawn into my world so quickly, and how they respond can be telling. Do they withdraw, or are they able to find a way to actively partici-pate? Does the unexpected situation make them nervous or uncomfortable? Even if it's a topic or experience they know nothing about, are they able to find common ground and enjoy the conversation?

Alternatively, I'll ask about something fascinating or newsworthy. If they are familiar with the topic, I'll look for how they approach the discussion. Do they have a point of view? Is their assessment logical and analytical? If they don't know what I'm talking about, do they admit it and find a way to move on, or do they try to fake it?

In reality, this is all an exercise in evaluating their ability to deal with uncertainty. Finance, and investing especially, is a dynamic world in which you must adjust to new information, people, and situations quickly. If a candidate doesn't demonstrate the ability to connect, engage, pivot, and change course within the bounds of a conversation, chances are that person won't fare well at Blackstone.

Our people are all different, but they share some common traits: self-confidence, intellectual curiosity, courtesy, an ability to adjust to new situations, emotional stability under pressure, a zero-defect mentality, and an unwavering commitment to behaving with integrity and striving for excellence in all we choose to do. Being nice—thoughtful, considerate, and decent—doesn't hurt either. I will never hire anyone who isn't nice regardless of his or her talent. It's also important to me that Blackstone remains free of internal politics, so if jockeying for position is part of your nature, we don't want you.

Here are my rules for how to have a successful interview:

1. *Be on time.* Punctuality is the first indicator of how much thought and preparation you have put into an interview.

2. *Be authentic.* Interviews are a mutual assessment, a bit like speed dating; everyone is looking for the right fit. Be comfortable and natural, and chances are you will be liked for who you are. If you share who you are and the interview results in a job offer, that's great. If it doesn't work, it's likely that the organization wasn't right for you either. Better to know and move on.

3. *Be prepared.* Learn about the company. Interviewers always enjoy discussing what's happening in their environment. Plus it's a good way for you to hear

how enthusiastic an employee feels about the place where he or she works. Describe what draws you to the company and why. An interviewer wants to understand your motives and whether they fit with the organization's culture.

4. *Be candid.* Don't be afraid to talk about what's on your mind. Focus less on impressing the interviewer and more on being open and striving for an honest conversation.

5. *Be confident.* Approach the situation as an equal, not as a supplicant. In most situations, employers are looking for someone who can hold the table. Provided they are not arrogant.

6. *Be curious.* The best interviews are interactive. Ask questions, ask for advice, ask your interviewers what they enjoy most about working for their organization. Find a way to engage interviewers, and always make sure the conversation goes both ways. Interviewers like to talk too, so that they can share what they know.

7. *Avoid discussing divisive political issues unless you are asked.* In which case, be straightforward. Describe what you believe and why, but don't be argumentative.

8. *Mention people you know at an organization only if you like and respect them.* Your interviewer will be judging your taste in people.

THE BEST WAY
TO LEARN IS BY DOING

My first assignment at Lehman came from Herman Kahn, a cantankerous old partner I had seen but not yet met. He wanted me to prepare a "fairness opinion" analysis on a manufacturer of airline seats. Companies ask banks for fairness opinions when they want an objective evaluation of the price to be paid in a transaction. In this case, the manufacturer had been sold three years earlier for a high price just as the market for airplane seats had peaked. Since then, sales of airplanes had declined and the company's value had decreased dramatically. Kahn asked me to figure out if the price paid in 1969 had been fair.

It was not an easy analysis. Today, we do the research and calculations using computers and relevant databases. Back then, it required days in Lehman's basement archives going through back issues of the *Wall Street Journal* and the *New York Times*. I'd come up after ten hours covered with newsprint ink, only to get to work with my slide rule making the calculations. It was kludgy and mind-numbing work, but it was essential to learning my craft.

I wrote a sixty-eight-page history of the company and its shifting value based not only on the trajectory of its stock price but on its prospects, the market trends, and everything else I considered relevant. I included appendixes and footnotes for clarification. Then I took this work of beauty to Herman Kahn on the partners' floor. He wasn't there, so I put it in the middle of his desk where he would see it as soon as he sat down. I went to my office and waited. A few hours later I got a call.

"Is this Steve Schwarzman?" Herman Kahn was hard of hearing and his voice was loud, nasal, aggravated.

"Yes, it is."

"Schwarzman! This is Herman Kahn! I got your memo! There's a *typo* on page 56!" And he slammed the phone down.

I looked at page 56. The only error I could find was a misplaced comma. *Jesus*, I thought. *This isn't Harvard Business School. These people don't fuck around. I'm living according to their rules. I had better learn to play by them.* I never heard from Herman Kahn again on the project.

A few months later, a group of us, including the deal teams as well as others at the firm, were summoned to the boardroom. Lehman was the lead underwriter in the initial public offering (IPO) of the Student Loan Marketing Association, the precursor to Sallie Mae. We were supposed to raise $100 million, a lot back then. So far we had only $10 million. Lew Glucksman, the head trader and number two person at the firm, wanted to know why. I was the most junior person on the team, the junior associate to a more senior associate, responsible for a couple of numbers. Lew glared around the table and settled his gaze on me.

"Who the fuck are you?" he screamed. "And why aren't you sitting up straight?"

I could feel my cheeks burn. Everybody around me was looking the other way. I went back to my office afterward, shaking. Later, people came up to me one by one to commiserate and assure me I hadn't done anything wrong. Two things came out of that meeting. First, to this day, I sit straight in important meetings. Second, I had caught Lew Glucksman's attention. He must have asked about me and heard good things, because shortly afterward, he called and told me to get to work on fixing this broken IPO. I had never raised money and had no idea how to do it, but I knew better now than to try figuring it out by myself. I reached out for help.

Steve Fenster, my senior associate, had become my closest friend at Lehman. Before entering finance, he had been one of Robert McNamara's whiz kids, the group of brilliant young men brought in to modernize the Department of Defense during the 1960s. He had a probing, provocative intelligence and the rare talent of looking at the same facts everyone else did but finding things no one else could see. We talked together almost every night, and he explained to me how IPOs and mergers worked—loan structures, debt instruments, mergers and acquisitions, the machinery of a financial firm.

Steve was also one of the firm's eccentrics. Every day he dressed in a dark suit, a repp striped tie, and wingtip shoes. Only on vacation did he wear loafers. One time he had to go straight from vacation to see a client and found he had packed two left wingtips by accident. The idea of wearing loafers to a business meeting was unacceptable, so he wore the two left shoes instead. The client noticed. But Steve was so brilliant that no one cared.

"It's not that hard," he said of my latest assignment, trying to settle me down. "You build a model of why this is a good investment. Everything's a spread." This company simply made loans and charged more for the loans than it cost them to borrow money to make the loans. All I had to do was calculate how many loans it could make and I could determine the company's profit potential. "Then you go to some financial institutions and show them why they would want to buy into this thing." I had to identify the investors and institutions that might be interested and then craft a pitch that persuaded them they needed the Student Loan Marketing Association as part of their portfolio of investments.

Since this was a company that made loans to students, I figured one place to start was with universities. Harvard had the largest university endowment, so as a recent graduate, I called and got an appointment with Harvard's treasurer, George Putnam. Putnam was the head of Putnam Investments, a giant mutual fund company he had founded in the late 1930s. For a first-year banking associate with his little road-show book begging for an investment, meeting Putnam was like meeting one of the gods of New England.

I opened my pitch book and began my windup.

"Mr. Schwarzman," said Putnam, interrupting me. "Can you please close your book?" I closed the book, nervously. "Mr. Schwarzman, have you ever heard of the UJA?" The UJA, the United Jewish Appeal, three letters it never occurred to me would be crossing George Putnam's lips.

"Yes, I've heard of the UJA."

"Have you ever heard of card calling?" Card calling was a common practice at the UJA's fundraising dinners. The chairman would call out the names of all potential donors, announce what they gave last year, and everyone would listen for what they were going to give this year. It was a way to create a level of expectation and apply peer pressure.

"Let's start this meeting over, Mr. Schwarzman. You say, 'Mr. Putnam, you're the treasurer of Harvard University, and I'm starting the largest—what will be the largest—student loan lending business in the United States, and I've got you down for $20 million.' Now, say that." I said it.

"That's a great idea, Mr. Schwarzman," he said. "I'm in for twenty." He had read up on the company before I walked into the room and would not be convinced by me one way or the other on its merits. He just wanted my help in making a quick decision on how much to invest. "Now what you do is take your book, get on the train, go to New Haven, and see Mr. So and So at Yale, and say, 'Mr. So and So, I'm raising money for the Student Loan Marketing Association, which is going to be the biggest lender to students in the United States. I've got Yale down for $15 million.' Try that. See what happens. After that, get back on the train, go to Princeton. Ask them for $10 million."

By the end of my university pitches, I had raised the better part of the $100 million, the money that founded Sallie Mae. Putnam gave me a lesson in raising money that would stay with me throughout my career as I raised fund after fund at Blackstone. Investors are always looking for great investments. The easier you make it for them, the better for everyone.

———

Steve Fenster and George Putnam were good teachers. But I also learned by making my own mistakes. Late in my first year, I was sitting on a plane with Eric Gleacher, a smart, no-nonsense ex-marine, a few years older than me, who had just been made partner. We were on our way to St. Louis to see a food processing company about spinning off its chain of convenience stores.

I had prepared the financials, laying out the various options. Eric would be presenting. Compared to the huge teams at investment banks today, banks then were much smaller. There wasn't the diligence, checking and rechecking of presentations. When we got settled on the plane, I handed my work to Eric. As he turned the first page, his brow began to furrow. He looked at the next page even more quizzically. After the third page he said, "Steve, I think you've made an error." I had gotten one number wrong early on, and it had affected my calculations on about half the pages. "This is a mess," said Eric. "But we can give the presentation anyhow. Just take out the bad pages, and I can talk my way through the rest of it. It's okay."

Herman Khan had been outraged because of a typo. Now I had messed up an entire deal book. Eric buried himself behind his newspaper while I tore out the offending pages in all the copies of the presentation. We landed in St. Louis and took a cab to the company, Eric still silent. We sat down at the board meeting, and Eric passed out our booklets. There was some introductory talk. Then he began his presentation.

"As you can see from the analysis . . . I think we have a statistical error." As he spoke, he all but launched himself across the table grabbing our presentation books from the board members. "I can talk you through this without any numbers."

I had been so freaked out by my mistake that instead of tearing out the bad pages, I had torn out the good ones. I could have melted under the table. We left the company, got in the cab, and rode back to the airport. Not a word. Right before they called the plane, Eric turned to me: "If you ever do that to me again, I'm firing you on the spot."

Painful as it was, Lehman was the school I needed. Like any other craft, finance has to be learned. As Malcolm Gladwell pointed out in his book *Outliers: The Story of Success*, the Beatles needed to go to Hamburg from 1960 to 1962 to transform themselves from a garage band into the Beatles, and Bill Gates spent hours as a teenager on the computers at the University of Washington close to his house before he could write the software for the first PCs. Similarly, people who succeed in finance must start with repetitive practice before they can ever hope to achieve mastery. At Lehman, I observed every step of the process and was trained in all details, any one of which, done wrong, can bring everything crashing down.

There are people who come to finance from other professions, from law or the media perhaps, but the best I've ever worked with grew up in it. They learned by doing the fundamental analysis. They established strong foundations for their careers by discovering that the smallest things matter and suffering the indignity of their early mistakes.

———

During my second year at Lehman, a new chairman and CEO arrived. Pete Peterson had been CEO of Bell and Howell, a maker of media equipment, and most recently President Nixon's commerce secretary. He had great CEO contacts and was widely respected in business and government. He arrived at Lehman to find it in financial trouble, struggling to survive, and rife with the kind of infighting that I had predicted in my Harvard Business School paper would kill it.

Pete had an ally in George Ball, a partner who had served as deputy secretary of state under Presidents Kennedy and Johnson, and eventually as ambassador to the United Nations. They worked their international contacts and persuaded the Banca Commerciale Italiana to provide capital to help Lehman survive. Once Lehman was off life support, Pete sent out a memo to the entire company asking for ideas. After a year at the firm, I figured I knew enough to write a strategic plan involving money management and investment banking. A week after I sent it, Pete called me to see him. At the end of our meeting, he said: "You seem to be a capable young man. You and I should work together."

The word on Pete was that he was smart but had no experience in finance or investment banking. He asked five times as many questions as anyone else, and people found him exhausting to work with. His relentless questions enabled him to get to the heart of the problems at the firm, but the process was trying.

If he didn't really know what he was doing and I still had so much to learn, it would be a case of the one-eyed leading the blind. I suggested we wait until I was better prepared. Pete took my candor well. But about two years later, he called again: he wanted me on his team. We were a good match. I knew what he didn't but was young enough not to get in his way.

One day, he invited me for lunch with Reg Jones, the CEO of General Electric. Pete and Reg were both on the board of General Foods and had become friends. Reg wanted Pete to meet a young executive he was grooming at GE.

"This is Jack Welch," said Jones.

"Hi, Steve. Nice to meet you." He had a kind of high-pitched voice, squeaky and with a strong Boston accent.

"Reg is here because Jack will be the next CEO of General Electric—but that's currently a secret," said Pete. "He'd like us to teach finance to Jack. So that's your job."

"Okay," I said, hesitantly.

"Yeah, yeah, yeah," Welch said. "It's good." This squeaky guy with his "yeah, yeah, yeah" is going to be CEO of General Electric? He's either got to be the smartest guy on earth, or else Reginald Jones was off base in choosing him.

When Jack came to learn finance, it took me about one minute to see that Reginald Jones wasn't off base at all: he had hit a home run. Having Jack Welch go to work on you was like having your brain connected to a dust-buster sucking out everything you know. I've never met anyone like him before or since. He never stopped asking questions—torrential, relentless questions—and he instantly grasped the links between one idea and another, even if they were entirely new to him. He was like Tarzan swinging through the trees at blistering speed, never missing a vine, learning more quickly than I could teach.

Getting to know Jack and watching him in action reinforced my growing belief that the most important asset in business is information. The more you know, the more perspectives you have and the more connections you can make, which allow you to anticipate issues.

Jack became CEO of General Electric in 1981 and began a run as one of the greatest CEOs in American history. Pete's introduction also led to a long friendship. After decades, I'm still amazed by Jack. Meeting him was one of the gifts of being part of a major firm so early in my career. Wall Street and business are small worlds. If you start at a great school or a big firm, crossing paths with the best people of your generation, you'll keep running into them. Many of the friends I made at Yale, Harvard Business School, the Army Reserves, and in those early years on Wall Street have remained my friends. The trust and familiarity of those early relationships have enriched my life in ways I could never have predicted.

ALL DEALS ARE CRISES

An investment banker's job is to deal with change and often high-stress situations. You suggest an acquisition or a sale of a division, identifying a target purchase or a buyer. You propose that a company borrow more debt to fund expansion or repurchase shares when its stock price is low. How you initiate and manage that change is the measure of your success.

By late 1978, I had been with Lehman for six years as an associate. My responsibilities had grown, and I was under consideration for partnership. One Friday, I was in Chicago on business when I got a call from Ken Barnebey, the CEO of Tropicana, the orange juice company. Earlier in the year, I had been to see him at the company's headquarters in Bradenton, Florida, to propose various financial ideas. It was a casual, get-to-know-you meeting. But naturally I had hoped that one day something would come of it.

"We've got a very sensitive situation I'd like to talk to you about," he said. "We've been approached by a company that wants to buy us, and we're considering what to do." Barring any conflicts, he said, he wanted me in Bradenton Saturday at 8:30 a.m. to speak to his board. I called our New York office. My colleague Teddy Roosevelt asked around and confirmed there was no conflict. If any other divisions at Lehman had been working on deals involving Tropicana, I wouldn't have been able to proceed. I called Ken back, and he described the terms of the bid. The price had been agreed in principle, but the buyer was presenting different packages of cash and securities the seller might accept, which would make the deal more or less valuable to them. My job was to assess these different structures on behalf of the board and make a recommendation.

Chicago was in the middle of a snowstorm. All flights to Sarasota-Bradenton airport were delayed. By the time I got on a plane, it was late, and the flight almost empty. As we headed south through several storms, all I had to help me understand the proposed transaction was a copy of the *Stock Guide*, which contained the basic financials of public companies. I looked up Tropicana and found its earnings and a few other ratios. I could see how much money it made, its profits as a percentage of revenue, and the amount of debt and equity on its balance sheet—the simple metrics of a company's financial health. I could also look up other food companies and see how they compared to Tropicana. But there had been little merger activity in the sector since the stock market crash of 1973, so I had no recent, comparable deals to guide me.

We landed at four in the morning, and it took another hour and a half to find a cab and get to my motel. I lay down on the bed for a few minutes, then took a shower. I had been planning to fly right back to New York from Chicago, so had only the clothes I had arrived in. I put them back on and tried to clear my head. At 7:30 a.m., I walked into Tropicana's offices.

"We're in a rush because we've already approved the deal in principle," said Ken. "Beatrice [the acquiring company] has too. We have to announce when the market opens Monday, which means we have to get everything in place right now. Beatrice is offering three different types of structures. One is a combination of common and straight preferred stock. One is common and convertible preferred. One is common and cash. We need you to advise us which of these to take, if any. We've got an hour before the board gets here."

I had had no sleep, had no partner with me, not even another associate, and I had never done a merger. *You are in such trouble*, I told myself. *What are you going to do?*

When I started in finance, I was ill prepared for the stress of the work. Every point in every negotiation was a fight, with a winner and a loser. People in this business weren't interested in carving up the pie so everyone got a slice. They wanted the whole pie for themselves. I observed that when I was the one making the decisions and the voices rose and tempers flared, my heart would beat faster and my breathing would become more shallow. I became less effective, less in control of my own cognitive responses.

The fix, I found, was to focus on my breathing, slow it down and relax my shoulders, until my breaths were long and deep. The effect was astonishing. My thoughts became clearer. I became more objective and rational about the situation at hand, about what I needed to do to win.

That morning in Florida, I slowed down my breathing until I could relate to everyone and figure out the issues at hand as if there were no stress at all.

In my relatively short career, I had learned that deals ultimately come down to a few key points that matter most to each side. If you can clear everything else away and focus on these points, you will be an effective negotiator. You cannot let all the voices, paperwork, and deadlines overwhelm you. What Ken and the board needed from me now was some clear thinking.

The equity portion of each of the structures would be tax free if Tropicana's shareholders accepted more than 50 percent of their payment in Beatrice stock. The simplest structure was for common stock and cash: Beatrice would pay Tropicana's shareholders 51 percent of the $488 million purchase price in its own stock and the rest in cash. The appeal of the other two structures depended on what you thought of the future of a combined Beatrice and Tropicana. If you felt reasonably confident, you might take the straight preferred stock, which came with no voting rights but a guaranteed dividend paid out before any dividends to common stockholders. And if you felt really good about the deal, you'd take the convertible preferred, which came with a lower dividend but the right to swap it at any time for common stock. If the stock went down, you'd still have the dividend. If it went up, your upside was unlimited. There was no way I could figure this all out for myself. Exhausted and bleary, I needed advice—and cover, if this deal went wrong. I called Pete.

"I'm seeing Tropicana's board in an hour. What should I do?" He advised me to call Lew Glucksman, and then Bob Rubin, one of the senior banking partners. I called Lew and woke him up. "Lew, here are the multiples, based on the *Stock Guide*."

"I think the price is fair," he said, and he recommended one of the three structures.

Then I called Bob Rubin. "Bob, I'm sitting here at Tropicana, I talked to Lew, I talked to Pete. Here's the situation. What should I do?"

"The price sounds okay," Rubin said. "In terms of the structure, it's a matter of taste."

As the five members of the board arrived, I felt at least a little more confident. Then I saw the stenographer and two tape recorders in the room. Everything I said would be recorded. The chairman, Anthony Rossi, looked and sounded like Marlon Brando in *The Godfather*, in the scene where he is playing with his grandson among the tomato plants, just before he keels over and dies. "Come, Mr. Schwarzman," he said, pointing to the chair next to his. "*Sit-a* here, next to me."

Rossi had emigrated from Sicily as a young man. When he arrived in Florida, he had opened a grocery store, then went into the citrus business and founded Tropicana. He ran it so tightly that he didn't allow anyone to have windows in their offices in case they might get distracted. He was the only one with a window, so he could watch the trucks bringing the oranges in and make sure no one was stealing. This deal was the consummation of a life's work. He was a Baptist and planned to give away a lot of the money he was about to make to a religious foundation. He wasn't a financier, but he was shrewd enough to have built a strong business. I owed it to him to be straightforward and clear.

"Tell us, Mr. Schwarzman," he said, "what do you advise us to do?"

Another trick I had learned for managing stress was to take a moment to slow myself down. People were always happy to let me have that extra moment. It even seemed to reassure them. They would be even more eager to hear what I had to say once I was ready. So I took a moment and then began.

"The first thing is that you do not have to sell the business." It was important that Rossi hear that. That he still feel in control. "But as you've decided, next you have to figure out whether the price is attractive. I understand you're already satisfied with that, which would be my opinion as well."

I told the board they should feel comfortable about Beatrice, given its financial health, and laid out the details of the various purchase structures, the issues of tax and timing, drawing on Lew's and Bob's insights. I explained to Rossi how the convertible preferred would give him a steady income, with the possibility of further upside if the stock went up. After an hour and a half of discussion, they chose the mix of convertible preferred stock and cash and asked me to finalize the deal terms with Lazard, Beatrice's bankers.

When I left the room I called Ellen. She had been expecting me home the previous night.

"Sweetie, I'm so sorry . . ."

"Where are you?"

"Bradenton, Florida. I just did this amazing deal." I couldn't quite believe it myself.

"What? We've got a dinner party tonight."

"I can't make it to the dinner party. I'm under enormous stress right now, and I have to finish what I'm doing. I'll catch up with you later."

Lou Perlmutter was one of Lazard's masters, a senior partner and expert in mergers and acquisitions. He could easily have tried to take advantage of my inexperience.

"Steve, this deal's meant to happen," he said. "I'll give you the standard down-the-center thing. Just say yes, because I don't want to overnegotiate. It would only make a mess."

Lou knew that Beatrice wasn't the only company interested in Tropicana. Others were circling. He didn't want a long negotiation with Tropicana's financially unsophisticated board and their young banker. All he needed from me was to convince the board quickly so we could print the deal and go home. Lou knew that if he jammed me, I would find out, or someone at Lehman would find out, and the deal would get held up. So he made it as easy as he could. We worked together the rest of the day.

As I was flying home, the snowstorm that had hit Chicago the previous night was slowing air traffic into New York. I made it home around 4:30 a.m., beyond exhausted, trying to get my head around what had just happened. $488 million! It was the second biggest M&A deal in the world that year. By the time I got home, I hadn't slept for forty-eight hours but still I couldn't go to bed. I put some logs in the living room fireplace and started a fire. I hardly ever drink, but I poured myself a glass of Courvoisier and put on the Bee Gees' *Saturday Night Fever* album. I sat back in the easy chair, imagining John Travolta strutting across the disco floor. $488 million. What had I just done?

At 7:00 a.m., the phone rang. It was Felix Rohatyn. He had spoken with Lou Perlmutter. My head was still full of Courvoisier, exhaustion, and *Saturday Night Fever* as Felix began. "I just heard about the Tropicana deal," he said. "First, I want to congratulate you. That's fantastic. Second, you're thirty years old and you've done something huge. And by yourself, I understand, without a partner or anyone else. So this is a huge breakout moment in your career. A lot of people are going to hate you. Don't worry about that. You are different from them. Do not let that bother you!

"The third thing is that you now have a responsibility to speak out in public. You will need to speak up when you see something wrong that can be corrected. Don't fear doing that, because certain people have an obligation to society to do that. I'm one of those people. You are now one of those people."

Felix had a particular vision of the contribution bankers could make. But all I could think about was who would hate me.

The phone rang again. It was Peter Solomon, Lehman's vice chairman.

"Who the fuck do you think you are? You sold Tropicana? I'm working on a deal to buy them for Philip Morris! We were going to make them a tender offer. Philip Morris is the biggest client we have. And you put yourself in the way? I'm talking to the executive committee on Monday. We're firing you! On Monday, you're history!"

"I know Teddy Roosevelt talked with you," I replied. "You never mentioned anything about Tropicana to him."

"Monday morning, Steve. Monday morning you're out of here!" Slam.

I knew the truth, though, and called Pete. I assured him that Teddy had specifically spoken to Peter about conflicts and he hadn't said a thing about Philip Morris's interest in Tropicana.

"That's ridiculous," Pete said. "Don't worry about it."

On Monday Solomon raged to the executive committee about his broken deal with Philip Morris. Everyone in the office speculated about my future. I was surrounded by jackals. But thank God for Pete. He wasn't having any of it.

MONEY IS A POOR CURE
FOR A BAD SITUATION

The Tropicana deal secured my promotion to partner, and I celebrated by redecorating my office. If I was going to be there twelve hours a day, I wanted it to be a cocoon against all the psychological stresses of my work, cozy, like a beautiful sitting room or library in an English house. I had the walls painted partly in reddish-maroon, the rest covered in the kind of grass cloth I'd seen at Lee Eastman's place. I installed a chocolate carpet, chintz chairs, and a partners' desk from the 1890s. It was exquisite. No one else at the firm had ever done this. It wasn't how they thought about work. But I didn't consider myself to be at work. This was my second home, and I wanted it to be beautiful, comfortable, and visually interesting.

When I arrived at DLJ in 1969, I had my face pressed up against the glass of a life I could only imagine. Nearly a decade afterward, I was living it. One day in 1979, I had just finished a deal when another partner stuck his head in my door and asked if Ellen and I would like to come with him to Egypt. Tomorrow. For dinner next to the pyramids. One of our clients was sponsoring the event, and Lehman had bought a table and needed to fill it. The next day, we left on a Pan Am plane with one hundred other guests. While we were in Paris refueling, the door opened and fifty of the most beautiful women I had ever seen in my life—models who were going to appear in a fashion show for us—boarded our plane. In Cairo, we went straight past customs, and a motorcycle escort cleared the way to our hotel next to the Sphinx. That night we attended the fashion show by the designer Pierre Balmain. The following afternoon, we went for tea with Anwar Sadat, Egypt's president, and his wife, Jehan. Sadat had won the 1978 Nobel Peace Prize for negotiating peace with Israel. On the final evening, we had dinner with five hundred people on the sand in front of the pyramids and the Sphinx. I sat at the table next to President Sadat. The night ended with Frank Sinatra singing *New York, New York*. It was one of the most memorable evenings of my life.

On our flight home, almost everyone came down with amoebic dysentery, including me. But it didn't take the shine off an extraordinary trip. It was the kind of astonishing experience I had hoped to have someday. Now I wanted even more.

In 1980, the *New York Times* profiled me on the front page of the Sunday Business Section with a large picture as Lehman's "Merger Maker." The reporter credited me with a "drive to succeed, a strong persistence (he once finished running a cross country course even after he tripped and broke his wrist) and an infectious vitality that make other people like to work with him." The cross-country race had been in ninth grade, and I had to be rushed to the hospital. She went on: "Mr. Schwarzman says he approaches problems by asking himself, 'What would I want if I were in their shoes?' That, he says, is what gives him his rapport with people. Still a student of behavior, he listens hard to what people say, believing that things that are said are said for a reason. This art of listening gives him an unusually high gift of recall."

It was a pretty accurate picture of me at the time. Listening to people seemed obvious. But it evidently marked me out on Wall Street. I didn't just try selling whatever it was I had to sell. I listened. I waited to hear what people wanted, what was on their mind, then set about making it happen. I rarely take notes in meetings. I just pay very close attention to what the other person is saying and the way he or she is saying it. If I can, I try to find some point of connection, an area of common ground, a shared interest or experience that turns a professional encounter into a more personal one. It sounds like common sense, but apparently in practice, it's relatively rare.

One effect of my intense listening is that I can recall events and conversations in detail. It's as if they are imprinted and stored away in my brain. A lot of people fail because they start from a position of self-interest. What's in this for me? They will never get to do the most interesting and rewarding work. Listening closely and watching the way people talk puts me much closer to answering the question I'm always asking myself, which is: How can I help? If I can help someone and become a friend to their situation, everything else follows.

There is nothing more interesting to people than their own problems. If you can find out what they are and come up with solutions, they will want to talk to you no matter their rank or status. The harder the problem and the scarcer the solution, the more valuable your advice is. It's in those situations, where everyone is walking away with averted eyes, that the field clears and the greatest opportunity awaits.

The early 1980s weren't just good for me. Five years in a row, Lehman notched record earnings. Our return on equity beat all our competitors. I rose to be chairman of the mergers and acquisitions department, advising some of the firm's biggest clients. At Lehman's Water Street offices, there were never enough hours in the day. Our department was second to Goldman Sachs in deal size, but we led them and the rest of Wall Street in deal volume.

By then Pete had been Lehman's CEO and chairman for ten years. He had pulled Lehman back from the abyss. Although he didn't enjoy finance in particular, his strength was his range of contacts in business and politics. He could get anyone on the phone. He was twenty-one years older than me, but we had developed a close working relationship. We complemented each other. He could bring people together and nurture relationships; I could originate and execute deals. He was a thinker, tolerant and reflective. I could be confrontational if necessary. I ran and closed many of the deals that Pete initiated. People around the firm considered us a team. We trusted each other implicitly. But it was Pete's tendency to trust people in the feuding castle of Lehman that eventually got him into trouble.

In the early 1980s, Lehman's traders were racking up huge profits in a bull market. Their leader was Lew Glucksman, who had been helpful to me during the Tropicana deal. But generally he was as volatile as the markets themselves. Self-restraint was not in his emotional vocabulary. He roamed the trading floor in a rumpled suit or in shirtsleeves, his shirttail hanging out, an unlit cigar clenched between his teeth. He once got so angry that he yanked a phone out of the wall and smashed it into a plate glass window. Another time, he got so pumped up, he ripped his shirt open, tearing off the buttons, and stomped around bare-chested.

In 1983, he went to Pete and asked for a promotion. Pete agreed and made him president of the firm. Pete thought that was only right and fair. But he didn't understand men like Lew Glucksman. A few months later, Lew walked into Pete's office and said that was just the first banana. Now he wanted the whole bunch. He wanted to be co-CEO. Pete didn't want to fight, so he acquiesced. Eight weeks later, Lew was back. "I need to be CEO myself. I want you gone." He had organized a putsch with the trading partners. Pete didn't tell me about Lew's ultimatum until he had caved in. I was appalled.

"Why didn't you fight?" I said. "You could have marshaled your own resources and pushed this guy out. You've got a lot of support among the partners. Why didn't you at least talk to me?"

"I knew what your advice would have been," he said. "You would have wanted to kill him. I know you. I'm not like you. I've been here for ten years already. I turned the place around. We were at the brink; now we're making a fortune. Why would I want to destroy it? It's just not worth the fight. Besides I don't know anything about trading. If I forced Glucksman out," he said, "what would happen to the trading division?"

"You don't need to know about trading," I said. "You hire the best guy from Goldman or JPMorgan."

"It would rip the firm apart."

"If somebody challenges you, you've got to be ready to rip the place apart. Then you put it back together."

"No, no," Pete said. "That's what you'd do. Not me. I've been fighting people here for ten years. I'm tired of it." And with that, he walked away. Pete was fifty-seven years old and had undergone surgery for a brain tumor, which turned out to be benign. The firm was going to require him to start cashing in his stock when he turned sixty. If he could get out with a good settlement, that seemed the best option for him and his family.

I knew things weren't going to turn out well for the firm. Only months after Pete left, Lehman was in deep trouble. Lew and some of his allies in the London office had made a huge trade in commercial paper—loans to companies with no collateral. If the borrower defaults, the owner of the paper cannot lay claim to any assets. These loans can be profitable if leveraged, and they are ordinarily short term (thirty, sixty, or ninety days), which means they aren't that risky. Usually you can be sure they will be paid back over such a short period.

Lew and his team had gotten greedy in a rising market and bought notes with five-year maturity dates, which had higher interest rates, making them a lot more vulnerable. The markets turned against them and the value of the securities plummeted. Their losses on the trade amounted to more than the firm's total equity. Lehman was back on the edge of collapse.

Lew had made these trades in secret, but word started to get around, first in London, then in New York. I had heard what was going on from a good friend in the London office, Steve Bershad, who had been sent to England to build the firm's corporate finance business. He had been so disturbed by what he saw in the trading room that he had called in auditors to take a look. "The firm's busted," Steve told me on the phone. "We have no equity."

Lew called a meeting of all the partners. With over seventy of us sitting in the thirty-third-floor large conference room, he said, "I know there are rumors about some position in London. These rumors are completely false. We have no problems. And I will instantly fire anybody who says that we do!"

Instead of sharing the problem and asking for help, Lew had decided to lie. I was expecting one of the senior partners on the firm's board of directors to challenge him. Instead, they listened in silence and left the meeting whispering to each other, visibly scared and confused. Lew's leadership had proved toxic, and immediately people were wondering how they could secure their stakes in the firm before it went bankrupt. Sheldon Gordon was head of Lehman's investment banking division and the firm's vice chairman. He had worked as a trader alongside Lew. People considered him to be one of his closest allies. But I knew he was smart and decent, and I heard he was exploring options with other members of the board. I went to see him.

"You realize this is going to blow up," I said. "There are a lot of people who know Lew is lying. I know the firm's busted, you know it's busted, and if the outside world finds out we have no equity, we're going to collapse. The partners won't take him on because they're afraid he'll fire them. If we don't sell the business and somebody learns about this, don't you think we're dead?"

"Yes," he agreed. "We'll be finished."

"Do you want to sell the firm?" As the head of mergers and acquisitions, I thought I might be able to find a way for a stronger firm to step in and rescue us. Even with all our problems, Lehman was still a great firm, with a global brand and talented people.

"Absolutely," said Shel. "If this gets out we're dead and gone. But you'll need to get the thing done in a couple of days. We don't have any time here." As he spoke, I was already thinking about potential acquirers.

The first name on my list was Peter Cohen, chairman and CEO of American Express's Shearson investment unit. He was my age, one of the youngest CEOs on Wall Street. American Express had the money to buy Lehman, and I knew that Cohen was ambitious to expand Shearson into the investment banking business. He was also my next-door neighbor in the Hamptons. We knew each other socially. It would be easy enough to make a quiet overture. I called him late that Friday. The next morning, I went to see him. We met in his driveway.

"We've had a big trading loss," I explained. "We're not really looking to sell the firm, but we probably should. If you're interested, this is a one-time special—if you can act on it in the next few days." Over that weekend, he spoke to American Express's CEO, Jim Robinson. On Monday, he called and said he'd like to do a deal. He offered $360 million. Salomon Brothers had been sold two years earlier for $440 million, but Salomon had a much bigger trading business and wasn't on the verge of bankruptcy. It was the best we could get, given the time constraints.

Shel told the partners. He said they would all receive rich payouts. If they waited, they might get nothing. The other partners excluded Lew from the discussions. All but one of them, one of Lew's closest allies, approved the sale. Two days later, the deal was announced on the front page of the *New York Times*. There were still details left to negotiate and a risk it wouldn't go through. But this way, we controlled the news, and we put American Express publicly on the hook in case they had second thoughts. The day of the announcement, investors and journalists clamored for information. Lehman Brothers, founded in 1850, had been an institution on Wall Street for over 125 years. The sale was a shock.

It wasn't until the early evening that I realized I still hadn't spoken to Lew. Shel and the other partners had outflanked him. The firm had been sold, and his failure as CEO was complete. I went down to his office, Pete's old office. It was dark. I thought he must have gone home but knocked on the partially opened door.

"Hello. Is anyone here?" A small voice answered, and I could just about see Lew sitting at the end of the couch over against the wall.

"Why are you sitting in the dark?" I asked.

He said he was ashamed. He had destroyed the firm he loved. "I'm thinking about blowing my brains out."

I asked if I could sit down. He waved me over.

"Lew, you didn't intend this. Sometimes things happen that weren't intended."

"I know," he said. "But I'm responsible, so it's my fault, whatever I intended."

"You were trying to do something good, and it turned out

wrong. And it *is* a terrible outcome for the firm. But people are going to have to go on with their lives. It's going to change nothing if you kill yourself. It'll just be another tragedy on top of a tragedy, and you're not that old, you know. There's always a future. You'll reinvent yourself in some way."

We talked for half an hour or so; then I went back to my office. I was thirty-six years old, and I had sold Lehman Brothers. I was now free to leave a firm I had come to find intolerable. I felt light, exhilarated. But then there was Lew Glucksman sitting there deciding whether to shoot himself, worrying how that would affect his daughter. He loved the firm, he said. The tragedy was that he undoubtedly did.

All I wanted was to get out of Lehman as fast as I could. I had told Peter Cohen early in our negotiations that I had lost faith in Lehman's partners when they had failed to fire Lew. He had agreed that I could go. Then during the negotiations, he called and asked me to stop by. He was insisting that all of Lehman's partners sign a noncompete agreement, barring them from working for a competitor for three years if they left the firm. I told him a noncompete was irrelevant to me. He knew I was leaving.

"The problem is the American Express board met yesterday," he said. "Since Peterson left and Glucksman's effectively gone, you're the person who's best known to the board members. What they said at the meeting was that we're buying talent, and if we don't keep the talent, there's no reason to do the deal. You exemplify the talent. So they're requiring a noncompete. That's the deal. If you don't want to do the deal, don't do the deal."

"The deal's been announced," I said.

"I know it's announced. But if you don't sign your noncompete, we'll unannounce it. Your firm will go bankrupt. I don't care one way or another. You decide."

"You've got to be kidding," I said. "You and I have an agreement."

"I'm not kidding." I was the only partner who hadn't signed the noncompete. The whole deal now hinged on me. If I refused, the deal would collapse, and Lehman with it. But three years was a high price when I was so desperate to be free. Ellen said three years was no big deal, and I would figure it out. My partners swarmed me to cooperate.

The day I started at Lehman, one of the partners had told me, "Nobody at Lehman will ever stab you in the back. They'll walk right up to you and stab you in the front." It was competitive, every man for himself. I had seen that in the architecture of the place and written about it at HBS. But I had loved that about it. There was a gallows humor to all the infighting. My friend Bruce Wasserstein, when he was running mergers and acquisitions at First Boston, once said to Eric Gleacher and me, "I don't understand why all of you at Lehman Brothers hate each other. I get along with both of you." "If you were at Lehman Brothers," I told him, "we'd hate you, too."

But with Pete gone and the firm sold, I wanted to go. I knew that I could always make money somehow. I needed some space to think. I booked a room at the Ritz Carlton on Central Park South. I went for long walks in the park. And I thought until I figured out a compromise. I called Peter Cohen and proposed I stay for one year, not three, and then start my own firm instead of joining one of his large competitors. He agreed. In the end, despite what he had said, he wanted the deal as much as I did.

Once the takeover was finalized, Jim Robinson, the CEO of American Express, asked me to come and see him.

"I hope we're going to have a very productive relationship," he said. "But I've heard you're not too happy."

"Why would I be happy?" I said. "I'm working at a place I

don't want to be." He said he had known nothing of my negotiations with Peter Cohen.

"This is a pretty terrible thing we've done to you," he conceded. "Why don't you come here and take the office next to mine? It's right between me and Lou Gerstner." Gerstner was then head of American Express's travel and credit card businesses and would later be president of American Express and CEO of RJR Nabisco and then IBM. "You can work on some deals for American Express and teach Gerstner something about finance. He's an operating guy."

That seemed better than sitting over at Lehman. So I had two offices and began spending a lot of my time at American Express next to Jim Robinson. I was grateful, but he could quickly sense how eager I was to get out. He proposed I take a job in Washington to complete my noncompete period. He even arranged an interview for me with Jim Baker, then President Reagan's chief of staff.

The opportunity to spend some time in the capital appealed to me. You could not do the kind of work I had been doing in finance and not be fascinated by Washington's influence over the economy. Averell Harriman and Felix Rohatyn had convinced me of the appeal of a life at the intersection of business and politics, linking two worlds that so often operated at cross-purposes.

I'd met Jim Baker at the White House in 1982 at a meeting about stimulating the economy. The borrowing cost for even the best rated companies at the time was 16 percent. There were about twenty of us in the room, and I will never forget how scared those guys looked, worried that they would never be able to return the US economy to growth. Baker, though, was impressive, smooth, and effective in the combative world of Washington.

Our meeting went well. We discussed my being the number four person on the White House staff. Then Baker became secretary of the treasury. The only job available there was to run the government's debt issuance. It had gone unfilled for two years, so I told Jim it clearly wasn't a job that needed doing. The moment for me wasn't right.

I still had six months left, but I began negotiating my exit. I suspected it wouldn't be easy. Peter Cohen hadn't been transparent with the board about how he had gotten me to stay. I needed a lawyer in my corner, but given the size of Shearson American Express, it was hard to find anyone who would take me as a client. Finally, I found one brave attorney, Steve Volk, the lead M&A attorney at Shearman and Sterling. He would go on to be vice chairman of Citibank. His associate was Philippe Dauman, who later in life would go on to be CEO and chairman of Viacom. They listened to my story and promised to fight for me.

My hunch about Cohen turned out to be right. Despite all his promises, he had no intention of allowing me to leave. He worried I would take clients with me and that if word got out to the other partners that I had gotten a special deal, all of them might demand the same. Shearson insisted I not compete for one group of clients and give them a percentage of my fees if I did business with another. Our negotiations were long and angry, but I wanted to get out and get on with my life. Pete intervened to help us get to a final agreement. Cohen and his team failed to show up to sign the agreement not just once but twice, leaving me sitting in an empty conference room with all the closing documents on the table. When at last we did exchange signatures, the anger and resentment were palpable. It was a terrible ending to a great run, but it was also the chance for a new start.

I had learned so much about myself by then. From high school, through Yale, HBS, and time and again at Lehman, I had proved to myself that I could survive almost any situation. I could create worthy fantasies and make them real. Coach Armstrong had taught me the value of persistence, of running those extra miles and making those deposits of hard work, so they were there when I needed a withdrawal. And I had figured how to invest them to advance my career.

My early mistakes on Wall Street, the typos and calculation errors, and the embarrassment that followed, had taught me the importance of rigor, eliminating risk, and asking for help. Today on Wall Street, you can do many of the calculations with a keystroke that we used to have to do by hand. But learning the way I did, I saw the intricate ways in which deals can be structured, the subtleties that must be negotiated. Mastery like that takes experience, endurance, and tolerance for pain. And it yields the greatest rewards.

The Tropicana deal had shown me that under pressure, I was capable of far more than I ever thought. Pete Peterson had shown me the value of a great mentor and partner. I had forged some treasured relationships with wonderful people—colleagues at the firm and executives like Jack Welch who would keep popping up throughout my career. I had experienced Wall Street at its best, the highs of executing complex deals, that sense of being at the center of the universe, exchanging information with some of the most interesting people in the world.

And my exit from Lehman had shown me Wall Street at its worst, everyone for themselves. Watching the Lehman partners fail to take on Lew Glucksman had shown me how morality and ethics can buckle under fear and greed. I had seen that some people are vindictive and jealous. My experience selling Lehman and being forced to stay against my will not only taught me the worth of a good lawyer but also that money is a poor cure for a bad situation.

PURSUE WORTHY
FANTASIES

THE HARDER
THE PROBLEM,
THE MORE LIMITED
THE COMPETITION

N ow that we were free of Lehman and could work together
again, Pete and I began talking in earnest about starting
something of our own. We had our first conversation at Pete's
house in East Hampton with our wives.

"I want to work with large companies again," said Pete.
Since leaving Lehman, he had started a small firm that did
small deals.

"I just want to work with Pete again," I said. I was thirty-eight, and the money I had made at Lehman had provided for
my young family. By now, we had two children, Zibby and Teddy,
both healthy and going to great schools. We had an apartment in
the city and a house near the beach. Professionally, I had reached
a point where I wanted to start my own business. I felt I had
learned enough and acquired enough personal and professional
resources to make a success of it. Ellen, who had seen how miserable I had been during that last year at Lehman, said, "I want
Steve to be happy."

Joan, Pete's wife, was the creator of *Sesame Street*, the children's television show. She had an objective even Big Bird could understand: "I want a helicopter."

"Okay," I said. "We know what everybody wants. Now, let's go."

Many great businesses in Silicon Valley, from Hewlett Packard to Apple, have been founded in garages. In New York, we have breakfast. In April 1985, Pete and I began meeting every day in the courtyard restaurant at the Mayfair Hotel on East Sixty-Fifth Street and Park Avenue. We were the first to arrive and the last to leave, talking for hours, reflecting on our careers and thinking of what we could do together.

Our main assets were our skill sets, our experience, and our reputations. Pete was a summa cum laude, Phi Beta Kappa, process-oriented, analytic person. There was nothing he couldn't figure out through method and logic. He knew everyone in New York, Washington, and corporate America and had an easy, casual way with all of them. I considered myself more instinctive, quick to read and figure people out. I could make decisions and execute fast and was now well known as an M&A specialist. Our skills and personalities were different but complementary. We were confident that we would be good partners and people would want our services. Even if most start-ups failed, we were sure ours wouldn't.

Observing my father at Schwarzman's and all the businesses and entrepreneurs I had advised subsequently, I had reached an important conclusion about starting any business: it's as hard to start and run a small business as it is to start a big one. You will suffer the same toll financially and psychologically as you bludgeon it into existence. It's hard to raise the money and to find the right people. So if you're going to dedicate your life to a business, which is the only way it will ever work, you should choose one with the potential to be huge.

Early in my career at Lehman, I asked an older banker why it was that banks had to pay more to borrow money than similar-sized industrial companies did. "Financial institutions go broke in a day," he told me. "It can take years for an industrial company to lose its market position and go bankrupt." I had now seen that happen up close at Lehman—that sudden reversal of fortune, a bad trade, a bad investment that can destroy you in finance. We weren't going to start this journey in a tiny rowboat. We wanted to build a reputation for excellence, not bravery.

From the outset, we strived to build a financial institution strong enough to survive multiple generations of owners and leadership. We did not want to be just another of those groups on Wall Street who set up a firm, make some money, fall out, and move on. We wanted to be spoken of in the same breath as the greatest names in our industry.

What we knew best was M&A work. At the time, M&A was still the purview of the big investment banks. But we believed there would be an appetite for the services of a new kind of boutique advisory firm. We had the reputation and the track record. M&A took sweat equity but didn't require capital, and it would provide income while we figured out what else we might offer. I worried about the cyclicality of M&A and that alone it wouldn't be enough to sustain us. If the economy sputtered, so would our business. Eventually we would want steadier sources of income. But it was a good place to start. To get big, though, and build a stable, lasting institution, we would have to do much more than that.

As we sat in the Mayfair evaluating ideas, one potential line of business kept resurfacing: leveraged buyouts, or LBOs. At Lehman, I had advised Kohlberg Kravis Roberts (KKR) and Forstmann Little, the two largest LBO firms in the world. I knew

Henry Kravis and played tennis with Brian Little. Three things had struck me about their business. First, you could gather assets and earn income from recurring fees and investment profits whatever the economic climate. Second, you could really improve the companies you bought. Third, you could make a fortune.

A classic LBO works this way: An investor decides to buy a company by putting up equity, similar to the down payment on a house, and borrowing the rest, the leverage. Once acquired, the company, if public, is delisted, and its shares are taken private, the "private" in the term "private equity." The company pays the interest on its debt from its own cash flow while the investor improves various areas of a business's operations in an attempt to grow the company. The investor collects a management fee and eventually a share of the profits earned whenever the investment in monetized. The operational improvements that are implemented can range from greater efficiencies in manufacturing, energy utilization, and procurement; to new product lines and expansion into new markets; to upgraded technology; and even leadership development of the company's management team. After several years, if these efforts have proved successful and the company has grown considerably, the investor can sell it for a higher price than he or she bought it, or perhaps take the company public again, earning a profit on the original equity investment. There are a lot of variations on this basic theme.

The key to all investing is using every tool at your disposal. I liked the idea of leveraged buyouts because they seemed to offer more tools than any other form of investment. First, you looked for the right asset to buy. You did your diligence by signing nondisclosure agreements with the owners and getting access to more detailed information about what you were buying. You worked with investment bankers to create a capital structure that gave you the financial flexibility to invest and survive if economic circumstances turned against you. You put in experienced operators you trusted to improve whatever you bought. And if all went well, the debt you put in place enhanced the rate of return on the value of your equity when the time came to sell.

This type of investing would be much harder than buying stocks. It would take years of effort, excellent management, hard work, and patience and require teams of skilled experts. However, if you did this successfully over and over, you could generate significant returns and develop a record the way Coach Armstrong did at Abington High School, 186–4, and also earn the trust of your investors. The returns these investments earned for investors—pension funds, academic and charitable institutions, governments and other institutions, as well as retail investors—would also have the benefit of helping to secure and grow the retirement funds of millions of teachers, firefighters, and corporate employees, among others.

Unlike M&A, LBOs didn't require a constant stream of new clients. If we could persuade investors to put money into a fund, locked up for ten years, we then had ten years to earn management fees, improve what we bought, and turn a big profit for our investors and ourselves. If a recession hit, we could survive it and, with luck, find even more opportunities as panicked people sold good assets at low prices.

Back in 1979, I had studied the prospectus for KKR's eye-popping buyout of Houdaille Industries, one of the first big LBOs. This deal was the Rosetta Stone of buyouts. KKR had put in just 5 percent of the cash to buy Houdaille, an industrial manufacturing conglomerate, and borrowed the rest. Leverage on that scale meant the company could grow at 5 percent, but the equity would grow at 20 to 30 percent. I had been keen to do a similar deal using Lehman's resources, but I couldn't muster the internal support.

Two years later, I was the banker for the legendary media and electronics company RCA when it decided it wanted to sell Gibson Greetings, then America's third biggest greeting cards company, an asset that didn't fit with RCA's other businesses. We contacted seventy potential buyers. Only two were interested. One was Saxon Paper, which turned out to be a fraud. The other was Wesray, a small investment fund co-founded by William Simon, a former treasury secretary. Wesray offered $55 million for Gibson, and we set a date to close the deal. Wesray's investors were putting in just $1 million of their own capital but assured us they would have the rest of the money by the closing date. When they didn't, we gave them a one-month extension. Still, no money. There were no other suitors. They pleaded for one more shot. I found out later that they were trying to finance the deal by arranging to sell and then lease back Gibson's manufacturing and warehouse buildings. That would have given them the cash they needed, but they couldn't get it done. That, I thought, was that.

In the meantime, Gibson's earnings started going up. Although we hadn't yet found a qualified buyer, I recommended to Julius Koppelman, the RCA executive handling the sale, that they increase the price they were asking for Gibson. He proposed an additional $5 million. I told them that wasn't close to reflecting Gibson's value given its rising profits, but they wouldn't budge: RCA was desperate to sell and wanted the deal done. They weren't interested in getting the highest price. When RCA asked me for a fairness opinion on a $60 million sale, I refused to give one, a controversial and highly atypical stance at the time. When the deal closed six months later, Koppelman left RCA to become a consultant for Wesray. After Wesray bought Gibson, I made sure to go to Pete and Lew Glucksman to tell them what I thought of it. Wesray would make a lot of money one day, I said, and we'd be accused of incompetence. When you disagree, it's important to get your opinions on record so you aren't blamed later when things go wrong. Sixteen months later, Gibson went public, valued at $290 million, and Lehman was highly criticized by RCA's investors and the press for selling it too cheaply. Wesray had made more money on a single deal than Lehman made in a year.

Gibson was widely publicized for being one of the first successful, highly profitable leveraged buyouts. It was also the perfect case study of the type of deal Pete and I hoped to do at our new firm.

The good news was that after the Gibson IPO, LBOs had Lehman's attention. Pete, then CEO, was all in. Before his next trip to Chicago, he asked me to come up with a list of possible acquisitions. I settled on Stewart-Warner, a maker of dashboard instrument panels and the scoreboards at sports stadiums. Pete, of course, happened to know the chairman, Bennett Archambault. We met him at his men's club, an old-school place with wood paneling and moose heads all over the walls. Pete suggested he take his company private. I walked Archambault through the process: how we could raise money to buy the stock, how we could pay the interest, enhance the value, make the company work better, what it would mean over time.

"I think you can make a lot of money personally," Pete said to him. "And your shareholders can do well. Everyone can profit." Archambault got it. The existing shareholders would be paid a premium for their stake. As the head of a private company, he could improve it over the long term instead of worrying about quarterly earnings to placate the stock market. And he would end up owning a lot more of the company. "There don't seem a lot of reasons not to do it," he said.

Back at Lehman, I rushed into action. I staffed the deal and asked Dick Beattie at the Simpson Thacher law firm to start designing a fund for Lehman to do LBOs. Dick had been counsel in the Carter administration and had since become an expert on the legal intricacies of LBOs. We were confident we could raise the $175 million to take Stewart-Warner private. Pete and I moved the deal through the Lehman vetting process and brought it to the executive committee. The executive committee turned us down.

They saw an inherent conflict. They didn't feel we could give M&A advice to our clients while at the same time trying to buy companies our clients might be interested in. I understood the basics of their position. But I was sure that there must be a compromise that could properly address the potential conflicts. Fine, we couldn't buy every company we wanted. But there must be a way to buy some of them. The opportunity in this business was too big to ignore.

In the years after the executive committee rejected our idea, a wave of LBO money transformed the way America bought and sold companies. More buyers had emerged, eager to buy assets they could never afford previously. Banks were developing new kinds of debt, with higher yields or novel repayment terms, to fund their acquisitions. Corporations saw the opportunity to sell businesses they no longer wanted to buyers who could do more with them. To be taken seriously as M&A specialists, we had to master this dynamic new area of finance. But the even bigger opportunity, Pete and I thought, would be to become investors ourselves.

As M&A bankers, we would be running only a service business dependent on fees. As investors, we would have a much greater share in the financial upside of our work. In private equity firms, general partners identify, execute, and manage any investments on behalf of limited partners (LPs), the investors who entrust them with their money. The general partners put their own capital up alongside the LPs, run the investment business, and tend to be rewarded in two ways. They receive a management fee, a percentage of the capital committed by investors and subsequently put to work, and a share of the profits earned from any successful investments, the "carried interest."

The appeal of the private equity business model to a couple of entrepreneurs was that you could get to significant scale with far fewer people than you would need if you were running a purely service business. In service businesses, you need to keep adding people to grow, to take the calls and do the work. In the private equity business, the same small group of people could raise larger funds and manage ever bigger investments. You did not need hundreds of extra people to do it. Compared to most other businesses on Wall Street, private equity firms were simpler in structure, and the financial rewards were concentrated in fewer hands. But you needed skill and information to make this model work. I believed we had both and could acquire more.

The third and final way we thought about building our business was to keep challenging ourselves with an open-ended question: Why not? If we came across the right person to scale a business in a great investment class, why not? If we could apply our strengths, our network, and our resources to make that business a success, why not? Other firms, we felt, defined themselves too narrowly, limiting their ability to innovate. They were advisory firms, or investment firms, or credit firms, or real estate firms. Yet they were all pursuing financial opportunity.

Pete and I thought of the people we wanted to run these new business areas as "10 out of 10s." We had both been judging talent long enough to know a 10 when we saw one. Eights just do the stuff you tell them. Nines are great at executing and developing good strategies. You can build a winning firm with 9s. But people who are 10s sense problems, design solutions, and take the business in new directions without being told to do so. Tens always make it rain.

We imagined that once we were in business, the 10s would come to us with ideas and ask for investment and institutional support. We'd set them up in fifty-fifty partnerships and give them the opportunity to do what they did best. We'd nurture them and learn from them in the process. Having these smart, capable 10s around would inform and improve everything we did and help us pursue opportunities we couldn't even imagine yet. They would help feed and enrich the firm's knowledge base, though we still had to be smart enough to process all this data and turn it into great decisions.

The culture we would need in order to attract these 10s would by necessity contain certain contradictions. We would have to have all the advantages of scale, but also the soul of a small firm where people felt free to speak their mind. We wanted to be highly disciplined advisers and investors, but not bureaucratic or so closed to new ideas that we forgot to ask, "Why not?" Above all, we wanted to retain our capacity to innovate, even as we fought the daily battles of building our new firm. If we could attract the right people and build the right culture at this three-legged business, offering M&A, LBO investments, and new business lines, all feeding us information, we could create real value for our clients, our partners, our lenders, and ourselves.

———

Businesses often succeed and fail based on timing. Get there too early, and customers aren't ready. Arrive too late, and you'll be stuck behind a long line of competitors. The moment we started Blackstone in fall 1985, we had two major tailwinds. The first was the US economy. It was in the third year of a recovery under President Reagan. Interest rates were low, and borrowing was easy. There was plenty of capital looking for investment opportunities, and the financial industry was meeting this demand with a supply of new structures and new kinds of businesses. LBOs and high-yield bonds were part of rapid changes in the credit markets. We were also seeing the emergence of hedge funds—investment vehicles with highly technical approaches to managing risk and reward in every class of assets, from currencies to stocks. The potential of all these forms of investment was just emerging and the competition was not yet fierce. It was a good time to be trying something new.

The second major tailwind was the unraveling of Wall Street. Since its founding in the late eighteenth century, the New York Stock Exchange had operated with a fixed-price commission schedule, granting a set percentage of every trade to the broker. That system ended on May 1, 1975, on the orders of the Securities and Exchange Commission (SEC), which determined it to be a form of price fixing. Under the old system, Wall Street's brokerage firms barely had to compete and certainly hadn't had to innovate. Now that commissions had to be negotiated, price and service mattered. Technology accelerated the process, punishing the small, high-cost brokers and rewarding those who could offer better services and lower prices at scale. In the ten years since the SEC's rule change, the firms that succeeded grew larger and larger, while those that stood still eventually died.

This change transformed Wall Street's culture. When I joined Lehman in 1972, it employed 550 people. When I left, Shearson-Lehman had 20,000 (when Lehman collapsed in 2008, it had 30,000). Not everyone liked being part of these giants. You lost the intimacy of knowing everyone by sight, that sense of working for a single, coherent entity. You went from being part of a nimble team to sitting inside a huge bureaucracy. As a new associate at Lehman, I had caught the eye of Lew Glucksman, who yelled at me for not sitting up straight. But that led to someone telling him I had potential and him giving me work. That can happen in a firm of 550. With 20,000 people, it's much harder to find the good, young talent. At Lehman in the early 1970s, we had people from the CIA and the military, all kinds of different fields, who learned finance on the job. They brought a wide range of skills, perspectives, and contacts to our work. But by the mid-1980s, banks were hiring armies of MBAs who could plug in and do the work immediately.

Pete and I believed that these changes to the culture at the big firms would lead to a shake-out of great people and great ideas. If they were anything like us, they would be searching for ways out. We wanted to be ready for them.

For months, we agonized over what to call ourselves. I liked "Peterson and Schwarzman," but Pete had already set up a couple of businesses that included his name and didn't want to use it again. He preferred something neutral so that if we added new partners, we wouldn't have to argue about adding their names. We didn't want to become one of those ungainly law firms with five names on the letterhead. I asked everyone I knew for suggestions. Pete's wife, Joan, talked sense into us: "When I started my business I couldn't think of a name. In the end, we just invented one: 'Sesame Street.' What a stupid name that is. Now it's in 180 countries all over the world. If your business fails, nobody will remember your name. If your business succeeds, everyone will know it. So just pick something, get on with it, and hope you succeed enough to be known."

Ellen's stepfather came up with the answer. He was the chief rabbi for the Air Force and a Talmudic scholar. He proposed we draw on the English translations of our two names. The German *schwarz* means black. Pete's father's original Greek name was "Petropoulos." *Petros* means stone or rock. We could be Blackstone or Blackrock. I preferred Blackstone. Pete was happy to go along.

After months of talking, we had a name and a plan to be a distinctive firm composed of three businesses: M&A, buyouts, and new business lines. Our culture would attract the best people and provide extraordinary value for our clients. We were hitting the market at the right time and had the potential to be huge.

We each put up $200,000 in capital—enough to get started, but not so much that we could be spendthrift. We took three thousand square feet at 375 Park Avenue, the Seagram building just north of Grand Central Station. The building was open, modern, and architecturally significant, designed by Ludwig Mies van der Rohe, the pioneering modernist architect. It was in midtown, far from Wall Street, but near many corporate offices. It was also in the same building as the Four Seasons restaurant, a famous networking location. In 1979, *Esquire* magazine had described it as the birthplace of the "power lunch." It would be easy for Pete to work his many corporate contacts. Had I used us as an exhibit in my business school thesis on the architecture of financial firms, I would have noted that we were straining for prestige.

We bought some furniture, hired a secretary, and divided up our roles. Pete had been a CEO twice before and told me that he didn't want the hassle of running a business again. He asked me to take the CEO role but with the title of president. One of my first acts was to design our logo and our business cards. I hired a design firm, had them come up with alternatives, and spent an enormous amount of time going over them. The design we chose is the one we still have: simple, black and white, clean, and respectable. I thought the time and money we spent when both were scarce were essential to getting this right. When you're presenting yourself, the whole picture has to make sense, the entire, integrated approach that gives other people cues and clues as to who you are. The wrong aesthetics can set everything off kilter. Our business cards were an early step in establishing who we wanted to be.

On October 29, 1985, six months after we had started having our breakfasts at the Mayfair, we took out a full-page ad in the *New York Times* and announced ourselves to the world:

WE ARE PLEASED TO ANNOUNCE

THE FORMATION OF

THE BLACKSTONE GROUP

A PRIVATE INVESTMENT BANKING FIRM

PETER G. PETERSON, CHAIRMAN
STEPHEN A. SCHWARZMAN, PRESIDENT

375 PARK AVENUE, NEW YORK, NY 10152
(212) 486-8500

CALL, THEN
KEEP CALLING

To get business rolling, we wrote to everyone we knew—more than four hundred cheerful letters introducing our new firm. We wrote about our track records and reminisced about the business we had done together. We laid out our plans and asked for work. Then we sat back and waited. I was expecting the phone to ring nonstop. But on the few occasions it did ring, it was only to congratulate us and wish us luck.

"How about some business?" I would ask.

"Not right now. But we'll think about you in the future."

The day after our advertisement appeared in the *New York Times*, I heard a knock at the door. I opened it to find a guy in leather pants, a black motorcycle jacket, and a little peaked leather motorcycle hat. We were waiting to hear from our familiar M&A clients, but we got the gang leader from *The Wild Ones*.

"Is there a Steve Schwarzman here?" he said.

"What are you delivering?"

"I'm not delivering anything. My name is Sam Zell. Leah told me I should meet you." In 1979, we had hired Leah Zell at Lehman. She had been an English major at Harvard and had just gotten a PhD. After talking with her for a few minutes, it was obvious she had an exceptional mind. Though she knew nothing about finance, I had decided to give her a chance. She had proved to be a terrific analyst. This biker was her brother.

"What's with the outfit?" I said.

"I left my motorcycle downstairs."

"Where downstairs?"

"I chained it up on Park Avenue," he said. "To a hydrant."

Our first day. *This is some future*, I thought.

He must have thought the same thing looking at me sitting there in my suit in our bare office, the phones silent.

"Look, I'm sorry. We just moved in today. We've hardly got any furniture yet."

"That's okay," said Sam. He sat on the floor, leaned against the wall, against our rolled-up rug, and began to talk. He owned some real estate and wanted to buy some companies, but he didn't know much about finance. "Why don't you teach me?" he said.

I later found out that I shouldn't have been misled by the outfit. Sam's version of "owning some real estate" meant he was building one of the largest portfolios of real estate in the country. All he told me that day was he bought bankrupt properties and wanted to build an empire. We spent two and a half hours sitting on the floor talking. In the years to come, we would do a lot of business together. This one unexpected visitor turned out to be worth more to Blackstone than all the clients we expected in those early days who never came.

To coincide with our launch, the *Wall Street Journal* had planned to run a major front-page article about our new firm—publicity that would have been a huge boost for our new business. The day before it was supposed to run, the reporter called to tell me his editors were yanking it. He apologized. "The Shearson people heard we were doing it," he said. "They called us up and said you were fired for a variety of bad reasons. We didn't feel we could run the piece if Shearson told us on background that you're a bad guy."

I should have known our launch would rile Shearson. I had wanted out of Lehman because the ethics there had become so awful—the greed, the fear, the gutlessness, the hunger for power, the dishonesty. But this counterattack was a new low. I sat there in our bare office with boxes of office equipment scattered around. How could people be so vindictive?

Despite these setbacks, we were still confident enough to think that our reputations, our experience, and those hundreds of letters would bring in a flood of business. Weeks passed. Nothing. Pete had a secretary who was drawing a salary. I was making my own calls and taking deliveries at the front door. Every day I would look around the space we had rented. It felt like watching an hourglass, the money just draining out as the business never came. Not so long ago, people fought to have us work for them. Pete and I hadn't changed, but now that we were out on our own, no one cared about us. As the days ticked by, I worried we would be just another failed start-up.

Finally, Squibb Beech-Nut, a pharma company we had worked with at Lehman, hired us for an advisory job for $50,000. In my previous life, that would have been less than the legal fees on a single deal. It was now a lifeline. Then another small job came in, from Armco, a medium-sized steel company in the Midwest and a client at Lehman. We were covering our rent and other basic costs, but we were still on the edge. By then it was the early summer 1986, and we had been in business for nine months. Pete was away, my family was at the beach, and I was alone in Manhattan working on these two insignificant pieces of business.

One sweltering evening, I went for dinner alone to a Japanese restaurant on the second floor of a building on Lexington Avenue in the thirties. As I was sitting there, I began to feel dizzy, as if my whole body wanted to collapse. I felt I was failing on every count. I was overwhelmed by self-pity. Wall Street loves nothing more than watching other people fail. To see Pete and me, who had been so powerful at Lehman, so sure of our success, take a beating would have given many people pleasure. I couldn't let it happen. I could not fail. I had to find a way.

———

Here, I realized, was a great truth. For all that we had accomplished, we were a start-up. There would be no easy jobs. What I didn't know was that all the grunt work, the hours I had spent in my career building my own financial models with a pencil and slide rule, learning the craft of finance from my colleagues, was about to prove invaluable.

Shortly after my lonely Japanese dinner, Hays Watkins, the chief executive of CSX, a large railroad company, called us. In 1978, I had overseen the sale of a newspaper company that CSX owned. The standard sale would have involved an English auction—the kind you see in auction houses where the bidders raise their hands, increasing their offers incrementally, until the second highest bidder drops out. All you have to do to win is bid a dollar more than the next bidder. The problem with these auctions is that you never know what the winner might have been willing to pay. Someone might buy a Van Gogh painting for $50 million, but perhaps if there had been another bidder, the buyer could have been pushed up to $75 million.

For CSX's newspapers, I had staged a two-round sealed-bid auction. In each round, the bidders submitted their bids in a sealed envelope, not knowing what others were offering. The first round weeded out the low bids, the people just fishing. The serious buyers then got to review the target company's financials and visit with management. After that they submitted another sealed bid. The magic of this kind of auction is that if the buyers are desperate to acquire the asset, they won't just try to offer a dollar more than the second-highest bidder. They will offer the highest price they can afford to ensure they win. This style of auction was little known in the M&A world when I began doing it, but it has since become standard practice. Watkins said he remembered me as an innovator and problem solver.

"We have a project," Watkins said. "We're just starting on it. We thought maybe you could work on it." Maybe we could work on it? We were sitting around worrying about going broke. But I knew that he wouldn't have come to us if the situation were simple. There were lots of advisers who could help. Watkins had a difficult problem, and he wanted an inventive solution. As an investment banker and later as an investor, I found that the harder the problem, the more limited the competition. If something's easy, there will always be plenty of people willing to help solve it. But find a real mess, and there is no one around. If you can clean it up, you will find yourself in rare company. People with tough problems will seek you out and pay you handsomely to solve them. You will earn a reputation for doing what others cannot. For a pair of entrepreneurs trying to break through, solving hard problems was going to be the best way of proving ourselves.

CSX wanted to expand into ocean shipping and had made a friendly and generous offer to buy Sea-Land Corporation, a container company. The management of Sea-Land was keen to accept it, but they were being held up by Harold Simmons, a crusty Texan investor. Simmons had no interest in owning Sea-Land. But he had been buying stock in anticipation of an outside acquisition, intending to hold up any sale until he got the price he wanted. He wanted to be overpaid to go away. The finance industry calls this practice "greenmail."

CSX's initial offer was a reasonable $655 million. At Lehman,

I'd have had a whole team to support me on a deal this size. Now I had to handle this work alone. Simmons owned 39 percent of the stock in Sea-Land. We couldn't force him to sell, but at the price CSX was offering, Simmons would have made a handsome profit. Still, he was in a strong position to hold out for more. I spoke to him on the phone, explaining how much he stood to make based on the current offer. I can still hear his Texan accent: "Mr. Schwarzman, Ah've told you many times already, Ah am *not* selling my shares. Ah am *not!*" I tried everything to persuade him, until I decided to fly down to see him with our attorney.

Simmons was thin, lanky, with a pock-marked face. He was in his mid-fifties but looked much older. His office gave no hint of his considerable wealth. It was in a cheap building outside Houston, the interior walls covered with peeling wood veneer.

"We'd really like to buy this business, and you're sort of getting in the way," I said. "We'd like you to move aside. We'd like to buy your stock. As you know, we're offering a premium."

"Ah know what you want," he said. "Ah've told you, mah stock is not for sale."

"I thought you were going to say that," I said. "So I've prepared a special arrangement I'm making available for stockholders who don't want to participate in our tender offer." He was the only one. "If you don't want the cash, I'm going to substitute a private issue, PIK [payment in kind, i.e., not cash] preferred stock with no maturity date."

What this proposal meant was that he could either take the cash, or we were going to turn his asset into a serious liability. If he wanted to take CSX hostage, I was going to do the same to him by using the tender offer to force a merger and freeze him out. His preferred stock wouldn't be listed on any exchange, so he wouldn't be able to sell it easily. It would also be junior to corporate debt in the capital structure, so if anything went wrong, he wouldn't get paid until after the creditors. And with no maturity date, he would never even have a chance to redeem his stock because it would never come due. He would just be stuck holding stock that generated ever-increasing tax bills for the indefinite future. The proposition was detestable and highly unusual.

Simmons looked at me, then looked at his lawyer. "They can do this?" Simmons asked.

"Mmmh hmm," the lawyer said bobbing his head up and down. "They can do it."

Simmons turned to me. "Get the hell out of my conference room!" My attorney and I walked out, got into the car, and drove back to the airport. From the pay phone in the lounge, I called my secretary. Simmons had just called to tell me he'd be selling his stock.

If the job had been easy, we would never have gotten it. It required creativity and psychological insight to identify Simmons's weakness and nerve to confront him with our solution to CSX's problem. This assignment was a breakthrough for us. It was the first major fee we received for our advisory business, and it made Blackstone's name as an M&A shop.

After we wrapped it up, Hays told me he was bringing in Salomon Brothers for a fairness opinion on the price they had paid. I had written dozens of fairness opinions at Lehman since my first assignment for Herman Kahn. I told Hays he didn't need Salomon. We could do it for him. I knew Sea-Land and CSX, having just done the deal. Hays agreed. I even waived the fee. Blackstone became the first major boutique advisory firm to write a fairness opinion.

In fall 1986, as we neared our first anniversary, we decided it was time to set about raising our first buyout fund. We would need to convince investors we could take their money; buy, fix, and sell businesses; and return their money to them with a substantial profit after several years. It was step two of our business plan: going from providing advice and transaction services to the more complex but (we hoped) more durable and profitable business of investing. Neither Pete nor I had ever run such a fund, let alone raised money for one. Though we tended to agree on everything, we disagreed on how much we ought to pursue.

I thought we should raise a billion dollars for our first fund, which would make it by far the biggest first-time fund ever launched. Pete thought I was dreaming.

"We've never done a single private equity deal," he said. "And neither of us has ever raised *any* investment money for ourselves."

"So what?" I said. "I know the guys who do this stuff. I represented them at Lehman. I've been in the room." If they could do it, I assured Pete, we could.

"It doesn't trouble you that we haven't done a deal yet?"

"No, it doesn't."

"It does me," said Pete. "I think we should start with a $50 million fund, learn what we're doing, and then do something bigger."

I told Pete I disagreed for two reasons. First, when investors put money in a fund, they want to know that theirs isn't the only money. So if you're raising a $50 million fund, chances are you'll have to raise it in increments of $5 to $10 million. And if you're going to all the bother of raising $5 to $10 million, you may as well save yourself some legwork and ask for $50 to $100 million. Second, investors would expect us to build a diversified portfolio. With only $50 million in hand, we'd have to do a series of tiny deals to get there. Since our expertise was in working with big corporations, tiny deals made no sense.

Pete was still apprehensive. "Why would somebody give us money when we've never done anything?" he asked.

"Because it's us. And because it's a moment."

When I began my career, I was like most other ambitious young people: I believed success was achieved in a straight line. As a baby boomer, I had grown up seeing only growth and opportunity. Success seemed a given. But working through the economic ups and downs of the 1970s and early 1980s, I had come to understand that success is about taking advantage of those rare moments of opportunity that you can't predict but come to you provided you're alert and open to major changes.

Demand for LBO deals was rising among investors, but the supply was limited and the people who could execute them even more so. It was the perfect scenario for a pair of entrepreneurs with our particular skills. Years earlier at Lehman, we couldn't get the bank's executive committee interested in LBOs. We were ahead of their conventional thinking. Now, if we waited any longer, we risked being too late. Others would attract the eager money looking for ways into buyout deals.

"I'm convinced that now is the right moment for us to raise a fund and that moment may never reappear for us," I told Pete. "We've got to hit it."

As a salesman, I'd learned you can't just pitch once and be done. Just because you believe in something doesn't guarantee anyone else will. You've got to sell your vision over and over again. Most people don't like change, and you have to overwhelm them with your argument, and some charm. If you believe in what you're selling and they say no, you have to presume that they don't fully understand, so you give them another opportunity. After many discussions, Pete, in his own way, gave in.

"If you feel that strongly, I'll sign on for it."

GO WHERE
OTHERS AREN'T

We honed our proposal into an offering memorandum— the legal document that explains the terms, risks, and objectives of an investment—and sent it to nearly five hundred potential investors: pension funds, insurance companies, endowments, banks, other financial institutions, and some wealthy families. We made calls and wrote follow-up letters. Once again, our telephones went quiet. We made the mistake of trying out our half-formed pitch on our best prospects, the people we knew best. Rather than being forgiving, they found it all too easy to turn us down. We received just two invitations to meet. Met Life committed $50 million and New York Life $25 million, but only if their investments did not exceed 10 percent and 5 percent of the fund, respectively. Until we raised at least $500 million, their commitments were worthless.

Pete suggested we wait a couple of weeks before making more follow-up calls and refine our approach. This time, I deferred to his counsel. Second time around, we had a better feel for our pitch and arranged meetings with eighteen potential investors.

The Equitable Insurance Company brought us in for two meetings, ten days apart. When we were called back, we hoped it was just a question of signing them up. At the second meeting, the person we had seen just ten days earlier didn't even recognize us. "Blackstone?" he said. He couldn't remember anything about us. It wasn't even a scheduling error. Pete and I left not just deflated but confused. Were we so irrelevant that people couldn't even remember who we were?

Delta Airlines's investment fund agreed to meet us if we came to their office in Atlanta. The night before our 9:00 a.m. appointment, Pete had attended dinner at the White House. I met him at Atlanta's Hartsfield-Jackson airport and we took a cab to our meeting. Pete always had a giant briefcase with him and now also carried a tuxedo bag. When we got out of the taxi, we were still several hundred yards from the Delta building, which was set back from the road. It was hot and humid. I helped Pete lug his bags. By the time we arrived, we were both sweating through our shirts.

A secretary took us down to the second-level basement, not up to the executive floors. The cinderblock walls were painted a bilious green. Pete and I were sticky and disheveled but did our best to straighten up. Inside the small conference room, we were offered coffee. Pete said no; hot coffee on a hot day didn't sound great. *We're in the South*, I thought. *We should be gracious.* So I said yes. Our host went over to a card table with a hot plate and a metal coffee carafe and poured me out a brown cup with a white plastic insert. "That'll be twenty-five cents for the coffee kitty." I dug into my pocket for a quarter.

We were trying to get $10 million from these people. They had read the material and invited us down. We were offering the kind of fund they usually invested in. We went through our presentation with all of our usual enthusiasm, emphasizing our expertise, our contacts, and the opportunities we saw in the markets. When we finished, I asked the executive who had poured me the coffee, "Do you find this of interest?"

"Oh, yes. Quite interesting, but Delta doesn't invest in first-time funds."

"You knew we're a first-time fund. Why did you ask us all the way to Atlanta?"

"Because you're both famous people in finance and we wanted to meet you."

When we left, it was steamier than when we arrived. We dragged our bags back toward the road. Halfway there, Pete looked at me and said, "If you ever do that to me again, I'm going to kill you."

The rejections were horrible and humbling. The setbacks seemed endless. We met people who lied to us or never showed up for appointments even after we had traveled across the country. People we knew well in positions of authority rejected us. Pete and I talked throughout these struggles. He was not someone who failed. He hated failure. But at the same time, he was sixty years old. He was at a different place than I was, with a different mentality. If I had the drive, he had the patience and equanimity. He picked me up and kept me going. He assured me that when you believe in what you're doing, overwhelmed or not, you have to keep moving forward, even when the quest feels hopeless. Which it did.

Pete was from an immigrant family. His parents had come to the United States from Greece and opened a restaurant in Kearney, Nebraska, where Pete worked as a boy. He went to college and graduate school and made his way in business thanks to his intelligence and personal skills. He understood the journey I was on, the need I had to make this work. It had been his journey too. We were just on different schedules.

"This is a high hill," he would tell me before a meeting. "This is really pushing it." But then he'd suck it up, and we'd go off to meet the next investor, where we'd get shot down again.

Six months after we started and had met almost every prospect who would see us, we hadn't raised a dollar since our original pledges from New York Life and Met Life. We were nearing the end of our list of eighteen when we reached Prudential. Prudential was the number one financier of leveraged buyouts, the gold standard. We didn't know anyone there well, so we had saved their meeting to be one of our last. By then we would have our pitch perfected. Garnett Keith, Prudential's vice chairman and chief investment officer, invited us for lunch in Newark, New Jersey.

As I began talking, Garnett took his first bite of a tuna sandwich on white bread, cut diagonally. As I spoke, he would bite off some more, chew, swallow, and not say a word. His jaw would move, his Adam's apple roll up and down. By the time he was three-quarters of the way through his sandwich, I had said all I had to say. Garnett put down the last quarter of his sandwich, stopped chewing, and spoke: "You know, that's interesting. Put me down for 100."

It was so sudden, so casual. There was nothing legal I wouldn't have done for that $100 million. If Prudential thought it was a good idea to invest with us, others would follow. I wanted to reach over and snatch away the last quarter of that sandwich to make sure Garnett didn't choke on it.

We were on our way.

———

After Prudential's commitment, Pete went to Japan as a speaker at the Shimoda Conference, a gathering of Japan's corporate establishment. He suggested mixing in some fundraising. In 1987, Japanese industrial companies were buying large numbers of American assets. Japan's brokerage firms, we figured, would follow, seeking opportunities in the US capital markets.

There were four large Japanese brokerages: Nomura, Nikko, Daiwa, and Yamaichi. We didn't have contacts at any of them and needed representation. I went to Bruce Wasserstein and Joe Perella, two of the top investment bankers at First Boston. They had excellent relations in Japan. Joe had been a friend since we were in the same class at Harvard Business School. Bruce and I had encountered each other regularly in deals, and we played tennis on weekends in the Hamptons. They set us up with one of their bankers who knew the Japanese market.

But when I laid out my plans to him, he told me there was no point approaching the brokerages because they never invested in our kind of fund. I asked him to try. He refused. Only when I threatened to fire him did he arrange a meeting with Nomura and Nikko Securities, a firm that was opening an office in New York. At Nikko, the Japanese barely spoke English. They looked disoriented. They hadn't a clue about American corporations or investing. I asked them what they were doing here. They told me they were hoping to do some M&A. As respectfully as I could, I told them they had no chance of succeeding in American M&A assignments if they didn't speak decent English. But a thought occurred to me on the spot. Why not form a joint venture? They could bring the Japanese companies to America, and Blackstone could work with them. A fifty-fifty split of revenues on condition they also invested in our first fund.

It was a creative way for both of us to get what we wanted. We needed money for our fund; they needed to build their M&A business. People in a tough spot will often focus on their own problems when the answer may lie in fixing someone else's. By paying attention to Nikko's needs rather than ours, a possible solution had materialized for both of us.

"Right now," I told them, "you're going to get 100 percent of no money. You're going to fail. I can make you successful. All I want is for you to invest in our fund. That's all I care about. You'll make plenty of money with it. But what's important for you isn't the investment. It's what I can do for you." They liked the idea in principle, and we agreed to meet in Japan.

A week later, Pete, a representative from First Boston, and I went to Nikko's Tokyo headquarters to meet with Yasuo Kanzaki, who ran its international business. The prospect of Blackstone working with Nikko to serve Japanese clients coming to America looking for acquisitions delighted him. "I know we will never be successful in America with our own people," he said. I thanked him and told him that in addition to the joint venture, we wanted him to invest in our fund. I explained our investment strategy and said I knew my pitch was most unusual.

"I will talk to my colleagues on our executive committee. I have only one request. Do not go to see Nomura before we make a decision." Nomura was their main competitor, the largest of Japan's brokerages. Nikko was a distant number two. We agreed. The next day Pete and I woke early for the rest of the meetings. Woozy from jet lag, we both fell asleep in the back seat of the car. When we stopped, I woke up and looked out the window and saw the sign on the building: Nomura.

"What are we doing here?" I said to the rep. "Didn't we tell you yesterday we can't go to Nomura?"

"It's on the schedule," he said.

"Then tell us how we handle this situation. We promised Nikko we're not going to meet Nomura. We can't make a promise then break it."

"But you can't insult Nomura. They're the most important broker. You have an appointment with the executive vice president for international business, the same as the other guy."

"We can't be in this position," I said. "What are our options?"

"You could cancel, but that would be bad manners. You could go and have a nonmeeting meeting, and hope that Nikko doesn't find out, where you present nothing, like just a courtesy call. Or you can go make your presentation."

None of these options seemed great. We needed to stop floundering. "We've got to call the guy at Nikko and tell him what's going on and get his advice. We don't know the customs here, and we don't want to offend him," I told Pete. He agreed and made the call. We had one of those giant built-in phones in the car, and we both pressed our ears to the handset, practically kissing each other, so that we could hear Yasuo Kanzaki. We explained that by accident, we were parked outside Nomura. We could hear that sound Japanese people often make when they don't like something, sucking air in between his teeth.

"You're at Nomura now?"

"It's a mistake," I said. "We're sorry. We haven't gone in, and we're asking your advice. What should we do? Should we just cancel the appointment? Have a nonmeeting meeting? We don't want to do anything that will offend you."

"Okay," Kanzaki said. "Nikko is very interested. How much money do you want for your fund?"

Pete covered up the phone and whispered. "Fifty?"

"A hundred," I whispered. "It's what we got from Prudential."

"We're looking for $100 million," said Pete.

"Okay, no problem. $100 million. We have a deal. Now you can go to Nomura and have a nonmeeting." As we hung up, I murmured to Pete: "We should have asked for $150 million." Recalling this on my sixtieth birthday, Pete said that one of my unique qualities is that my "goals are so demanding and dynamic that sometimes it is even hard for me to accept yes for an answer."

Inside at the reception desk, we asked for Junko Nakagawa, head of Nomura's international investments. There was a lot of muttering and confusion until they found someone who spoke

English. "I'm so sorry," he said. "You are not at Nomura head-quarters. You are at a brokerage branch."

We were half an hour late for a nonmeeting we didn't want in a country where being late is a gross discourtesy. We raced to the Nomura headquarters, asked for Mr. Nakagawa, and apologized.

Fifteen minutes passed. Very un-Japanese. Finally someone came. "I'm sorry," he said. "Mr. Nakagawa is not in Tokyo today. There must have been a mistake with the appointment. But I'm the general manager. I'm no one really, but I can have a courtesy meeting with you." Which is what we did: a nonmeeting courtesy meeting, during which all we could think of was the $100 million from Nikko.

Their pledge transformed our fortunes. Nikko was the investment bank for the Mitsubishi group, Japan's largest *zaibatsu*, or family of related companies. Once Nikko said yes, all the other companies in the zaibatsu said yes too. Everywhere we made our pitch, people said yes. I loved Japan. After months of rejections, we couldn't stop selling. We flew home with a further $325 million in our fund. Our luck flew home with us.

For months, I had been pitching General Motors's pension fund, the biggest in America at the time. I had come at them five times through different people in different ways, but kept getting the same answer: we lacked a track record. Then one of the partners at First Boston introduced me to Tom Dobrowski in GM's real estate division, whom he knew through his church.

When I met Tom, he was wearing Sunday school medals. Strange for an adult, I thought. But my First Boston colleague was right. Tom was smart, and we hit it off. After listening to Pete and me make our pitch, he said, "Jeez, that's really interesting. Maybe we *should* do something with you guys." GM came through with $100 million.

We were rolling. It was as if all the lights along the way had been switched from red to green. I called my old friend Jack Welch, now CEO of General Electric.

"You guys don't know what you're doing, do you?" Jack said.

"No," I said, "but it's us. We're the same."

"Yeah, yeah, yeah. I love you guys. Listen, I'll give you $35 million. Why? Because you are great, both of you. That way you can use the GE name to help get some other people. Maybe we'll do some business together. Wouldn't surprise me."

When we got up close to $800 million, we began to run short on possibilities. I'd wanted a billion. But it had been a year since we had sent out our initial placement memoranda, a year that had felt like *The Perils of Pauline*, one heart-stopping event after another. We had persevered through rejection, disappointment, and despair.

There is a saying in finance that time wounds all deals. The longer you wait, the more nasty surprises can hurt you. I like to finish work quickly. Even if tasks are not urgent, I like to get them done to avoid the unnecessary risks of delay. I determined to do the same with the fund. By September 1987, stock markets were hitting record highs, and I did not want to get caught if they turned. We decided to push hard to close the fund and wrap up the legal details as soon as possible.

Each of our thirty-three investors had a team of lawyers, and each lawyer wanted everything done right. It was like fighting thirty-three fights in thirty-three foreign countries all at the same time. But we pushed hard to have everything signed and sealed by Thursday, October 15, and we did it. Caroline James, our only associate, who was handling the closing, left soon afterward to become a therapist. She would have a lifetime of case material just from working with me on the closing.

I arrived at the office after the weekend, on the morning of Monday, October 19, with our fund closed and the money committed. That day, the Dow dropped 508 points, the largest one-day percentage drop in stock market history, bigger than the one that triggered the Great Depression. If we had taken an extra day or two to close the fund, we would have been caught in the downdraft of Black Monday. The money could have slipped away, all our efforts gone to waste. Our urgency had saved us. We were ready to start investing.

DON'T MISS THE CAN'T
MISS OPPORTUNITIES

O ur first leveraged buyout was the kind of large, complex but potentially rewarding deal we had sought. The kind of situation begging for a solution where conventional wisdom had thinned the field. Since we weren't yet either the biggest or the best in our business, we had to pick spots where the problems were toughest and we were the only ones offering a way forward.

USX started as U.S. Steel, the company created in 1901 by J. P. Morgan when he bought Carnegie Steel from Andrew Carnegie and his partners, including Henry Clay Frick, in what was then the biggest leveraged buyout in history. By 1987, U.S. Steel had been an iconic American name for more than three-quarters of a century. But steel production was vulnerable to sharp rises and falls in commodity prices and fluctuating demand from customers. The company had diversified into energy, buying Marathon Oil, and changed its name to USX. But its problems were multiplying. A labor strike paralyzed its plants, and Carl Icahn, a corporate raider in the Harold Simmons mold, had bought enough shares to launch a proxy action or a hostile takeover bid. He had demanded the company make changes to raise the share price. Management decided it would rather pay him off than do what he wanted. To raise the greenmail money, they planned to sell the railroads and barges they used to transport their raw materials and their finished steel, divesting them into a separate company. That was the business we were going to buy.

From the start of Blackstone, Pete and I had agreed that we would never do hostile deals. We believed that businesses were made up of people who deserved to be treated with respect. If all you did as an acquirer was slash costs and take out money until a business collapsed, you would be hurting employees, families, and their communities. Your reputation would suffer, and decent investors would be scared off. But if you invested in improving the companies you bought, not only would their employees benefit from working for a stronger company, but your reputation would be enhanced and you would earn much higher long-term returns—"Friendly Transactions in a Hostile Environment," as we put it in a *Wall Street Journal* advertisement. USX would test that.

If Carl Icahn hadn't come along, USX would not have been trying to sell its transport system. The company depended on this network, from freighters on the Great Lakes to barges in the South, with railroads in between to haul iron ore, coal, and coke into their plants and take the finished steel products out to customers. They wanted the money from divesting it but feared losing control.

To us, the transport system looked like a good asset going through a bad time. The steel strike had idled the railroads and barges. They were generating no income. But the strike would be settled eventually, and we thought the trains and shipping would get back to making a significant profit. The deal could be good for both sides, provided USX trusted us to respect their concerns. Trust would be at the heart of the negotiation.

Roger Altman, who had just joined Blackstone as vice chairman, brought us the deal. He had gone from being co-head of investment banking at Lehman to the assistant secretary in the

US Treasury under President Carter, and would later serve as deputy secretary under President Clinton. When Pete, Roger, and I went to the headquarters of USX in Pittsburgh, our main goal was to satisfy the company's managers that we could be good partners. We were not Carl Icahn; we were a friendly buyer. But it was one thing for us to say it, another to demonstrate our intent through the deal's terms.

We proposed a partnership in which we would buy 51 percent of the transportation business and USX would keep the rest. By selling over 50 percent, USX would relinquish responsibility for the business's debts, making their own balance sheet considerably healthier and boosting the value of their stock. But to reassure them that this wouldn't come at the cost of losing control of their essential transport network, we proposed a five-person board with two directors from our side, two from theirs, and an arbitrator, whom we would agree on, would attend all board meetings, and would serve as the tie-breaking vote. They liked our price: $650 million.

Now we had to find the money. Though we had raised an $850 million fund, our intent was to do as many deals as possible with that money. The less equity we used in each deal, the more deals we could take on, borrowing the balance of what we needed from banks. We could use our entire $850 million to buy one $850 million asset, taking on no debt, or treat it as a 10 percent down payment on $8.5 billion worth of assets, borrowing the rest. The second option, assuming we borrowed responsibly, had the potential for much higher returns. Safety also demanded diversification.

I called the banks then financing leveraged buyouts, but all I heard back was, "We don't like steel. We don't like strikes. Everybody in steel goes broke ultimately. Steel is a nonstarter. So, no." I told them they were wrong. We had analyzed the opportunity in depth. Steel was a commodity, vulnerable to shifts in the price of its inputs, iron ore, coal, and nickel, and supply and demand in the market. The price for shipping steel, though, was based on volume, and the Interstate Commerce Commission set the tariffs. For every ton you shipped, you were paid a certain amount. Once steel started moving again, even at lower prices, the transport business would rally. "No," said the banks, still confused by the difference. "It's all the steel business."

If steel was a red flag and strikes were a red flag, so was our inexperience. Only two banks showed the slightest interest: JPMorgan and Chemical Bank. I wanted JPMorgan, the most prestigious commercial bank in the United States. Its name would boost our standing and help build the Blackstone brand. Plus, going back to J. P. Morgan himself, the bank knew steel. They had made their fortune in steel. I was thrilled they were willing to do the deal until I heard their terms: they wanted to charge an unusually high rate of interest and wouldn't put up their own money to underwrite it. When banks issue loans to companies, they typically raise the money by raising money from other banks as well. But they also underwrite the transaction, promising to cover the balance if investors don't buy all the securities. If a bank won't underwrite its own transaction, that hesitation typically signals a lack of faith in the deal.

I challenged them. They said that for JPMorgan to put its name on a deal was as good as underwriting it. But if it's as good as underwriting it, I asked, why not just underwrite it? That would guarantee us the money. They told me not to worry. They were JPMorgan. But their explanation didn't ring true. They were clearly worried about something and not telling me. When I pushed them, they said, "Don't work with us, then. It doesn't make any difference to us. JPMorgan does not change its approach. That's how we do business."

I hadn't wanted to go to Chemical Bank. It was not the prestigious banking partner I had in mind. It was known as "Comical Bank," the sixth or seventh largest bank in the United States, always striving but never quite achieving. But JPMorgan had proved so rigid and condescending, I had no choice. Like us, Chemical had never done an LBO. And also like us, they wanted to get one done. They turned out to be the opposite of JPMorgan: enthusiastic, entrepreneurial, open, and collaborative. At our first meeting, Walt Shipley, the bank's CEO; Bill Harrison, the head of corporate lending; and an investment banker my own age, Jimmy Lee, all greeted me. They had studied our proposal, examined our needs, and lined up an excellent package. The interest rate they planned to charge would fall as the steel strikes ended and the transport business picked up. It made sense. As the business got healthier, the company would seem less risky to lenders, and the interest rate we paid would change to reflect that. They also promised to underwrite the entire deal themselves. "Our underwriting, our money," they said.

I went back to Pete feeling torn. I liked the team at Chemical Bank—their creativity and energy. Their promise to underwrite the whole deal meant we would get all the money we needed the moment we signed. No risk at all. But I was still hung up on JPMorgan. I gave them one more chance to meet Chemical Bank's offer. When they passed, I went back to Shipley, Harrison, and Lee, the three "Comical Bears." We shook hands.

We carved the transportation division out of USX and called it Transtar. Blackstone put in $13.4 million in equity; USX put up $125 million in vendor financing, lending us money to take the division off their hands; and Chemical raised the rest. It proved to be a phenomenal deal. The market for steel did recover, as we predicted. The transport business came back, and the investments we made in Transtar improved its cash flow. Within two years, we had made nearly four times our equity. By 2003, when we sold our final stake in the business, we had made a total return of twenty-six times our investment, or 130 percent a year.

For the next fifteen years, we financed almost every deal with Chemical Bank. Our businesses grew together. The erstwhile Comical went on to swallow Manufacturers Hanover, Bank One, Chase Manhattan, and eventually JPMorgan itself, whose name they adopted. Walt Shipley became CEO of Chase Manhattan, Bill Harrison CEO of JPMorgan Chase, and Jimmy Lee its head of investment banking and my best friend in business. In all our years of collaboration, we never lost a dime together. Pete was happy, I was happy, the three Comical Bears were happy. We had gotten off to a good start. Now we just had to keep doing it.

In spring 1988, I read in the newspaper that one of First Boston's star bankers, Larry Fink, had left. When he was still in his twenties, Larry and a small group of traders had figured out how to package mortgages into securities and trade them like stocks and bonds. Mortgages were the second biggest asset class in the world after US Treasuries. Larry at First Boston and Lew Ranieri at Salomon Brothers controlled around 90 percent of this fast-growing market in mortgage-backed securities. Larry's success had propelled him onto his firm's management committee and put him in line to be its eventual CEO. He was only thirty-five. I had met him through our mutual friend Bruce Wasserstein and found him to be plain-spoken, intelligent, and energetic.

Not long after I heard the news of Larry leaving, we got a call from Ralph Schlosstein, who had run the small mortgage area at Lehman, saying that he and Larry were going into business together. Could they come by and see us? They were in our conference room the next day. Larry looked shocked.

"What happened?" I said. "You're a genius."

Two years earlier, he told me, he had made a bet that interest rates would rise. They had fallen. Mortgage holders had paid down their loans in the hope of refinancing at lower rates, affecting the value of Larry's portfolio. He had hedged his bets perfectly, he thought, so that even if rates went down instead of up, he would be protected. But a guy from the back office who ran Larry's computer models had made a mistake, and the hedges were wrong. Larry had made his calculations based on the wrong numbers. In a single quarter, his department lost $100 million. It wasn't his fault; he didn't control the back office. But he took the blame and he left.

I couldn't believe it. Larry was their most profitable guy.

"What do you want to do now?" I asked. He told me he was done with packaging securities and trading them. He wanted to invest in the mortgage securities market that he had done so much to create. No one else knew it better.

"Sounds like a good idea," I said. "Bring us a business plan. What do you need?"

A few days later Larry and Ralph were back.

Their plan included a list of the assets they wanted to buy and sell, the people they needed, and the profits they could make. They wanted $5 million to get going.

"That's it?" I asked.

"That's it. I want five people from the mortgage department at First Boston, and I need to pay them. I can work for nothing." His financial reward would come from his stake in the new business.

Blackstone didn't have any spare cash lying around at that point and certainly not millions. Our buyout fund was for investing in buyouts on behalf of our investors, not new businesses. But our first new business line had just popped up in front of us, and it ticked all the boxes: an amazing opportunity, beautifully timed, in a giant asset class, with one of the two top people in the world to manage it. We had prepared ourselves to expect the unexpected, and here it was. We would be fools to let it slip. Pete and I decided we would each invest a further $2.5 million personally in Blackstone to fund Larry's new venture. We would own half of the new company, Blackstone Financial Management, and Larry and his managers would own the other half.

Not long after Larry and his team came onboard, we decided to sell a 20 percent stake in our advisory business to Nikko for $100 million, valuing that subsidiary at $500 million, though its revenue was just $12 million. Nikko was already our partner on M&A deals for Japanese firms and had invested in our first fund. We had a good, trusting relationship. We could return their capital in seven years. In the meantime it would help us hire and build our organization more quickly. The transaction validated what we had built and strengthened us as we continued to grow.

By 1991, we had invested most of our first private equity fund and were trying to raise a second fund when a recession broke the momentum of the US economy. Panicked regulators cracked down on the insurance companies that had been the core investors in our first fund and limited their ability to invest in equities. Garnett Keith, the chief investment officer of Prudential, who had invested $100 million in our first fund, called to say that much as he wanted to, the change in regulations meant he could no longer invest with us. He said he might be able to find

$1 million to show he supported us. I told him not to stretch and subject Prudential to criticism.

We had to find a fresh source of capital. Our first target was the Middle East. I set off with my colleague Ken Whitney, our treasurer who was also running investor relations for us. We stopped for a day in London. As we rushed out of our hotel to catch our connecting flight, we bumped into Teddy Forstmann, the founder of a rival firm, Forstmann Little, and his beautiful date, both with cashmere sweaters draped over their shoulders and heading to Wimbledon. In the car, I told Ken I wouldn't trade places with Teddy for anything. I wanted to be working, building the firm.

Our meetings in the Middle East were mostly a bust. Late June and early July was the worst time of year to visit. In Kuwait, we took a taxi without air-conditioning in 120 degree heat and arrived at our meeting dripping like we'd just stepped out of the sea. All the senior people knew better and had left for the summer, and the junior staff we met didn't understand what we did. At one meeting, we had presented for an hour when a young Kuwaiti asked the difference between investing with us and buying US Treasuries. Still, we obtained several small commitments. A few months earlier, Kuwait had been liberated from Iraqi occupation by a US-led military coalition. We could see the bullet holes in the buildings.

Next, we headed to Saudi Arabia. After five days of doing six presentations a day, we didn't have a single commitment. Exhausted, on our last day in Dhahran, floating around in the hotel pool, I started telling Ken how successful we would be. I laid it all out for him. To be successful you have to put yourself in situations and places you have no right being in. You shake your head and learn from your own stupidity. But through sheer will, you wear the world down, and it gives you what you want. The money had to be out there. I told him to forget about what had just transpired in Saudi Arabia. It was done. Wasted. We were going to be successful, enormously so.

Ken is a balanced, sensible guy and couldn't hide his disbelief. He told me years later that he didn't want to offend me, but at the time he thought I was out of my mind.

If the insurance companies were out and the Middle East was a bust, we had to keep looking. The next obvious target were pension funds, vast pools of capital, many controlled by states and employees' unions, which had to be invested to generate retirement income. Pension funds were typically conservative and had not yet begun investing in alternative assets. I had never met anyone from a pension fund. They were as foreign to me as Japan had been. Once again, we needed someone to get us in the door.

A few big firms promised introductions, but these placement agents were expensive, and I wasn't sufficiently impressed with anyone we met. We were getting desperate, though, and were about to sign with one of them when Ken brought in a couple of guys just starting out in the placement business. One of them was Jim George, who was wearing a suit but looked as if he would much rather have been out West in jeans and a flannel shirt than stuck in an office in midtown New York. He told me he had never done this kind of work before. He was modest and soft-spoken. I had to crowbar out of him the reason he was sitting in front of me. For years he had been sitting on the other side of the desk as chief investment officer for the state of Oregon, where he had overseen the first investment by a state pension in private equity. A few years earlier, he had invested with KKR. "It worked out nicely," he said. "After that, whenever any other state fund wanted to think about this asset class, they'd call me and they'd come up and see me. I'd tell them what we were doing. You know, that type of thing."

He was barely out of the room when I grabbed Ken and told him Jim was our man. He was the opposite of the smooth placement agents we had seen. He was perfect for what we needed. I didn't care that he was new to the work. Jim George was going to lead us to the promised land, I was sure of it. Another can't-miss opportunity. We put together an offer.

A few days later, I called Jim's partner and invited them both in for another meeting in New York. I was jumping out of my chair promising that if we could agree on a fee, they could get to work immediately. Jim, though, was out of town. His partner said he would try to reach him, but called back later and apologized. Jim couldn't fly up for a meeting the next day.

"This may be the biggest thing in your careers. He can't see me?"

"Jim just got off a Disney cruise in Fort Lauderdale. He doesn't have a suit with him."

"I don't care whether he has a suit," I said. "Just tell him to get on a plane and fly up to New York."

"I told him that, but he won't do it. He only wants to come in a suit."

"Please," I said, "just buy him a suit and get him up here."

Jim's personal dignity was unimpeachable. It was why people trusted him. He had rules, and wearing a suit to a business meeting was one of them. When we met, I told him how much I intended to pay him. He was shocked. It was a big leap from his government salary in Oregon. "You deserve it," I told him. "You've given great service to Oregon and to the other pension funds in the country. We're going to see every one of the state funds. And we're going to sweep the table." He agreed to help us.

What Jim had was far more important than a business card from one of the big placement firms: he had the credibility and temperament for the work. Visiting pension funds with Jim turned out to be like going around Japan after Nikko invested with us. When the pension managers saw him, they saw one of their own, from the smallest to the biggest of all, the California State Public Employees Retirement System, which has invested with Blackstone ever since. With Jim leading us, we raised $1.27 billion for our second fund, the biggest private equity fund in the world at the time.

———

At around the same time we were raising our second private equity fund, we also began considering another new opportunity: real estate. In the late 1980s and early 1990s, the US real estate market collapsed. First, bad loans overwhelmed the savings and loan associations. These small financial institutions across America had lent more than they should have to fuel a nationwide building boom. Then in 1989, when the extent of their problems emerged, the federal government created the Resolution Trust Corporation (RTC) to liquidate their assets, their mortgages, and the buildings these loans had been used to build. But when the country tipped into recession in 1990, the value of all those newly built offices and homes collapsed. The RTC came under pressure to move the assets off their books at almost any price they could get, forcing massive amounts of real estate onto the market.

In 1990, all I knew about real estate came from my personal experience as a home owner. One of the partners at Blackstone suggested I meet Joe Robert, a real estate entrepreneur from Washington, DC, who was looking to raise money. I had read in the newspapers that the market was frozen: the buyers had all fled. Joe, though, saw the market differently. He had built a property management firm in Washington and developed close ties to the government. Watching the RTC's struggles, he had lobbied hard for them to involve private sector investors and real estate experts to help work through their backlog of distressed property. In 1990, his efforts resulted in a deal with the RTC for him to sell a $2.4 billion portfolio of property acquired by the government from collapsed savings and loans during the 1980s.

"I'm selling $5 to $10 million buildings to doctors and dentists," he told me. "They have savings and enough credibility in their communities to borrow whatever they need from the banks." What he wanted from Blackstone was the money to buy these buildings for himself. He had done well enough on brokerage fees, but now he saw the chance to make much more as an owner and developer. It seemed a perfect match: our money and his expertise. He proposed working together on the next RTC auction, which was coming up in just a couple of weeks. "Trust me," he said. "The country's in a complete mess. There won't be many people bidding."

When the RTC released the details of the auction, it included a package of garden apartments in Arkansas and East Texas, about three years old and 80 percent occupied. As investments go, this collection of buildings couldn't have been further from the deals I was used to working on. It would not require a lot of capital and the risk seemed modest. It seemed a great way to learn the business and probe for a bigger opportunity in the future.

I called Bob Rubin, then CEO of Goldman Sachs and a future US treasury secretary, and proposed working together. Goldman had significantly more experience in real estate than we did. He agreed.

When Joe and I went to meet Goldman's real estate team, though, we found they had a different view of the risks of this deal. Goldman wanted to bid as low as possible to avoid overpaying. For me, the biggest risk was not offering enough and missing out on a tremendous opportunity. I wanted to make sure we beat Bankers Trust's expected bid. You often find this difference between different types of investors. Some will tell you that all the value is in driving down the price you pay as low as possible. These investors revel in the transaction itself, in playing with the deal terms, in beating up their opponent at the negotiating table. That has always seemed short term to me. What that thinking ignores is all the value you can realize once you own an asset: the improvements you can make, the refinancing you can do to improve your returns, the timing of your sale to make the most of a rising market. If you waste all your energy and goodwill in pursuit of the lowest possible purchase price and end up losing the asset to a higher bidder, all that future value goes away. Sometimes it's best to pay what you have to pay and focus on what you can then do as an owner. The returns to successful ownership will often be much higher than the returns on winning a one-off battle over price.

At the price I suggested, I calculated that we would lock in a 16 percent annual yield. That meant every year we would receive 16 percent of our purchase price back in profits from rental income. And that was just the start. These apartments were producing a steady flow of cash. They were almost new, so we wouldn't have to spend a lot of money fixing them. If we added some debt to the acquisition, we could lift the return on our investment to 23 percent a year. This concept will be familiar to anyone who has taken out a mortgage. Let's say you paid $100,000 for a house by putting down 40 percent in cash and borrowing 60 percent. If you sold the house immediately for $120,000, your profit would be $20,000, or 50 percent of the $40,000 in cash you initially put down. Alternatively, if you paid for the same house by putting down only $20,000 in cash and borrowing the remaining $80,000, then the return on your original $20,000 investment would double to 100 percent. Taking on debt, assuming you can pay it back, can substantially increase your return on equity.

In addition, we thought we were close to the bottom of the real estate cycle. In 1991, we felt real estate had bounced off the bottom. As the economy recovered, the vacant 20 percent of apartments would fill up, lifting the 23 percent return to 45 percent. And rents would then rise, taking the 45 percent to 55 percent. If all we had to do for this 55 percent compound return was buy the asset, I reasoned, we shouldn't be worrying about getting the lowest possible price at the auction. I told Goldman, "I'm happy with 55 percent a year. I don't need 60." They conceded, we placed our bid, won, and over time our first investment in garden apartments yielded a 62 percent annualized return, even better than I'd imagined. After that auction, I asked Joe how much of this stuff was out there. "There's a whole country full," he told me.

We were new to the real estate game, but that was our edge. We came without baggage, no failing properties or underwater loans. I could scarcely believe it. A country full of value and no competition. But as we prepared for the next auction, Joe told me that Goldman Sachs had offered him the chance to invest a billion dollars. Though he had committed to us, he wanted to take them up on it.

"The only way you know these people is thanks to me," I said to him. "How can you just run over there?" He said he felt bad about it, but Goldman was offering him what he wanted. If I could raise a similar-sized fund in the next month, though, he'd reconsider.

Under the terms of our main investment fund, we could use the money for real estate deals. But I wanted our investors' consent before we committed such a significant portion of their money to this new strategy. I felt it was our duty to explain what we were doing. At our annual investors' meeting, I laid out the opportunity, expecting our limited partners to jump at it. But to my surprise, all except General Motors turned it down. One after the other, our investors told me, "We know you're right. But we're loaded to the gills with these terrible real estate deals." They all agreed with us that prices were low and must eventually go up. But still they couldn't act. We had a huge opportunity but no money for it. I could have held Joe to his promise to keep working with us, but since we could not offer him a competitive platform, the right thing to do was to let him go.

We were determined not to give up, even without Joe. A few times in every investor's life, an immense opportunity appears. I asked Ken Whitney to find me someone else to develop our real estate business. We needed a 10 to build a great new business. As I worked through a list of names, checking references, I spoke to a man in Chicago, John Schreiber, whom Ken had identified as a reference. We talked for a while about the candidate he was supposed to be recommending. (He wasn't enthusiastic but was too polite to say so.) And the longer we talked, the more I was intrigued. In the 1980s, John had worked for JMB, a real estate investment firm in Chicago, which had been an active and aggressive buyer. Over the previous decade, he had bought more real estate than anyone else in America. He had seen the collapse coming and told JMB to sell everything. They told him he was crazy and paid him out so he could leave. Then came "the thousand year earthquake" that proved him right.

"So why don't you come and work with us?" I said. He had worked so hard in the 1980s, he told me. He had eight kids and his family wanted to see more of him.

"You built the largest real estate firm in America and had eight kids? When did you ever get to see your wife?"

"Obviously I found the time," said John.

I kept pressing, and eventually he promised to give us twenty hours a week. He said he'd hire a couple of younger guys and mentor them for us, and use his connections to open some doors. We'd see how it went. In no time, his twenty hours were seventy hours. It was the 1980s all over again for him. I wasn't sure how his wife felt about it, but we were delighted to have him. He stayed in Chicago, working from home, an éminence grise to those who didn't know him. But he did much more than just hire a couple of younger guys and oversee them. He went in person to check out every single property we contemplated buying. Blackstone's partners were investing their personal money, and the deals were so good they had us talking to ourselves. But months in and without a fund, we couldn't get to real scale. It was driving me crazy.

Even as the real estate market began to recover, investors still felt burned by the crash. We needed to come up with a sweetener, some incentive to calm their fears and help get them over their misunderstanding of the risk. In the same way I had used a sealed bid auction for CSX's newspapers and pressured Harold Simmons with an endless flow of taxable yet unredeemable stock, we invented a novel structure designed to address a particular psychological state. It had to convey our confidence in the opportunity while giving investors a safety valve if they felt scared. We decided that for every three dollars an investor pledged to our real estate fund, two dollars could be discretionary. They could make a pledge, but if they didn't like the specific deals we were presenting, they could hold back two-thirds of it.

The first investor to express interest was a friend of Jim George. Steve Myers ran the public pension fund for the state of South Dakota. Jim told us Steve was a clever, courageous investor. Jim, Pete, John Schreiber, and I flew out to see him in Sioux

Falls, South Dakota. When I explained what we were trying to do, Steve lit up. Real estate had come off the bottom, and the market was rising. It was a great time to get in. He persuaded his board to commit $150 million.

For the first time in my life, I was nervous about taking money. It was a big check for South Dakota's $4 billion pension fund, a lot for a single investment representing a lot of people's retirement funds. I asked Steve if he was sure. Under the terms of the deal, he said, he was only committed to investing $50 million of his pledge. He could invest the remaining $100 million if he liked the deals he saw and hold back if he didn't. For an opportunity with this kind of potential, that was a risk he could take. Steve's decision gave us our second new business line, real estate, which would eventually become Blackstone's largest business.

CYCLES:
INVESTING THROUGH UPS
AND DOWNS

The success of any investment depends in large part on where you are in the cycle when you make it. Cycles can have a major impact on the growth trajectory of a business, the valuation, and, of course, the potential rate of return. We routinely discuss cycles as part of our investment process. Here are my simple rules for identifying market tops and bottoms:

1. Market tops are relatively easy to recognize. Buyers generally become overconfident and almost always believe "this time is different." It's usually not.
2. There's always a surplus of relatively cheap debt capital to finance acquisitions and investments in a hot market. In some cases, lenders won't even charge cash interest, and they often relax or suspend typical loan restrictions as well. Leverage levels escalate compared to historical averages, with borrowing sometimes reaching as high as ten times or more compared to equity. Buyers will start accepting overoptimistic accounting adjustments and financial forecasts to justify taking on high levels of debt.

Unfortunately most of these forecasts tend not to materialize once the economy starts decelerating or declining.

3. Another indicator that a market is peaking is the number of people you know who start getting rich. The number of investors claiming outperformance grows with the market. Loose credit conditions and a rising tide can make it easy for individuals without any particular strategy or process to make money "accidentally." But making money in strong markets can be short-lived. Smart investors perform well through a combination of self-discipline and sound risk assessment, even when market conditions reverse.

All investors will tell you that markets are cyclical. Yet many behave as if they don't know this. In my career, I have seen seven major market declines or recessions: 1973, 1975, 1982, 1987, 1990–1992, 2001, and 2008–2010. Recessions happen.

Market bottoms can be difficult to detect as markets are declining and the economy weakens. Most public and private investors buy too early and underestimate the severity of recessions. It's important not to react too quickly. Most investors don't have the confidence or discipline to wait until a cycle fully plays out. These investors suffer by not maximizing the profit they would have otherwise made from executing the same idea at a later point.

Timing the bottom of a cycle isn't easy, and it's often a bad idea to try in any case. The reason is that it typically takes a year or two for an economy to really emerge from a recession. Even when a market starts turning around, it still takes time for asset values to recover. This means you could be investing at the bottom with no return for some period of time. This happened to investors who started purchasing Houston office buildings in 1983 after oil prices collapsed and the market hit bottom. Ten years later, in 1993, these investors were still waiting for prices to recover.

The way to avoid this type of situation is to invest only when values have recovered at least 10 percent from their lows. Asset values tend to increase as economies gain momentum. It's better to give up the first 10 to 15 percent of a market recovery to ensure that you are buying at the right time.

While most investors say they are interested in making money, they are actually interested in psychological comfort. They would rather be part of the herd, even when the herd is losing money, than make the hard decisions that yield the greatest rewards. Doing what everyone else is doing seems like a way to avoid blame. These investors tend not to invest aggressively near market bottoms, but instead do it at market tops, where it makes little sense. They like the comfort and reassurance of watching assets go up. The higher prices go, the more investors convince themselves that they will continue appreciating. This same phenomenon explains why it's almost impossible to bring an IPO to market near the bottom of a cycle. But as a cycle grows riper, the number, size, and valuations of IPOs explode.

Cycles are ultimately powered by all types of supply and demand characteristics. By understanding and quantifying them, you can be well positioned to identify how close you are to a market top or bottom. In real estate, for example, building booms are stimulated when existing buildings are being valued at significantly more than replacement cost because developers understand that they can build a new building and sell it for more than they paid. This is a brilliant strategy if only one building is being constructed. But almost every developer can see the same opportunity to make what they think will be easy money. If a large number of them start building at the same time, you can easily predict that supply will overwhelm demand and the value of buildings in that market will decline, most likely precipitously.

The idea that no one can see bubbles, as one former chairman of the Federal Reserve once announced, simply isn't true.

THERE ARE NO BRAVE, OLD PEOPLE IN FINANCE

As Blackstone was expanding, we hired a young banker from the corporate finance division at Drexel Burnham Lambert. He was smart and ambitious and soon after he arrived in 1989, he had a deal for us. Edgcomb, based in Philadelphia, bought raw steel and milled it into products for car, truck, and airplane manufacturers. This young partner had worked on a couple of Edgcomb deals at Drexel, so he knew the company, and its executives knew him. Now it was up for sale, and we got an exclusive first look at buying it.

An exclusive always warrants attention, and the deal looked promising. Edgcomb was making a lot of money. Its customer base was growing, and the company looked as if it could expand. They were asking around $330 million, which, based on our analysis, seemed like a decent price. I was ready to offer. Before I did, though, another of our new partners, David Stockman, came into my office spouting doom. David was a hybrid of Washington, DC, and Wall Street and had been director of the Office of Management and Budget under President Reagan. He had been with us less than a year, and had a fierce intellect, analyzed deals closely, and expressed his opinions without reservation.

"This Edgcomb thing is a disaster," he said. "We absolutely cannot do it."

"The other guy thinks it's great," I said.

"It's not great," David said. "It's awful. The company is worthless and poorly managed. All of its profits are coming from the increase in steel prices. They're one-time profits, and the basic business just has the illusion of profitability. It's going to end up going bankrupt. If we leverage it the way we're going to, we're going to go bust ourselves. It's a disaster in the making."

I called Edgcomb's champion and chief critic into my office to debate the investment, so I could hear them argue it out face-to-face and then make a decision. I sat there and listened to their pitches as if I were King Solomon. I thought the younger man got the better of it. He had worked with Edgcomb for years. He had an insider's knowledge and could answer all the questions. Stockman was analyzing the deal as an outsider. He had a strong argument but didn't have the same level of information. We thought we understood steel after our success with Transtar, the transportation business we had bought from USX. And somehow we thought we could now predict the commodity cycle, so I decided to go ahead. We made the offer, gathered money from investors, and closed the deal.

And right on cue, a few months after we closed, steel prices began to nosedive. Edgcomb's inventory was now worth less than they had paid for it and dropping in value every day. The profits we anticipated, which were to pay our borrowing costs, never materialized. We couldn't make our debt payments. Edgcomb was imploding, just as David Stockman predicted it would.

I got a phone call from the chief investment officer of Presidential Life, which had invested in our fund. He wanted to see me. I took a cab to his office in Nyack, on the Hudson above New York. He asked me to sit down and started screaming at me. Was I a complete incompetent or just stupid? What kind of imbecile would squander his money on something so worthless?

How could he have given a dime to someone as inept as I was? As I sat there absorbing the punishment, I knew that he was right. We were losing their money because our analysis was flawed. I was the person who had made the decision. I don't think I have been as ashamed as that in my life before or since. Even messing up those deal book numbers for Eric Gleacher as a first-year associate at Lehman didn't compare. I wasn't capable. I wasn't competent. I was a disgrace.

I also wasn't used to being yelled at. My mother and father never raised their voices. If we did something wrong, they let us know about it, but they never screamed or shouted. I felt tears welling up and my face turning red and hot. I had to force myself not to cry. I said I understood, and we would do better in the future. As I found my way to the parking lot, I vowed to myself, *This is never, ever going to happen to me again.*

Back in the office, I worked like a demon to make sure that even if Blackstone and our investors lost money on Edgcomb, our creditors—the banks we had borrowed from to fund part of the deal—didn't lose a nickel. Edgcomb was just one deal in one fund. We would make other deals with the money from that fund and ensure that, overall, our investors did well. But our creditors lent us money deal by deal. If we failed to repay them even once, I feared, it would damage our reputation. Banks would lend us less money on stricter terms, making business harder.

We then examined our decision making. For all our entrepreneurial strengths, our drive, our ambition, our skills, and our work ethic, we still weren't building Blackstone into a great organization. Failures are often the best teachers in any organization. You must not bury your failures but talk about them openly and analyze what went wrong so you can learn new rules for decision making. Failures can be enormous gifts, catalysts that change the course of any organization and make it successful in the future. Edgcomb's failure showed that the change had to start with me and my approach to investing and evaluating potential investments.

———————

I had fallen into a trap common to many organizations. When people have to pitch ideas, they tend to address the great man or woman sitting at the end of the table. If their idea is no good, the great man or woman rejects them. Regardless of the quality of their proposal, they leave the room with their heads down. A few weeks later, they go through the same routine with a new proposal and leave the room even more slowly than before to show what they think of the decision. The third time, they're gritting their teeth. The fourth time, the person at the end of the table now feels bad. The proposers aren't horrible employees, just not that good. But if that fourth idea is near-okay, the boss will end up green-lighting it just to keep everyone happy.

In my enthusiasm to give a new partner a shot with the Edgcomb deal, I had made myself and the firm vulnerable. I had succumbed to a good sales pitch. I learned later that one of the analysts on this new partner's team had opposed the deal. He couldn't see it ever working. But the partner had told him to keep his doubts to himself.

I should have been more wary of my emotions and more scrupulous with the facts. Deals aren't all math. But there are a lot of objective criteria to consider, and I needed to do that at length, in peace, not with two people pushing their views, and me sitting there deciding between them.

Finance is full of people with charm and flip charts who talk so well and present so quickly you can't keep up. So you have to stop that show. Decisions are much better made through systems designed to protect businesses and organizations than through individuals. We needed rules to depersonalize our investment process. It could never again rely on one person's abilities, feelings, and vulnerabilities. We needed to review and tighten our process.

I had always been maniacal about not losing money, and the trauma of Edgcomb pushed me further. I began to think of investing as like playing basketball without a shot clock. As long as you had the ball, all you had to do to win was just keep passing, waiting until you were sure of making the shot. Other teams might lose patience and take those off-balance, low-percentage shots from behind the three-point line, the way we had done with Edgcomb. At Blackstone, I decided we would keep moving and passing until we could get the ball into the hands of our seven-foot center standing right underneath the basket. We would obsess about the downside of every potential deal until we were certain we could not miss.

We decided to involve all of our senior partners in our discussions of investments. We would never again allow one person single-handedly to green-light a deal. During my career, I had gotten things more right than wrong, but Edgcomb had shown that I was far from infallible. My colleagues had decades of experience. By working together, arguing and applying our collective wisdom to evaluate an investment's risks, we hoped we could examine our deals more objectively.

Next, we insisted that anyone with a proposal would have to write a thorough memorandum and circulate it at least two days before any meeting so it could be carefully and logically evaluated. The two-day requirement would give readers time to mark up the memo, spot any holes, and refine their questions. No additions could be made to the memo at the meeting unless there was a significant subsequent development. We did not want extra sheets of paper going around the room.

The senior partners would sit on one side of the table and the internal team presenting a deal on the other. Around us would be the junior members of our teams, who were expected to watch, learn, and contribute.

These discussions had two fundamental rules. The first was that everyone had to speak, so that every investment decision was made collectively. The second was that our focus should be on the potential investment's weaknesses. Everyone had to find problems that hadn't been addressed. This process of constructive confrontation could be challenging for the presenter, but we designed it never to be personal. The "only criticism" rule liberated us to critique each other's proposals without worrying that we might be hurting someone's feelings.

The upside of the potential investment should be included as well, but that was not the focus of our early investment committee discussions.

Once this group dissection process concluded, whoever was running the deal now had a list of problems to address and questions to answer. What would happen to the company they were proposing we buy if a recession hit? Would its profits decline gently or plummet? Were the best managers likely to stick around following a buyout? Had we thought hard enough about the likely response from competitors? Or the effect on profitability if commodity prices collapsed, as they had after we bought Edgcomb? Did their financial model take account of all these eventualities? The presenter's team would go back and find answers to our questions, and in doing so, they could implement fixes or figure out how to manage the downside, or they might uncover new risks, new probabilities of loss that they might never have seen before. And back they would come for another round of discussion. By the third round, we hoped, there would no longer be any nasty surprises lurking in the deal.

I also resolved that I would never talk to just the lead partner on any potential investment. If I had detailed questions, I would call the most junior person, the one working the spreadsheets and closest to the numbers. If I had done that on Edgcomb, I might have heard from the analyst who hated the deal. Breaking through the hierarchy would allow me to get to know the junior people at the firm and get a different read. The risk may not be obvious on paper, but it came through in the analysts' tone of voice when I asked them, "Just walk me through this deal from your perspective." You could hear if they liked it or felt anxious. Psychology would be one of my strengths as an investor. I didn't need to remember each number in an analysis. I could watch and hear the people who knew the specifics and tell how they felt from their posture or tone of voice.

The final change we made to depersonalize and derisk our investment process was to encourage a greater sense of collective responsibility. Every partner on our investment committee needed to participate in assessing the risk factor of a proposed investment. In this way, the internal team presenting could not target the senior person at the table or lobby him or her for a positive decision. Everyone in attendance would share responsibility for whatever decision was made. And we made every decision in the same predictable manner.

As we have added new businesses to Blackstone and ventured into new markets, we apply this same process to all our investment decisions. Everyone contributes to the discussion. Risk is systematically broken down and understood. Debate is full and robust. The same small groups of people, who know each other well, go over each investment applying the same rigorous standards. This unified approach to investing has become the backbone of the Blackstone way.

For all that was going on at Blackstone in its early years, the rest of my life didn't stop. Ellen and I divorced in 1991, but we continued to raise our children, Zibby and Teddy, together. It had been a painful decision to separate. Before we did, I remember going to see my internist, Dr. Harvey Klein, for a checkup. Physically I was fine, but at the end of our meeting, Harvey asked me how I was doing. I told him I was under a lot of stress at work, and I couldn't make a decision on my marriage. I was unhappy but frightened by the prospect of divorce. Harvey jotted down a telephone number and handed it to me.

Dr. Byram Karasu is a psychiatrist who spent twenty-three years as department chair at the Albert Einstein College of Medicine in New York. He is the author of nineteen books; runs a small, private practice in Manhattan; and is regularly called on for his opinions in Washington. When I stepped into his office for the first time, I made it clear that I wasn't there for therapy. I just couldn't make my mind up about divorce. He asked me what was holding me up. Four fears, I told him: the fear of losing my relationship with my children, the prospect of signing away half of what I had worked so hard to make, the fear of losing half my friends, and terror at having to date again.

Four reasonable anxieties, Byram said, but all ultimately unjustified. My children were well past the imprinting stage of childhood, when divorce might traumatize them. If I wanted a good relationship with them and worked on it, they would want the same. As for my money, yes, it would be a big check to have to write, but if it cleared the way for a new chapter in my life, I would soon forget about it. The friends we had made as a couple would likely split fifty-fifty, and that was just a fact of life. And as for dating? As a wealthy, single man in Manhattan, I wouldn't be short of options.

Byram was warm, thoughtful, insightful, experienced, and

My great grandfather William Schwarzman immigrated to the US from Austria in 1883; he later met and married Jenny Whartman in Philadelphia, PA. Portrait c. 1925.

My great grandparents William and Jenny Schwarzman with my father, Joseph, as a boy, c. 1925.

My grandfather Jacob Schwarzman, the founder of Schwarzman's Curtains & Linens, with my father, Joseph, as a boy, c. 1921.

With grandparents Jacob and Rebecca Schwarzman, in Philadelphia, PA, c. 1951.

My father, Joseph Schwarzman,
during WWII, 1943.

My mother, Arline Schwarzman,
c. 1943.

With my parents at 1113 Gilham Street, Oxford Circle, Philadelphia, 1947. As soon as we could afford it, my mother moved us to the suburbs.

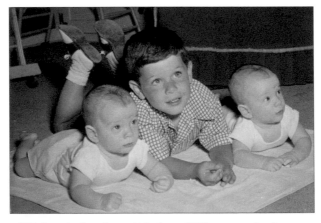

With twin brothers, Mark and Warren—the future lawn-mowing crew, c. 1950.

Schwarzman's Curtains & Linens, Frankford, Philadelphia, c. 1960.

Running the first leg of the
440-yard relay, 1963.

Mile relay champions at the Penn Relays, 1963. FROM LEFT:
Bill Grant, Bobby Bryant, Richard Joffney, and me.

R&B vocal group Little Anthony & The Imperials, c. 1964.
Michael Ochs Archive/Getty Images

My first significant gift to Yale's students: an end to the parietal rules that banned members of the opposite sex from visiting each other's dorm rooms, 1967. *Yale archives*

Yale senior yearbook photo, 1969. *Yale archives*

3038 N STREET
WASHINGTON, D. C. 20007

September 26, 1969

Letter from Averell Harriman responding to my request for career advice, 1969. Harriman's encouragement set me on my path to Wall Street and later to philanthropy and advising leaders around the world.

Dear Steve:

Thanks for your letter of September 19th. I am now living in Washington but come to New York occasionally. I find that I will be in New York on Thursday, October 16th and will be glad to see you at 3:00 p.m. if that is convenient, at my home at 16 East 81st Street. Let me know if that is convenient for you.

I am not sure that I can be of much help to you in making your decision but will be glad to discuss it.

Looking forward to seeing you.

Yours in 322,

W. Averell Harriman

Mr. Stephen A. Schwarzman, bsc
D-167
Donaldson, Lufkin & Jenrette, Inc.
140 Broadway
New York, New York 10005.

At army training in Fort Polk, Louisiana, 1970.

My roommate and oldest friend, Jeffrey Rosen (with glasses), now deputy chairman of Lazard, and me in class at Harvard Business School asking the tough questions, 1971.

Stephen Schwarzman, Lehman's Merger Maker

By KAREN W. ARENSON

Felix Rohatyn of Lazard Frères, J. Ira Harris of Salomon Brothers, Robert Greenhill of Morgan Stanley and Stephen Friedman of Goldman Sachs may still be the reputed kings of the merger and acquisition world, but a new generation of younger investment bankers is coming up behind them.

Of the newcomers, probably none has been as hot recently as Stephen A. Schwarzman, a 32-year-old partner at Lehman Brothers Kuhn Loeb. In recent months he has played an instrumental role in the Bendix Corporation's winning bid for the Warner & Swasey Company, RCA's $1.35 billion acquisition of C.I.T. Financial, and ill-fated talks between Macmillan and ABC. Other deals that bear his mark include the Beneficial Corporation's $72 million purchase last month of the Southwestern Investment Company and the Beatrice Foods Company's $488 million acquisition of Tropicana Products Inc.

"Steve has a special instinct that puts him in the right place at the right time," says Martin Lipton of Wachtell Lipton Rosen & Katz, one of the most active lawyers in mergers and acquisitions. "It's a very special instinct that you find in a Rohatyn or a Harris, but not in very many other people."

Being in the right place at the right time is as important a trait for a successful investment banker as knowing how to structure a securities transaction. The Wall Street wizards who facilitate the concentration and diversification trends that shape American industry are a cross between the ancient matchmaker and the modern financial expert. It is the investment bankers with the right clients and contacts who do the big business, who know what deals can get put together and who get called in when a deal starts to jell. One thing that separates the junior bankers from the big players is the size of their networks of contacts.

And Mr. Schwarzman's circle clearly has been growing quickly. His

two phones rang constantly on a recent morning in his maroon-walled second floor corner office overlooking Hanover Square: An executive interested in acquiring a company be represented. A potential new client setting up a lunch meeting. A client pledging money for Lincoln Center, for which Mr. Schwarzman has been helping to raise funds. An arbitrageur congratulating him on his latest deal. An associate checking the details on an assignment.

Mr. Schwarzman fielded each call with rapt attentiveness, eyebrows arching for emphasis, walking back and forth behind his desk in excitement.

According to those who have worked

Continued on Page 13

Schwarzman of Lehman Brothers: "I'm an implementer."

My first profile in *The New York Times* at 33 years old, 1980.

With son Teddy and daughter Zibby, 1987. However busy I was at work, I always tried to be there for my family.

With Blackstone partners at our Park Ave. offices, 1988. FROM LEFT: James R. Birle, Laurence D. Fink, me, Pete Peterson, David A. Stockman, and Roger C. Altman. *James Hamilton*

My parents, Arline and Joseph Schwarzman, c. 1990.

Sunday Times coverage of Blackstone's first European investment in the Savoy Group of hotels, including the Savoy Hotel, Claridge's, the Berkeley, and the Connaught, 1998. *The Sunday Times/News Licensing*

Cardinal Edward Egan, President George H. W. Bush, me, and Mayor
Michael Bloomberg at the Al Smith Dinner in New York, 2004.

Congratulating 2005 Kennedy Center honoree Tina Turner as
Oprah and Caroline Kennedy look on. *Margot Schulman*

With my partner, Pete Peterson, on Blackstone's 20th anniversary, 2005. Blackstone had grown into more than we ever dared imagine, but the best was yet to come.

Tony James and me celebrating Blackstone's 20th anniversary, 2005.
Tony was key to institutionalizing and transforming Blackstone
into the well-run business it is today.

With President George W. Bush at my apartment in New York City in 2007. I have known George since Yale, and the course and intersection of our respective lives never ceases to amaze us.
Reflections Photography/Washington DC

At the 2008 Kennedy Center Gala. FROM LEFT TO RIGHT: Me, Christine, Katie Holmes, Tom Cruise, Kennedy Center honorees Steven Spielberg (2006) and Martin Scorsese (2007), and president of the Kennedy Center Michael Kaiser. *Carol Pratt*

With President Bill Clinton at the White House, 2009. *Margot Schulman*

With Senator Ted Kennedy at the Kennedy Center, 2009. Ted's character, friendship, and support were one of the best parts of my time at the Kennedy Center.

convincing. His advice changed the direction of my life in the most positive way. I have been to see him once or twice a week ever since to talk about work mostly, and he always thinks with that same objective clarity he showed me at that first meeting. He understands my brain, the intensity with which I experience and respond to the world. He helps me test my intuitions and strip away the psychological, social, emotional, and intellectual filters that can obscure the truth.

Byram was also right about my divorce clearing the way for a new chapter in my personal life. My friends were kind enough to set up dates for me, and one was with a recently divorced attorney, Christine Hearst, who had a job lined up and her boxes packed to move to Palo Alto. Not the most promising setup. We were both busy, and Christine was already thinking about her new life on the West Coast. But my friends were insistent that I meet her, and I had promised I would try.

I thought our first date was great. She thought it was weird. She was expecting me to pick her up, but I was working late and we were going to a party close to my office, so I sent a car over to get her instead. She looked surprised when I finally did get in the car. I glanced over and said, "Hi, I'm Steve." And then proceeded to flip down the visor mirror and run an electric shaver over my face. We went from a book party at Rockefeller Center to see George Michael perform at the new Sony Plaza building on Madison Avenue to a dinner party with friends. Debbie Bancroft, the mutual friend who introduced us, called me the next morning to ask how the date went.

"Great," I told her. I liked Christine and we had done all these exciting things. Christine, though gregarious, is a private person. She had told Debbie she felt like an accessory as we went from place to place, socializing with lots of people I knew and she didn't. She had had a miserable time. The date was so busy

155

that we never had a proper chance to talk at all. Debbie told me I was to call Christine, apologize, and invite her out for a quiet evening at a restaurant, someplace where we could actually get to know each other. I did as she suggested, and our next date was a long dinner at an Italian restaurant on First Avenue. I had such a good time that by the end of the dinner, I had my trusty calendar out. Christine looked surprised as I ran through various dates and tried to schedule when we might meet again. She wasn't used to anyone in finance as precise as I can be.

"We can do this thing fast or slow," I said. "I prefer fast."

Thankfully, I didn't put her off. Once we started dating, one of her first orders of business was to bring some order to my bachelor habits. I was living in an apartment at 950 Fifth Avenue with my son, Teddy, and had hired a chef, Chang. Night after night we'd have those familiar father–teenage son conversations over dinner. "How was school?" "Fine."

The first time Christine came over, she went into my kitchen and opened the fridge. It was more than I ever did. There she found box upon box of Stouffer's ready meals all stacked up. For two years, Chang had been heating them up and serving them to me and my son, and we hadn't even noticed.

A couple of years later, after Christine and I were married, I wanted to hire a chef. Christine has many skills, but none of them include meal prep. And everyone who knows me knows that after a long day's work, I like a proper dinner. So we put out an ad and were particularly impressed by a résumé from a chef called Hymie. We invited him for an interview, and Christine recognized him the moment she opened the door. It was Chang! He had simply changed his name and hoped we might have forgotten the bad Stouffer years. That's New York for you.

DON'T LOSE MONEY!!! DEVELOPING AN INVESTMENT PROCESS

People often smile whenever they hear my number one rule for investing: Don't. Lose. Money. I never understand the smirks, because it is just that simple. At Blackstone we have established, and over time refined, an investment process to accomplish that basic concept. We have created a framework for assessing risk that has been incredibly reliable. We train our professionals to distill every individual investment opportunity down to the two or three major variables that will define the success of our investment case and create value. At Blackstone, the decision to invest is all about disciplined, dispassionate, and robust risk assessment. It's not only a process but a mind-set and an integral part of our culture.

This is how we do it:

The concept of an investment committee is commonplace across Wall Street and other industries. A handful or more senior leaders from a given firm invite deal teams to present a new opportunity that has usually already been summarized for them in the form of a memorandum. The deal team will try to sell a potential investment to the committee, listing all the reasons a deal is great and quantifying the potential for profits. If the committee members like what they hear, they bless the deal, and the presenting team is relieved to know they can proceed. If not, it feels like a loss, and the deal team usually skulks out of the room feeling defeated, memos in hand and perhaps muttering to themselves. Not at Blackstone.

We structure our investment process to democratize decision making and encourage intellectual engagement by everyone involved—the deal team and committee members. There is no "us" and "them," no seeking of approval from a group of elders. Instead, there is only a collective sense of responsibility for identifying the critical drivers of a deal and analyzing the extent to which those drivers could affect the financial performance of an investment in various scenarios.

Everyone around the table, from the most junior to the most senior person, is expected to have an opinion and participate. No one person, or subset of people, dominates the conversation or holds the power for approval. It's team ball. Everyone must debate and agree on the variables and decide the range of possible outcomes. In some cases, the variables are obvious, and in others, it takes a few rounds of rigorous debate and discussion to determine what they are. But we don't move forward without agreement.

It's a subtle point, but this approach removes a lot of the noise and emotion that often affects investors' ability to make sound decisions. It also eliminates individual risk and the pressure for a deal team to be "right" on the ultimate outcome. In instances when we talk about investing billions of dollars, this pressure can be psychologically intense and overwhelming if concentrated on just a few people. You could ruin the firm or your reputation with one bad investment.

At Blackstone, investment committees are about discussion and discovery, not about getting a deal approved. Because the decision to move forward or not is made together, no one feels pressured to sell a deal just because he or she brought the idea. Similarly, there is no pressure to approve a suboptimal deal as consolation for a deal team's hard work in sourcing and analyzing the investment in question. If we make an investment and it goes wrong, we all got it wrong, and we are all responsible for fixing it. And when we are right, which is more often the case, we reap the rewards together.

Our process forces every person, no matter anyone's seniority, to act like an owner of the firm, as if our LP's capital was their own. This arrangement results in an extremely powerful alignment of incentives, and it also turns every deal evaluation into a teaching moment. The success of our process speaks for itself.

SPINNING THE
WHEEL FASTER

Pete and I always resolved to hire 10s. Today, Blackstone gets to choose from the very best young graduates. For our 2018 class of junior investment analysts, we received 14,906 applications for 86 spots. Our acceptance rate is 0.6 percent, much lower by far than the most selective universities in the world. If I had to apply for a job at my own firm today, I seriously doubt I'd be hired.

But it took many years of trial and error to get here. Early on there were challenges to finding and keeping the people we wanted. The first was not our fault. Under the terms of my departure from Lehman, we could not hire our former colleagues. These were the people we knew best, whom we trusted, and with whom we had worked well. They would have been the ideal partners in our new venture. The second problem was that the big firms on Wall Street at that time were more like tribes than businesses. For someone to leave Goldman Sachs to join Morgan Stanley was like a Comanche leaving to join the Mohawks. And back then, Blackstone barely constituted a hunting party, let alone a tribe. The scale and systems at Lehman had largely spared me from having to fish through Wall Street's hiring pools. But now there were no bureaucratic layers to protect me from the truth that finance is an industry that encourages self-delusion. People think they're great and tell you they're great, never that they failed at their last job, only that they are looking for "more opportunity." You hire them, and they often fail. So then you have to fire them and go looking for more candidates. Then you have to work through that second group as well, until with the third group, you might just have the people you want. Then the first and second groups go around telling everyone how difficult your firm is as a place to work, making hiring even more difficult.

The third problem was me. While I was good at raising money and doing deals, scrambling to keep the cash flowing into the firm, I was hopeless when it came to hiring and managing people in our first five years. Pete was bringing in friends even when we didn't have work for them. The partners who did have work would do their own deals with no sense of what the rest of the firm was up to. Information came to me, but I didn't always make sure to pass it on. We were more a collection of individuals than a team. I excused myself on the grounds that we were in a hard, competitive business with little time for worrying about people's feelings. I was wrong.

I saw the opportunity to begin optimizing our hiring and training in 1991 when we hired our first class of MBA graduates. I knew at this moment that Blackstone would succeed. These promising young people, who were entrusting their careers to us, would be Blackstone's future. In return, we owed them a culture in which they could realize their ambitions.

The Wall Street culture that I had grown up in was not going to work. At Lehman, people were smart and tough, and they made a lot of money. But everyone had complex relationships with each other. They were sometimes verbally abusive. In the early years, Blackstone's culture echoed the places we had all come from. Despite our efforts to create a new kind of firm, we still had a few midlevel people who were exceptionally hard on their staff. They would occasionally shout at them, insult them, and push them around. They would wait until the last moment on Friday to give people work, ensuring their subordinates lost their weekends. One young analyst got so frustrated that he kicked in a photocopying machine and destroyed it. When I heard about it, I thought, *This is insane.*

To purge the firm of its worst behavior, we turned to Respect at Work, a group that came in and interviewed people throughout the firm to find out what was going on. They put on skits to small groups, showing them what their behavior looked like. They made our employees take roles as bullies or victims. I went to every one of these performances and sat in the front row. To see these actors playing my colleagues was shocking, absurd yet horribly undeniable. Confronting our shortcomings was the first step to eradicating this kind of behavior. We made clear that if there was any more of it, the perpetrators would be fired. It was up to me to say what I believed, to stand behind it and show everyone at the firm that I was serious.

Just as we had rethought our investment process in the wake of Edgcomb, we now put ourselves in the shoes of these young people joining Blackstone and considered what they would want from us. At DLJ, I was never trained properly. I would cower in my office hoping no one noticed me, scared I would be found out as ignorant or incompetent. I must have been the biggest buyer of antiperspirant on the East Side of Manhattan. At Lehman, I had to learn from my own mistakes. Learning in that environment was a slow, uncertain undertaking that led to a high rate of burnout and attrition. So at Blackstone we invested in a thorough training program to make sure our recruits knew what to do before we put them to work. We expected them to be active and useful as soon as possible, flawless on the basics of finance and deal making, alert to our culture, not hiding to conceal their ignorance. The cost of an efficient, effective training program was minimal compared to the benefits of having our newest people, our greatest resource, feeling informed, confident, valued, and ready to work.

We formulated a clear set of expectations, which I laid out in a welcome speech to our new analysts. It boiled down to two words: *excellence* and *integrity*. If we delivered excellent performance for our investors and maintained a pristine reputation, we would have the opportunity to grow and pursue ever more interesting and rewarding work. If we invested poorly or compromised our integrity, we would fail.

To ensure my message got through, I defined excellence in narrow, practical terms: It meant 100 percent on everything. No mistakes. That is different from school or college, where you can get an A with 95 percent. At Blackstone, that 5 percent of underperformance can mean a massive loss for our investors. It is a lot of pressure, but I suggested two ways to relieve it.

The first was focus. If you ever felt overwhelmed by work, I said, pass on some of your work to others. It might not feel natural. High achievers tend to want to volunteer for more responsibility, not give up some of what they have taken on. But all that anyone higher up in the firm cares about is that the work is done well. There is nothing heroic or commendable about taking on too much and then screwing it up. Far better to focus on what you can do, do it well, and share the rest.

The second way to maximize your chances of achieving excellence was to ask for help when needed. Blackstone is full of people who have worked on a lot of deals. If you are spending all night trying to solve a problem, chances are there is someone a few offices away with more experience who could solve it in far less time. Don't waste your time trying to reinvent the wheel, I advised. There were plenty of wheels all around you, ready-made, just waiting for you to spin them faster, further, and in new directions.

As for integrity, the easiest way I could explain it was in terms of reputation. To earn a great reputation, you think long term. I had been building my reputation since growing up in suburban Philadelphia, true to those middle-class values of honesty, hard work, respect for others, and always doing what you say you will. If those values sound simple, it is because they are. Anything more complicated can get lost amid the traps and temptations of our work. So my message to our new analysts was simple: stick to our values and never risk our reputation.

During my career, I had brushed up against the worst of Wall Street. I had seen people compromise their integrity with disastrous consequences for themselves, their firms, and their families. In the early 1980s, when I was running M&A at Lehman, Dennis Levine had the office next door. Dennis was a banker with a young family and seemed like the rest of us. But in 1986, he pleaded guilty to insider trading, securities fraud, and perjury. He had been taking confidential information on planned corporate takeovers and bought stock in the target companies. When the takeovers were announced to the public, the stock went up, and Levine made large, illegal profits. His most famous conspirator was Ivan Boesky, a trader in a three-piece suit who had made millions of dollars sitting at the heart of Wall Street. Everyone knew Boesky, and everyone spoke to him.

One day in the early 1980s, Boesky had invited me for a drink at the Harvard Club on Forty-Fourth Street. He began by asking me how I liked Lehman. I told him I enjoyed the work and the size of the deals. Then he asked me, "Wouldn't you like to earn more money?" I said I was earning plenty, and more would come. "But wouldn't you like to get it a lot sooner?" he said. I thought he was offering me a job, so I told him I was happy where I was. But he kept on with this same weird and ill-defined proposition: "Wouldn't you like to have more?"

Finally, I asked him if he had anything else to discuss. He said no and gave me a lift home. I didn't think much of it until Boesky was arrested in 1986 based on Levine's testimony. The *Wall Street Journal* ran a story about how Boesky had lured another conspirator, Marty Siegel, the head of M&A at Kidder Peabody, with a meeting at the Harvard Club and that same odd language: Wouldn't you like to have more money sooner?

Boesky, Siegel, and Levine, as well as a more junior banker, Ira Sokolow, all went to jail. Though, reading the news, I realized that Levine must have been getting some of his inside information straight from my desk. He must have been coming into my office, taking it, and passing it on to Ivan Boesky.

I tell our first-year associates at Blackstone this story as a warning. These men—Boesky, Levine, Sokolow, and Siegel— looked like any of us. They walked, talked, and acted like us. And they went to jail for trading on inside information. If I ever caught anyone at Blackstone doing what they did, I warned, I would take them to jail myself. I didn't say it to frighten anyone. I said it to help them, to eliminate doubt and make their decisions simpler.

When we hired the class of 1991, Pete and I were looking decades ahead. We hoped that one day, this would be the group to which we could turn over the firm. They would ensure that Blackstone thrived long after us. They represented our future. We were training them not just to be great players, but future coaches for the classes that followed them. All the theories we had about building an information machine, adding new business lines and achieving significant scale, depended on these twenty-somethings living up to the promise we saw in them. Only time would tell if we had made the right bets.

And as it turned out, we did. Many in that first class, and the ones that immediately followed, stayed with us for years, becoming some of the most successful investors and managers in our industry.

SEEING AROUND CORNERS

EXPAND

By 1994, Larry Fink had raised two big funds for Blackstone Financial Management and was managing around $20 billion of mortgage-backed assets. But as the Federal Reserve began raising short-term interest rates more than expected, long-term rates also moved up sharply and many bond investors were caught off-guard. Bond prices crashed in what subsequently became known as the "great bond massacre," driving down the value of Larry's funds.

Larry wanted to sell the business. One of the funds was maturing soon, and he was concerned that investors wouldn't want to reinvest with him given the downturn in performance. I tried to reason with him. It was true that we, along with the rest of the market, were having a tough time, but in the case of Larry and his team, I thought we had the best in the business and I wanted to continue growing. Even if performance decreased for a while and there were redemptions from investors, I was sure the asset class would eventually recover. Give it time, I told Larry. I have no problem selling an asset or business when the time is right, but this wasn't the right time. This business could be huge if we stuck with it.

But I couldn't persuade him. "Why do I have more confidence in you than you have in yourself?" I asked him. He told me that the business represented 100 percent of his net worth, but only 10 percent of mine, hence our differing appetites for risk. We went back and forth for months.

The other disagreement we had was around equity in the business. Under our original agreement, Blackstone owned half of Blackstone Financial Management, Larry and his team the rest. We had agreed to reduce our stakes to 40 percent each, leaving 20 percent to be distributed as stock to employees. If there was any further dilution to be had after that, it would have to come out of Larry's side. That was the deal. But before long, they asked us to give up more stock. I refused. Larry and his team were furious, saying they did all the work. I believed that once you signed something, you stuck to it, but in retrospect, I should have put the contract aside and accommodated Larry's request.

Blackstone, Larry, and his team ended up selling its stake in Blackstone Financial Management to PNC, a medium-sized bank in Pittsburgh. The only humor in it all came from the process of renaming the firm once it was owned by PNC. It could not be called Blackstone anymore. Larry thought there might be a way of retaining some institutional connection through a new name. He suggested Black Pebble or BlackRock. Black Pebble sounded puny to me. We settled on BlackRock.

Selling that business was a heroic mistake, and I own it. Larry's troubled funds recovered from their lowest point in 1994, and PNC has made a fortune from its investment. Larry has done what I always imagined he would and built a huge, successful business, the largest traditional asset manager in the world. I see him often, and he's an unbelievably happy man. It's extraordinary to think of what Blackstone and BlackRock have become. Two firms, hailing distance from each other in midtown Manhattan, starting with a few people in the same office. I often imagine what we might have been together.

If I were in the same situation today as I was in 1994, I would have found a way not to sell Blackstone Financial Management.

Larry was an 11, and his business was exactly the kind we wanted to build at Blackstone. Not only did it have the opportunity to be huge and highly profitable, it also generated the kind of intellectual capital that would inform and strengthen everything we did. Moreover, Larry's skills were complementary to my own, and he was an extraordinary talent and manager. I specialized in illiquid assets; he knew liquid securities. We could have worked both sides in the same business.

But I made the mistakes of an inexperienced CEO: I let the differences between us brew. I stood my ground on the dilution of our equity because I considered it a moral principle to respect the terms of the original deal. Instead, I should have recognized that when a situation changes and a business is doing extremely well, sometimes you have to make accommodations.

When we first thought of adding business lines to Blackstone, our idea wasn't to enter just any area. We wanted to build businesses that were great in their own right but also made our whole firm smarter. We believed that the more we learned from different lines of business, the better we would become at everything. It was the one thing they taught at Harvard Business School: everything in business is connected. We would see opportunities and markets in unusual and different ways from our competitors. Our perspective would broaden and deepen. The more feeds we had running into the firm, the more we'd know, the smarter we'd be, and the better the people who'd want to work with us.

In 1998, we did our first big deal in Europe, buying the Savoy Group in the United Kingdom, owners of four treasured London hotels: the Savoy, Claridge's, the Berkeley, and the Connaught. We had no permanent presence in London at the time, and it was a difficult deal because the owners had been fighting for years. So I flew over for the signing. Afterward, I went to Claridge's in Mayfair, sat down on a sofa, and sank so far into it that my knees were up around my ears. The whole place desperately needed an overhaul.

Who were we to do it? The British press greeted us as barbarians, Americans who would ruin these national treasures. I knew we were going to be judged in London by how we handled the redecoration of Claridge's, one of the grandest and most traditional of the city's hotels, a favorite of the Queen Mother. If we did a beautiful job, it would make our future there much easier. It would be better than any advertising. I considered it so important, I took on the task of overseeing the revival and redecoration myself. I like having a hand in creating beautiful things.

The best way to make the English happy, I figured, would be to hire an English decorator to renovate the hotel. I called Mark Birley, who had created a succession of stylish and popular clubs and restaurants in London, including Annabel's and Harry's Bar, and suggested he open a club at Claridge's. He warned me off a collaboration, saying, "I'm very unreasonable." When he was creating Harry's Bar in London, he told me, a supplier sent him the wrong sconces for the main dining room. The project was already months behind schedule, and his family and business partner were all pushing to get it finished. Put up something temporary, they urged. Don't hold up the opening for the sake of a few sconces. But Birley wouldn't budge. He didn't want to open until everything was perfect. "We lost a lot of money," he told me. "But I don't care about money. I care about perfection. That compromises the way I look at things." I told him I understood his choice of excellence over an easy life.

I then got the names of the five top English decorators and invited them to present to a panel of society women who I thought would know good taste from bad. It took nine months of planning to get the decorators and the panel together. At the end of the day of presentations, I told the panel that we would have a vote. One of the women put up her hand and asked, "Do I have to vote for any of them?" The verdict was unanimous. They didn't like any of what they had seen.

The next day, I got a call from one of the panelists, my friend Dorrit Moussaieff. The person I needed wasn't English at all, she said. He was French, and lived in New York. *Not the ideal pedigree for an English hotel in London*, I thought, but I was out of ideas.

A few days later, Thierry Despont came to my office, immaculately dressed and charmingly French. He gave me two books of his designs and said, "Thierry does not do auditions. If you want to hire me, just hire me. Also, I do not do commercial work, so zees project is ze wrong one for me."

Naturally I was intrigued. This was going to be a very different kind of negotiation, so I started sending out probes, searching for a way past this formidable facade. If Thierry didn't do commercial work, I asked, what did he do?

"I do ze big house. The library of one of ze houses I just do is bigger zan ze lobby of ze Claridge hotel." And he added with emphasis, "I work wiz no budget."

"Sounds fun."

"It is very fun."

"Out of curiosity, have you ever done any commercial work?"

"Yes, for my friend Ralph Lauren." Ralph had been redesigning his store on New Bond Street and asked Thierry to copy the stairwell at the Connaught. "I told Ralph I could not copy the stairwell of ze Connaught, but I can give maybe ze essence of ze stairwell." While he had been going back and forth to London to create that essence, he told me, he had stayed at "ze Claridge" on seventeen separate occasions. It was a "confused hotel," some of it Georgian, some Victorian, lacking any sense of a whole. He had redesigned the entire hotel in his head because "zat's how I zink. If I stay in some place, I zink how it should be better."

In any conversation with someone you don't know, you should always be patient and keep asking questions until you find a place of common ground. That Thierry had not only stayed often in Claridge's but thought about its design told me that his initial salvos about not doing commercial work were true, but perhaps not accurate in this situation. He had the confidence it would take to fix up Claridge's against potentially hostile public opinion. Now I had to persuade him.

"I know you don't do commercial work, but it sounds like this wouldn't even be work," I said. "You've already redesigned the place in your head." What is more, it would be the greatest advertising any decorator could have. I knew a lot of designers and decorators, but I had never heard of him. His reputation could be transformed with one project. "Every wealthy person visiting London will know you did Claridge's, and if they like it, they'll try to hire you."

"Thierry will zink about it and call you."

Two weeks later, he was back in my office. "I have zought about what you said and it would be easy for me to do zis. It could be a good project." I asked if he had any storyboards or preparatory drawings to show me. "Thierry does not do zis. Here is the rule. I will talk to you about colors and concepts and show you what I'm zinking. I'll lay it out and you can say if you like it or not. I'll work with you, you can veto any-zing, and we'll come up with ano-zer solution."

Then I dropped my bomb. Given how much we had ended up paying for the hotels, there wasn't much left over to pay an expensive decorator. The cash mattered to us, because we were trying to squeeze a profit out of the deal, but that mattered less to him. The hotel would be terrific advertising for him. Fair for him and fair for us, the perfect outcome.

"Do you talk to everyone like zis?" he asked.

"It's just the reality of this particular situation."

"Zere is only one answer I should give you. It is no. But I shall say yes."

Thierry did a beautiful job. Not long after the renovation, I received a letter from the exiled king of Greece who lives in London. After we had bought Claridge's, he had written to one of the British newspapers saying these uncouth Americans would destroy his favorite hotel. Now that he had seen what we and our French decorator had done, he was kind enough to write to me to tell me he had been wrong.

———

The success of our London hotels deal was one reason we decided to open our first overseas office there. In the late 1990s, many of our competitors began opening international offices. The most pressing argument for global expansion was that it would give us access to more investment opportunities. We could raise new funds and find new ways to reward our investors. If the United States entered another recession, we could turn our focus to other developed markets such as Europe or the developing markets of Asia, Latin America, and Africa. But even though we began doing a few deals outside the United States, like the Savoy Group, we did not move faster for two reasons.

First, our most important investment rule: don't lose money. We were comfortable in the United States, where there were plenty of deals to do. We understood the risks and knew how to minimize them. In new markets, we would have to learn much of this from scratch.

Second, overseas expansion risked compromising the investment process we had developed after Edgcomb. Its success depended on the same people being in a room together scrutinizing dozens of deals over time, reading each other's levels of confidence. I needed to hear a deal explained to me in person before I reached a conclusion. Hearing the nuance in someone's voice or seeing that person's body language told me as much as anything he or she said. I couldn't see us retaining the rigor our investment process demanded if we spoke only by telephone from offices scattered around the world. The evolution of video-conferencing technology changed my mind. By 2001, you could interact with people thousands of miles away in real time. That year, we opened an office in London.

The United Kingdom was an obvious choice for our first foreign outpost in private equity. It was the most active country for deals in the European Union, and we had done a few of them, like the Savoy Group, without moving a team there. The language, the legal system, and the general environment for doing business made it an easy place for an American firm to expand. But still, I felt we needed something to help us stand out. We looked at the American deal makers there, masquerading as Brits in their custom suits and shoes. And we looked at the Europeans, with centuries-old animosities. And then we decided that our edge was being unabashedly American, unabashedly Blackstone. We would offer the connection to American money and American business know-how, no cultural baggage attached. Just straightforward Americans, there to do business.

Most firms looking to start a new venture put a senior person in charge, someone with gravitas and experience. As we weighed our ambition to grow with our need to retain our culture, we decided it was much more important that we send someone who embodied our culture. Someone we could trust absolutely, someone hungry to build a business of his or her own within Blackstone.

David Blitzer had joined us in 1991 straight out of Wharton, a member of our first class of graduates. He had been one of the junior analysts I used to surprise with calls as I dug into the details of a deal. He loves Coca-Cola, hamburgers, and the New York Yankees and would never wear a custom suit. He is likable and sociable, smart and entrepreneurial.

The only problem was that David didn't want to go. He and his wife, Allison, were newlyweds and hadn't had any children yet, and they were worried about the care in British hospitals. So Christine and I took them out to a French restaurant on Central Park South. I promised David and Allison that we would fly them back for any medical care they wanted, even bring them over for a month before any child was born. It was a lot of money for the firm at the time, but I wanted David there. And I assured them that everyone I knew who had ever moved to London loved it. So off they went.

David chose Joe Baratta to go with him as his associate. Joe had also come to Blackstone in his twenties after working at Morgan Stanley. Joe had a strong entrepreneurial streak and a fascination with business, not just finance. He was a fierce worker who had suffered under some of our worst-behaved partners. But he had come through it all and was developing a great reputation. Like David, he understood our investment process and our culture intuitively.

They arrived in London with capital but no office and squeezed into a space sublet from KKR. The deals they pursued built on our unusual expertise in both private equity and real estate. They bought pubs, hotels, and theme parks and expanded into the rest of Europe. They were creative and aggressive and did some of the most successful deals in our history, building our first global outpost without sacrificing the culture and discipline central to our firm. As it turned out, David and Allison ended up having five children in London.

At around the same time back in New York, we were expanding as well. I asked Tom Hill, whom I had known since the Army Reserves and worked with at Lehman, to build out a new hedge fund business, Blackstone Alternative Asset Management (BAAM). Tom took over our nascent operations in this area and developed them into the largest discretionary investor in hedge funds in the world, increasing assets under management from less than $1 billion when he started, to more than $75 billion when he retired in 2018.

Within a year of David and Joe's arrival in London, Blackstone had outgrown its shared office space there. When you enter a market, you send signals with every choice you make, from the people you hire to the offices you rent. They are an important piece of your brand. I was determined that our new European headquarters exude the values of the firm: excellence, integrity, and care for all the people associated with us, those we employ and those whose money we invest.

I was on vacation in France when the realtor we had hired called and said he had five locations in London for me to see. I flew up and still wearing jeans and a polo shirt went to see five dark, dingy sets of offices, all with low ceilings and small windows. I told our realtor they were dreadful. He said they were the best to be found in London, outside of the City. I can see him now, with his slicked-back hair, his tightly fitting, blue, chalk-stripe suit, and taps on his wingtips, which clicked as he walked.

But as we were driving through Mayfair in central London, I noticed a construction site in Berkeley Square, covered in barriers. It was a great location.

"How about that?" I asked the realtor.

"Not available," he said. It was a hole in the ground. But the realtor asserted that the owners were refusing to sign any leases until the building was finished. Still, I insisted we take a look.

I stopped the car, and we walked back to the construction site office, where I found the site manager. I told him it looked like he was working on a terrific project. He said they were proud of it. I asked him who owned it. I wanted to figure out if it was an insurance company or a couple of smart entrepreneurs. It turned out to be the former.

At the time, London real estate seemed to be going down in value. Rents were down to £60 per square foot. I guessed that the owners probably started out expecting rents of £70 per square foot. If the market kept falling, this building would soon be a money-losing project. I asked the site manager to call the owners and tell them that I would take at least half the project at £80 per square foot. If I paid £80 for half, assuming the world did not melt down, they could rent the other half at £60 and still get the £70 per square foot they had in their projections.

"I know I don't look like a proper businessman," I told the site manager. "But I don't report to anybody. If I tell you I'll pay £80, it's just me. We'll pay. So please let the owner know. If he wants us to take more than half, we'll take more than half."

As we walked away, the realtor started criticizing me for my manners. He said he had told me the owners weren't ready to sign leases and I'd wasted his time, not to mention ruined any chance we might have had of getting space in the building. Fortunately, he was wrong on both counts. The owners called back the next day and said they liked my offer. We could have half the space. Today we have every floor but one.

I was never going to settle on offices that were less than perfect. The rewards of having a beautiful space that attracted the best people and gave our clients greater confidence in our abilities would far exceed the cost of paying a little extra to close the deal. And the best way to get what you want is to figure out what's on the mind of the person who can give it to you. By addressing the developer's concern about falling rents, we got the space I wanted.

We delegated the decoration at first to our facilities department. They hired a design firm who came to present to us in New York. This firm proposed putting a giant piece of natural wood in the lobby. We would look like a branch of Timberland.

"We are not a shoe store," I told them. "This is awful."

"What don't you like?" they asked.

"Everything."

"We can fix it."

"No, you can't. If you came up with this design, you can't fix it. The concept is so wrong. I don't want you even to try and fix it. You might be able to half-fix it. But I think we should settle up and move on."

One of the best features of the office was the amount of space and the large windows. I sent Stephen Miller Siegel, a designer I knew in New York, who came up with a beautiful design that we have to this day in all of our offices around the world: a thin ribbon of stainless steel running through walnut paneling. The only difference between London and New York is the light, so we have slightly different carpets, adjusted to the light, that in fact look the same. You never see decor this pretty in finance. Back then it was really something.

At Lehman, I had realized that I spent more time at the office than at home, so I wanted a beautiful environment. It made me feel happier. I wanted the same for everyone at Blackstone: warmth, elegance, simplicity, balance, and natural light pouring in from huge windows. When people come to a Blackstone office to work or for meetings, I want them to feel as blown away as I am by the experience.

One night in 2004, I was traveling in eastern France. My driver couldn't speak English, and I was exhausted from a European trip. My cell phone rang and it was a headhunter who asked if I would have an interest in being chairman of the Kennedy Center for the Performing Arts in Washington, DC.

The call surprised me; at the time I didn't even know what the Kennedy Center did. She said it was Washington, DC's version of Lincoln Center. The role was part time. I told her that much as I loved the performing arts, I had a full-time job running Blackstone. But she insisted on sending me some information.

Several days later, Ken Duberstein, who had been Ronald Reagan's chief of staff, called me. He told me that in Washington, the Kennedy Center, named in honor of President John F. Kennedy, is an incredible place to meet people. There are cabinet members on the board, and I'd get to meet the president whenever he visited. Lobbying was not permitted, so the center was bipartisan. It was also the social capital of Washington. The chairman must bridge the many worlds of Washington—politics, business, law, and culture—to bring the best of America and the world to the capital.

I had always been fascinated by politics, as a student running for office in high school to my meeting with Averell Harriman to my interviews at the White House when I was preparing to leave Lehman. From Blackstone's perspective, we were facing an increasing number of issues related to regulation and taxation. Our investors now included state, national, and international investment funds, so politics at every level was of increasing relevance to our business. Having an official position in Washington would allow me to meet new people and learn more. I called my old friend Jane Hitchcock, a playwright and novelist who lives in Washington, for advice. "Stevie," she said, "you have to do this."

Ken arranged for me to meet the board. I asked them about the center: its goals, its challenges, and what it needed from a chairman. Ken called me later and said the board was surprised. They thought they were supposed to be interviewing me, but instead I had interviewed them. My objective, I told Ken, had been to learn. I wasn't trying to persuade anyone I was right for the job. It was the same way I thought about interviews at Blackstone. If both sides could be easy, open, and direct with each other, the fit, or lack of it, would become apparent. From our conversations that day, it seemed the fit was there.

Next, Ken asked me to meet Senator Ted Kennedy, who had to approve any new chairman on behalf of the Kennedy family. He came to see me in New York and told me that after his brothers Jack and Bobby were assassinated in the 1960s, the family divided their public legacy. Ted looked after the Kennedy Center, and Jack's daughter, Caroline, the Kennedy Presidential Library in Boston.

"I have a simple rule with the Kennedy Center," he told me. "I'll support you and make sure you get the funding you need from Congress. I'll support you even if you screw up. And anything you need here in DC, call me and I'll make it happen for you." I had imagined there would be more political complexity in the process. Ted's promise pushed me closer to accepting.

One more thing, I told Ted. I wanted Caroline to get involved. She represented the next generation of Kennedys, but she never came to the Kennedy Center. He said he'd speak to her. A few days later, Caroline called, and we set up a meeting. I told her I wanted her to be the symbol of change and new life at the Kennedy Center. I realized that this wasn't something she wanted to do for herself, but it would be right for the institution. Her absence would be a deal breaker for me. Happily for me, she agreed and began a run of hosting each year's Kennedy Center Honors television show wearing her mother's famous diamond earrings.

The Kennedy Center also put me back in touch with George W. Bush, who had been a year ahead of me at Yale. I had met George's father, who became the forty-first president, at Parents' Day in 1967. To mark my appointment, the first lady, Laura Bush, hosted a lunch in the private quarters of the White House complete with a cake baked as a replica of the Kennedy Center. The building itself was frosted in chocolate, the stage made of sorbet, the orchestra members slices of peach, and the audience raspberries.

Another time at the White House, George and I were waiting for an event to start and had a moment to ourselves.

"How did you get here?" I asked.

"What?"

"How did you get here?"

"I'm president. That's how I got here."

"I mean, how did *you* ever get to be president?" He laughed and agreed that if you'd met us both in the late 1960s at Yale, you would have been surprised to find either of us at the White House, decades later, pillars of the establishment. It was a real pinch-me moment and another reminder of how people you meet accidentally early in life keep popping up to surprise you.

Being in Washington on a regular basis turned out to be more fulfilling than I had imagined. It gave me the chance to meet almost everyone of importance in our government, from Supreme Court justices to the leaders in Congress and members of the administration.

The role of chairman satisfied the producer in me. Whenever I was at the Kennedy Center, I had to go onstage and introduce the performance. And when we handed out awards, I welcomed and hosted our honorees. During my tenure, these included Dolly Parton, Barbra Streisand, and Elton John, among others. But the highlight for me was in 2005, when we awarded Tina Turner the Kennedy Center Honors. I had loved Tina's music since I was in college. Now I had the opportunity to host her and four other honorees for an entire weekend of celebrations. Tina came with her good friend Oprah Winfrey, who toasted her at an event at the State Department and came with us on a tour of the White House. As we walked around, Tina kept saying, in her surprisingly small voice, "I can't believe I ever got to the White House from where I came from." For the main event at the Kennedy Center itself, Beyoncé and a group of backup singers sang "Proud Mary," wearing the original short dresses that Tina and the Ikettes had made famous. Looking along our row in the balcony, with the other honorees and the president, I could see tears in Tina's eyes.

Several years after that night, I was at a charity event at Cipriani on Forty-Second Street in New York when I saw someone at a nearby table waving at me. I couldn't quite make out who it was because of the lighting, but my wife nudged me to go say hello. It was Beyoncé and her husband, Jay-Z. We talked for a few minutes, reminiscing about her Kennedy Center performance in 2005. It turns out that night was just as memorable and special for her as it was for me. As I walked back to my table, I shook my head in disbelief. What a remarkable life I was privileged to be living.

It's important to always be open to new experiences, even if they don't completely fit your agenda. My role at the Kennedy Center allowed me to use my experience—running organizations, fundraising, hiring talent—to give back to an important American cultural institution. In return, I learned more about Washington, DC, and developed interesting new relationships in almost every area of the entertainment business: comedy, theater, music, movies, television, opera, and dance. This included meeting the stars, directors, choreographers, musicians, and writers involved with each relevant art form. For someone from the financial world, chairing the Kennedy Center was a once-in-a-lifetime opportunity. Although I didn't know it at the time, the connections I made would eventually prove immensely important to me, even leading to several future opportunities to develop institutions in this area.

ASK FOR HELP
WHEN YOU NEED IT

As the firm grew rapidly, the burden of maintaining a zero-defect culture and managing our expansion was crushing. By 2000, Pete was in his late seventies and spending most of his time running the Council on Foreign Relations and focusing on domestic and international economic issues in Washington. When we started the firm, he told me he didn't want to be involved in the investment area. He said he would help us raise money, stay involved in the advisory business, and help in any way I asked him. Watching me now try to do everything, he told me, "Steve, you're going to drop dead; you're just working too hard." He was right. The day-to-day management of the business was not my strength. I needed help.

I had known Jimmy Lee since the late 1980s, when we had hired him at Chemical Bank to finance our first deal, Transtar. We had done a huge amount of business together since. He was exceptionally high energy, a model of integrity, a great friend, and someone I trusted. He knew capital markets, M&A, and the buyout business and was a great salesman. I felt we could achieve a lot together at Blackstone and have a lot of fun doing it.

The first time we discussed it, he told me he loved the idea, but it would be tough to leave his colleagues at JPMorgan. I told him to think about it. A while later, he came back to me. "I want to do it," he said. "I want to make the change."

As we were negotiating the legal arrangements, I got a call from Bill Harrison, the CEO of JPMorgan, another great friend. "Jimmy came in to see me about the discussions he's been having with you. You know it's my job to fight to keep him."

"Of course, Bill, I know that," I said. "Jimmy's incredibly loyal to you. I asked him to think this through, without any pressure from me, because it's about what he really wants to do with his life. This isn't just a job. The bank's been his life, as Blackstone's been mine. He's got to figure it out."

"Whatever he decides, we'll both have to live with it," said Bill. "I just wanted to give you a heads-up that he and I talked." A few days later I was at the Ritz Carlton in Sarasota, Florida. The legal agreement and press announcement between Jimmy and Blackstone was finalized. We were going to make the announcement the next day. I was walking on the veranda when my cell phone rang.

"Steve," said Jimmy, "I can't do it."

"You can't do what?"

"I can't leave the bank. I know I'm totally disappointing you. You gave me all the rope anybody could need, and I told you I'd do it. But I realize I just can't."

"Jimmy, we've spent months on this, and I really want you to do it. But I said at the beginning that it was your call, your life. You don't need to be emotional. If you are going to join, you have to be all in. If you can't do that, it's not a good thing. You definitely shouldn't join us because you feel guilty about me. If you need more time to think, that's absolutely okay."

"No," he said. "I've thought about it. I have to stay."

It was a terrible setback and disappointment. But I knew Jimmy's strengths, and I knew his weaknesses. A man who in many ways dominated Wall Street was at heart a modest, dutiful Catholic boy who had to do the right thing.

It took me a year to muster the energy for another search. When the search company gave me their list, I saw the same tired old names. Of the couple of new ones, one stood out. A decade or so earlier, we had agreed to buy Chicago Northwestern Railroad for $1.6 billion. DLJ, my first employer, had given us a bridge loan to pay part of the purchase price. We planned to issue bonds to pay it back. But as credit seized up in the late 1980s, we would have to pay a higher rate on the bonds than we wanted just to get the deal done before the markets slammed shut.

Early one morning, a violent storm was raging outside. I had to catch a flight to London a few hours later. Pete, Roger Altman, and I were sitting opposite the team from DLJ arguing over the rate. DLJ wanted a floating rate with no limit. I couldn't agree because the interest rate could theoretically go extremely high if the company got into difficulty. DLJ countered by proposing a floating rate that could range between a minimum and maximum based on what some Wall Street experts would determine was fair. I knew that the rate would never float down, only up to that high cap. They argued it was necessary to sell the bonds. We wanted a fixed lower limit on the rate, so we could be sure we could pay it back. We weren't getting anywhere, and our flight was waiting, assuming the weather didn't ground us entirely.

"I'll bet a million dollars of my personal money that whatever higher cap you set on the rate, that's where these bonds will end up. Anybody willing to take me up on that?" I asked, knowing full well that they wouldn't. Nobody.

"Half a million?"

Nobody. These DLJ people assumed I didn't know we would end up as victims under the structure they were proposing. They weren't confident they could sell the bonds without the cap.

"How about a hundred thousand? No? Anyone in for ten thousand?"

One hand went up, Tony James's. To move forward, I agreed to the structure they wanted, but sure enough, the bonds were eventually reset and their rate floated up to their highest possible point. I told Tony he could send his $10,000 to the New York City Ballet. And I always remembered him as the only person ready to stand by his firm's position.

I asked the headhunter for his file. At DLJ, Tony had run corporate finance and M&A and started the firm's private equity business. Over the past decade, DLJ had the best-performing private equity funds, and Tony had been the trigger puller, its head investor. Everything we did at Blackstone, he had been doing at DLJ. In many cases, he had done it better. I invited him for dinner at my house.

Tony is tall, patrician, and reserved. He had grown up in a wealthy suburb of Boston and gone to all the best schools. He had spent most of his professional life at DLJ, but since its acquisition by Credit Suisse, he had become frustrated. I could empathize, having gone through a similar experience when we sold Lehman. He didn't like the new hierarchy and bureaucracy. His record at DLJ was remarkable, but he didn't boast. He laid out the facts, what he had done, why and when.

Over the next few weeks, we had a succession of meetings and meals. Getting to know each other went well beyond the usual hiring process. I knew this decision was going to be the most important hire I ever made. We kept talking about interesting deals, the complexities, the decisions, why we had made one rather than another, whether that had been right or wrong. We talked about deals neither of us had been involved in and how they had been handled. What did he think? What did I think? How should it have been handled? We agreed on almost everything.

I called some of my old friends at DLJ, including Dick Jenrette. And they all said the same thing, as if they had met and drawn up a script: "Tony is perfect for you, absolutely perfect. He's the smartest guy we've had here. He's a completely dedicated, loyal, hard-working person. Nobody works harder. He doesn't have a political bone in his body. He'd be a perfect complement to you. He'd never undercut you. He'd be a great, great partner." I trusted my friends, I trusted him, I trusted myself. I was done.

As Tony and I finished our discussions, I told him, "Listen, we agree on virtually everything. There's only one disagreement we'll ever have. I only like to do big things. I don't like getting diverted. I like taking on huge opportunities and making them happen. You have a different philosophy. You like doing what works. You'll do huge things and small things. You don't care as much about scale, as long as they're well constructed and you can make them work.

"You'll be unhappy with me when I don't want to do things that aren't consequential, things you know you can set up and that are going to make money. You won't understand why I won't do it. But I'm always going to want to keep our firepower for something that's worthy."

Tony joined as my partner and chief operating officer in 2002, and, as predicted, those are the only type of disagreements we have ever had. Every other aspect of running Blackstone, every personnel question, every management problem, every deal decision, every investor issue, where we go, where we do not go—we talk, we figure it out, and we always agree. It is an amazing partnership.

———

I'm not a natural manager, but I've improved over the years. Tony, by his own admission, is the opposite. He is a great manager. I phased him in so that our partners could get used to his style and his direction without creating the kind of resentment that proud insiders often feel toward a person brought in from the outside. First, he was chief operating officer; later he became president. It took a year of introducing him into an important role in each of our businesses. But by the time we finished, everyone understood his capabilities and accepted his leadership. In time, he was running the business, directing investments and handling the day-to-day managerial challenges of a growing organization.

When he arrived, he found a culture in need of a refresh. It had been over a decade since the sweeping changes we had introduced after Edgcomb. We had just avoided the excesses of the dot-com bubble. Despite our younger partners urging me to invest more aggressively in technology firms, I had resisted. Investors seemed to have abandoned all logic in valuing tech firms. Our investment discipline kept us from joining the herd.

There were many other great aspects to our culture. Every Monday morning, for example, all of our investment teams gathered to talk about their deals and their context, starting at 8:30 a.m. and running until early afternoon. We discussed the global economy, politics, conversations with our investors, media, any issues that might affect the business. Then we went through a list of live deals, sharing our insights and ideas from our different activities around the world. Everyone could attend. Those who had something relevant to say were encouraged to say it, whatever their age or rank within the firm. All that mattered was the quality of their thinking. To this day, Monday mornings remain the clearest demonstration of our commitment to transparency, equality, and intellectual integrity.

But our reputation as a place to work had suffered as a result of personnel turnover. Many of our partners had become complacent. Sometimes they didn't work on Fridays or refused to spend enough time training and mentoring their junior people. In 2000, I had tried to reenergize the firm by adding five new partners, all in their early thirties, to our existing twelve. Many of the support functions of the firm, from HR to compensation, weren't working the way they should and I had been too busy to fix them.

Tony started by literally breaking down walls. He took down the partitions shielding the partners' offices from the rest of the firm and replaced them with glass. Sunlight now poured in where the analysts and assistants sat. Tony kept his own door open, and he expected others to do the same. He reached out to families and invited our employees to bring their children to work to learn about what their parents did all day. He instituted 360-degree performance reviews to assess everyone at the firm. He overhauled the compensation system toward one based on group bonus pools, written feedback, and open reviews.

Knowing the machinery of the firm was now operating properly and that Tony had their backs, our people felt more confident to speak up, especially young people. The number of people now attending our Monday morning meetings made our lawyers nervous. They worried that too many people knew too much. But Tony and I refused to change what we were doing. If we started eliminating people, how would they ever absorb our investment process? Almost everyone else in finance was stovepiped: they could see only what was going on in their own narrow slice of the industry. Our Monday morning meetings allowed people from every part of the firm to see how the specialists in other parts thought and acted, and we've never had a breach in confidentiality.

A few years after we introduced the 360-degree reviews, I learned that one of our most senior people was yelling at and demeaning people, behavior I had tried to eliminate years before. I realized that I could not delegate this problem. I met privately, one by one, with the fifteen people who worked most closely with the person under review and guaranteed the confidentiality of what they told me. I wanted them to trust this process and know that by being open, they were helping the whole organization reaffirm our core values. I learned that the partner was deceitful and vindictive. I called him to my office and explained what I had done. Every single person who worked with him was scared. Given his position, I assumed he could not help himself. It must be something out of his control. I was ready to give him one chance.

"I know you're appalled by this meeting," I told him. "That's either because you've been discovered or because you're learning about yourself. But if I ever see or hear about this kind of behavior again, you're gone. Regrettably, because I don't want you gone." He did change, for about a year. But then he reverted back to his old self. We let him go.

I was never a founder who needed to hang on to power at all costs. Lifting the day-to-day management burdens energized me for the deal making I loved. Tony brought a discipline and orderliness to each of the firm's functions that we had not had previously. I knew that bringing in and empowering someone of Tony's caliber would institutionalize the firm and give us an edge to complete some of the largest deals in Wall Street history.

———

In 2006, Angela Merkel invited me to meet her at the German Chancellery in Berlin. We had made substantial investments in German companies, but the country's vice chancellor, Franz Müntefering, had called private equity investors "locusts" who devour companies. This began a national debate for Germany that dominated daily headlines and television news.

"I've read some things and want to learn more," said the

chancellor, who, thankfully, wanted to hear the other side of the critics' argument. "They say you are locusts," and she raised her fingers above her head and waggled them like a locust's feelers.

"But I'm a good locust," I said, making the same gesture.

"But why would they call you a locust?"

I gave her the explanation I give to everyone who asks what we do. We are in the business of buying, fixing, and selling. We are managers and owners as much as we are investors. We try to improve the companies we buy and help them grow faster. The faster a company grows, the more someone else will pay for it. The perceived problems arise when we buy a company that is poorly managed and we have to fire people to make room for better ones, or change strategy. Even once we've improved the company, grown it, and hired more people than it ever had before, the people we fired tend to stay angry at us and become our critics.

Merkel told me that when she was growing up in East Germany, she had never learned about business or finance. Her father had been a pastor. She had trained and worked as a physicist. But she was a quick study. Why, she asked, aren't all companies run like private equity–owned companies? Some, I said, need access to bigger pools of capital, which exist only in public markets. A mining company, for example, has to invest huge amounts in exploration and extraction before it can earn any cash flow. As for the rest, maybe they should.

The chancellor's questions cut to a frequent debate on private equity, and one that would intensify with the financial crisis. Do investors like us help or harm the economy? The argument against us has always been that private equity is no more than financial engineering practiced by a small bunch of people far removed from the factories, shops, buildings, and labs where the real work is done. That is not us.

We step into markets when we see a dislocation. A great company hits a rough patch and needs financing and operating intervention to help it through. An infrastructure project needs capital. A corporation wants to sell a division and invest its capital elsewhere. A terrific entrepreneur wants to expand or acquire rivals, but banks won't lend to him or her. We enter these situations with financing, a strategy to transform the business, and expert operating professionals, and we invest the time needed to turn them around.

ENTREPRENEURSHIP:
NO ONE TELLS YOU ABOUT
THE PAIN

I once attended a meeting of student entrepreneurs at a top American university. A professor of entrepreneurship showed a slide illustrating all the steps a start-up must take, from hiring people and raising money to developing a product and going to market. His slide showed the business on a predictable, upwardly curving trajectory hitting various milestones. *If only*, I thought to myself. My experience of entrepreneurship was anything but a smooth, upward curve. It was so grueling that I have never understood the idea of people wanting to be "serial entrepreneurs." Doing it once is hard enough.

By the time the professor stopped talking and passed the microphone to me, I had decided these students needed a reality check. If you are going to start a business, I told them, I believe it has to pass three basic tests.

First, your idea has to be big enough to justify devoting your life to it. Make sure it has the potential to be huge.

Second, it should be unique. When people see what you are offering, they should say to themselves, "My gosh, I need this. I've been waiting for this. This really appeals to me." Without that "aha!" you are wasting your time.

Third, your timing must be right. The world actually

doesn't like pioneers, so if you are too early, your risk of failure is high. The market you are targeting should be lifting off with enough momentum to help make you successful.

If you pass these three tests, you will have a business with the potential to be big, that offers something unique, and is hitting the market at the right time. Then you have to be ready for the pain. No entrepreneur anticipates or wants pain, but pain is the reality of starting something new. It is unavoidable.

Real companies don't just happen. Raising money and recruiting good people is very hard. Even when you are small, though, and your resources most constrained, finding the right people is the most important thing you can do. You typically won't have access to the best, who are working elsewhere at much higher compensation levels. You have to make do with the people you get. That means, at a minimum, you must reduce your criteria to a simple question: Does this person have the same zealous commitment to the mission of this business as you do?

When Phil Knight was building Nike, he hired other distance runners to work with him because he knew that whatever they lacked in terms of business knowledge, they made up for in stamina. They would never give up. They would take the pain and make it to the end of the race despite the difficulties.

When you start a company, you are usually happy to find anyone of quality willing to go on the journey with you. But as you grow, you realize that some people are like wide receivers in football with hands of stone. You throw to them, and the ball just bounces off them. Others have hands like glue. As a decent person you think your role is to coax the bad ones along, to find workarounds. As employees, these are

6s and 7s out of 10. If you keep them, you will end up with a dysfunctional company, where you do all the work, staying up all night with the few people who can make it happen.

You have two options: either run a middling company going nowhere or clear out the mediocrity you created so you can grow. If you are ambitious, you have to fill your company with 9s and 10s, and give them the difficult tasks to do.

Finally, to succeed as an entrepreneur, you have to be paranoid. You always have to believe your company, regardless of size, is a little company. The moment you start to become big and successful, challengers will appear and do their best to take your customers and defeat your business. You are never more vulnerable than at the moment you think you have succeeded.

Many founder-led companies stumble trying to make the transition from scrappy start-up to a well-managed machine. Entrepreneurs often prefer to trust their instincts rather than the more orderly systems that professional managers use. Entrepreneurs often resist any limits placed on those instincts and the energy that brought their company into existence. But eventually it is those limits that create the foundation for the next phase of growth. The turbulence of starting a firm must at some point permit systems to be implemented that allow other people to help drive the organization forward.

LISTEN FOR
DISCORDANT NOTES

One Monday in fall 2006, I settled into my seat at the long conference table that fills the boardroom of our New York office. Colleagues filled every seat, even the benches along the walls. Video screens embedded in the walls showed our teams in London, Mumbai, and Hong Kong. We talked about politics, the macroeconomy, and trends in our businesses. Forty-three stories above the streets of Manhattan, these meetings always gave me the sense of manning a mission control center, navigating Blackstone through a fast-changing and uncertain environment. What I heard that morning scared me.

The discussion had turned to Spain, where we were looking at buying several blocks of condominiums. Someone said that there was now so much construction going on in southern Spain that you could move most of Germany there and still have units to spare. Developers were ignoring the basic laws of supply and demand.

As our European team laid out their concerns, a disembodied voice interrupted us. "We're seeing the same thing in India. Raw land here is up ten times in eighteen months." I almost choked on my coffee.

"Who is that?" I said, looking around the room. I thought

everyone was connected via monitor, and it took me a moment to realize the voice was coming from a telephone speaker.

"This is Tuhin Parikh," said the voice. "I recently joined the firm to look at real estate in India." We had opened our India office only a year before and had made no investments in real estate there. It was a surprise to hear from him. The line had static. But what Tuhin said was so startling, I asked him to repeat it.

"Yes, Steve," he said. "In the past eighteen months, we've seen land prices multiply ten times. Prices were much too high already. And now they have gone completely crazy." India was a fast-growing, emerging economy, which was why we had decided to open an office there. But it was not growing at anything like the rate that would have justified that kind of explosion in land prices. In fifteen years of real estate investing, I had never seen anything go up ten times in eighteen months.

Even more concerning, this was just raw land. When you buy land, you are betting that you can build something valuable on it. But that could take years. You are betting that you can get the approvals you need from the government; that construction goes smoothly; that there will still be demand for whatever you build whenever you finish it; and that the economic conditions remain strong enough for you to earn a yield higher than your cost of borrowing. When land prices are skyrocketing ten times in a year and a half, you know that investors have succumbed to a kind of madness, blinding themselves to all the obvious risks.

On the spot, we decided that we would not be doing the Spanish housing deal. There were some confused looks around the table. What did land prices in India have to do with Spanish condos? In an increasingly globalized economy, you had to be able to make connections that a decade or two earlier might not have existed. Cheap, readily available credit was now virtually borderless, flowing around the world in pursuit of opportunity. If we were seeing real estate bubbles in Spain and India, chances were that it was happening elsewhere. This was no time to reach for high-priced real estate deals in overheated markets.

The following weekend, I was at my house in Palm Beach reading the newspapers over breakfast and spotted a story about Palm Beach house prices rising 25 percent. The population growth in Palm Beach could not have been more than 1 or 2 percent a year. Yet here was the local paper describing the abnormal strength of the local real estate market. As in Spain and India, the basic link between supply and demand was broken.

All my life, I have been looking and listening for patterns. It is like the old TV show, *Name That Tune*. The more songs you know, the more likely you are to be able to identify the song from just one or two notes. You become like an experienced clinician, who can tell what's wrong with a patient long before seeing the results of all the tests. The suspicions raised by that real estate meeting earlier in the week now grew into outright fears of an imminent collapse. As I sat there in the Florida sunshine, I began to have serious concerns about the risk of a global collapse.

The Monday after I returned from Florida, I opened our 8:30 a.m. private equity meeting by asking about the environment for doing deals. It was tough. There were interesting opportunities to buy companies, but the prices were far too high. "It's not like we're losing the deals by a few dollars," one of the team told me. "People are bidding 15 to 20 percent higher than our highest valuations. We're not even close."

We had been doing private equity deals for almost two decades. Either we were missing something, which seemed unlikely given our experience and expertise, or other investors were taking too much risk.

I asked what kind of deals we were looking at. When they

told me we had just been approached with two deals for home-building companies, I almost jumped out of my seat.

"We're not touching housing," I said. If home builders were trying to sell us their companies, they were probably seeing what I was seeing. It would be a terrible time for us to buy.

At the 10:30 a.m. meeting with the real estate team, I said we had to eliminate any exposure to housing, not just condos in Spain, but anything, anywhere—in the United States too. Later, I instructed our credit group to reduce their positions in any real estate loans or mortgage-backed securities they might own and not buy any more. Our hedge fund team got the same directive. They listened to my warnings, and my partner, Tom Hill, the head of our hedge fund investment business, bet that the value of subprime mortgages, home loans made to the least creditworthy borrowers, would fall. He was right, and we made more than half a billion dollars for our investors.

If I had walked out of the office that morning onto Lexington Avenue, I would have seen an economy operating at full throttle. Shops were busy, the stock market was hitting all-time highs. People had gotten used to the value of their homes going in only one direction: up. Even in my own industry, all the talk was of endless growth. Our competitors kept outbidding us on deals. They saw a rosier future than we did.

Changing your behavior in the face of changing information is always hard. But when people are doing well, they don't want to change. They choose to ignore the discordant notes and the tunes you are hearing. They feel threatened by bad news and dread the uncertainty of change and the hard work it demands. This tendency makes them passive and rigid at the very moment they should be most active and flexible.

I have always regarded worry as an active, liberating kind of activity. Worrying allows you to articulate the downside in any situation and leads to action to avoid it. We had set up Blackstone to give us reasons to worry, to absorb reams of raw data, so we could develop our intelligence by looking for anomalies and patterns. At its best, worrying is playful, engaging work that requires that you never switch off.

My concerns about eliminating risk rippled across our portfolio. We did not just get out of Spanish housing; we got out of Spain entirely. The oversupply in condominiums identified by our real estate team suggested a credit bubble that could overwhelm the entire economy. No business, however robust, could compete against a systemic collapse.

Not long afterward, I was in Madrid visiting friends and had gone to look at Picasso's *Guernica*. We were about to close a giant deal to buy Clear Channel Communications, an American media company, in partnership with two other firms, Providence Equity Partners and KKR. I remember thinking as I looked at the painting that we shouldn't be doing it. Perhaps it was just being in Spain, and all the doubts I was having about its economy. Or maybe it was Picasso's gruesome subject matter, the bombing of the small town of Guernica during the Spanish Civil War. But I felt uneasy. As I came down in the elevators outside the Reina Sofía Museum, my feelings grew stronger, a physical sensation provoked by the evidence. By the time I got back to my hotel room, I had decided we had to pull out of the deal. I called Jonathan Nelson at Providence. It wasn't just nerves, I told him. It was judgment. All of us were in deal heat and eager to get something done. But if this deal went wrong, it could seriously damage our investors and our firms.

Across the firm, we were selling assets we had bought following the collapse of the tech bubble in 2001 and owned through a robust recovery. These were cyclical companies whose fortunes rose and fell based on the health of the overall economy. In 2003, we had bought Celanese, a big German chemical manufacturer, which had grown unwieldy and inefficient through multiple acquisitions. We shut the German headquarters and moved it to the United States, where it was making 90 percent of its sales. Just making it an American company transformed its multiple. By the time we sold our last shares in Celanese in May 2007, we had made nearly five times our money. It was our single most successful investment up to that point.

In 2005, 70 percent of our investments had been in cyclical businesses. By the following year, this share had fallen to 30 percent. We effectively closed shop for private equity deals, cutting our deal volume in half. I was determined that if the markets did collapse, our people wouldn't be tied up trying to clean up messes from bad deals. But of course, just as we were locking down the firm, we ran straight into a situation that embodied another of our investment principles: don't miss a can't-miss opportunity.

———————

We weren't the only ones seeing trouble. In October 2006, we got word that our old friend Sam Zell, our first visitor to Blackstone, was thinking of selling his office property business. Since the day when we had sat on the floor of our empty office and talked, we had stayed in touch. In 1994, we bought a company from him, Great Lakes Dredge and Dock, and our real estate team in particular had watched him closely. Sam is a true entrepreneur and never one to settle for the status quo. Since the early 1990s, he had been arguing that the public should be able to buy and sell shares in portfolios of commercial real estate, the way they can with other companies. He had created Equity Office Properties (EOP) as a real estate investment trust (REIT). It was the first of its kind to be traded as part of the S&P 500 index. By the time we were evaluating it, the EOP REIT was the largest office company in the world, with over 100 million square feet in nearly six hundred properties across the United States, many in prime urban locations. Everyone in the real estate business knew it was a rare collection of assets.

Sam wanted to get out of real estate at the top. If he felt the time had come to sell, you could bet something bad was on the horizon. The only way we thought we could make a profit on the deal was to break up the company before the crash we all felt coming.

———

Our real estate business by this time had grown beyond all recognition. Since that first deal for apartment buildings in Arkansas, we had raised and invested billions of dollars. We had also had to apply our own culture, focused on reputation and integrity, in an industry used to very different standards.

A few years after we began investing in real estate, we were in a meeting trying to price an asset with a team leader who had come to work for us from a pure real estate firm. When I asked him for the numbers, he said, "Which numbers do you want?"

"What do you mean?" I said.

"Well, there's the set of numbers for the bank, there's the set of numbers for taxes, there's the set for when you're raising equity. Then there are the numbers you believe."

I looked at the guy. "You've got four sets of numbers? You would actually tell somebody something you don't believe? At Blackstone, we have one set of numbers. For the banks, for the limited partners, for taxes. They're what we believe. We tell them what we believe. We're not in the con job business. We do the right thing. Get out of here. And if you come back with your team, it's what you believe. That's all I ever want to see."

When he left, I said to the partner who was running our real estate group, "Where did this person come from? You train this person or else we're going to shoot him out of a cannon."

Another common practice we found in real estate was retrading. Late in a deal, after terms had been agreed, even at the closing, we found buyers would threaten to pull out unless they got a lower price. This behavior put sellers in a terrible position. To get to the table, they may have agreed to terms requiring that the deal close by a fixed deadline, or spent a lot of money in transaction costs and turned away other potential buyers. Now they would have to start again from scratch or accept the lower price.

If I had tried that as an investment banker, I would never have had a career. In corporate deals, you agree on your price, and unless something big changes, you stick with it. You don't screw around, or else no one will ever take your word again. In real estate, guys who had been in the business forever told me that it was normal to make a high bid to get the deal, then slash it at the closing. That didn't work for me. We were going to do our real estate deals to the same standard we demanded in our private equity business: the same analytical rigor, the same discipline, the same level of trust. We might lose some deals in the short term. But in the long run, we would maintain our reputation as a firm that meant what it said.

Jon Gray joined Blackstone in 1992. By 2005, at just thirty-four years old, he was running our real estate business. He had started in private equity. But in 1995, we were bidding on Worldwide Plaza, an entire city block of mixed-use property on Eighth Avenue in Manhattan, and the real estate team needed help. We sent them Jon, who excelled in navigating a deal's complex details and helped push it to a successful close. He forged a close relationship with John Schreiber, and his prodigious run as a real estate investor began.

In the years after that, Jon developed two major insights that accelerated the growth of our real estate business. The first was to use collateralized mortgage-backed securities (CMBS) to make bigger acquisitions. CMBS were new securities. Traditionally, if you needed a loan to buy a commercial property, you borrowed from a bank or another big institution. With these new securities, a lender could package your loan with other loans into a tradable security and sell them to investors. It turned your loan into a more liquid and tradable asset. The easier it became for banks to sell their loans, the more loans they made and the less they charged us to borrow money. In practice, we could borrow more money at lower rates to make bigger acquisitions.

Jon's second insight was that public companies containing lots of properties were frequently valued at less than the sum of their parts. Real estate investors tended to be individual proprietorships or small family firms without our intellectual or financial resources. They might have accumulated lots of buildings over decades that had different uses and were in different states of repair. If you offered a good price for the whole lot at the right moment, they might take it because they did not have the people or patience to go through the entire portfolio, putting precise values on every piece of it and finding different buyers willing to pay the highest price. We had experts who could value a piece of real estate, fix it up, and then find the perfect buyer from our network of relationships. We also had the financing available to be patient. By doing all the work that other owners either couldn't or wouldn't, we could earn the difference between the "street value" of these properties and the "screen value," the value we could establish through our disciplined analysis. This increased our reward while lowering our risk.

When we appointed Jon co-head of our global real estate business, we were once again putting our faith in our next generation. He may have been short on years and experience compared to his peers at other firms, but he embodied our culture and had earned his chance. In June 2006, he closed our fifth and largest-ever real estate fund, $5.25 billion in committed capital.

As Sam Zell's Equity Office Properties deal developed, we would need Jon's leadership, our unique culture, our approach to financing, our flair for deal making, and a large chunk of that $6 billion fund. We were about to go straight into the eye of the gathering financial storm.

TIME WOUNDS ALL DEALS

E quity Office Properties was six or seven times larger than any other real estate deal ever done. This deal was so big that a miscalculation could be disastrous: we risked being stuck with buildings we couldn't sell and debt we couldn't pay. But if we got it right, the upside could be tremendous. Jon understood the pressure and moved quickly. We had to get inside the company and understand it before our competitors did, which meant we had to make a serious opening bid. On November 2, 2006, we offered a premium of 8.5 percent over the market price, and EOP opened their books to us. The whole real estate industry lit up, with various consortia of investors assembling to try to top us. Sam had what he wanted: an auction with multiple bidders.

Ordinarily in deals like this one, potential buyers will negotiate a breakup fee with the seller, meaning that the seller will agree to compensate a potential buyer for all the expense of a bid—the time and the legal, accounting, and diligence work—in case he decides to sell to someone else. If there is not much interest, the seller might agree to pay a high breakup fee to attract risk-averse buyers. But if there is a lot of interest, the seller can insist on a low breakup fee. The standard fee in transactions like this is 1 to 3 percent of the total deal size. There was so much serious interest in EOP that Sam was able to insist on a break-up fee of just one-third of 1 percent.

As the bids went up, we looked for ways to stay in the contest. The higher the price, the more resourceful we would have to be to turn a profit. We asked Sam for permission to presell properties from the company. If we could lock up buyers now for certain assets, we could feel more confident about paying a higher price for the whole portfolio. He refused. He had decided to unload EOP in its entirety, one large check for his decades of work, and he did not want us unraveling his firm before the sale was complete. We asked him to raise the breakup fee from $100 million, ⅓ percent of the deal, to a more reasonable 1⅓ percent, which was about $550 million, to cover all the costs we were incurring and deliver a return for our investors. He agreed, grudgingly. Just as we needed justification for a higher price, he needed to keep us at the table.

For a deal this big, we needed a lot of financing from the major banks—around $30 billion. We couldn't get a sum that large from just one bank, so we had gone to several, as is standard practice, committing them exclusively to our bid and tying up their resources. When Sam heard that other bidders couldn't get money from the banks that had agreed to lend to us, he summoned Jon to the Waldorf Astoria and explained in the most vivid terms what he would do to him personally if we locked up the banks.

Eventually almost all the other bidders dropped out. It came down to us and Vornado, a large, publicly traded real estate company owned by Steve Roth, a friend of Sam's. Jon, Tony, John Schreiber, and I met to decide whether we should just take the $550 million breakup fee and walk away or if we should stay in the competition. After all, $550 million was a good payday for our investors. But a successful deal for EOP could be worth much, much more. We decided to raise our bid to $52 per share, 9 percent higher than where we had opened, but with one big caveat. "This deal is so dangerous," I told Jon and his team, "I want to sell half of it immediately at a profit to make the price for the rest of it more conservative. I want to sell it on the day we close. I don't want any daylight. We need to execute the exact same day we buy." Everyone around the table froze. Who did that? Even thinking about doing it was surreal. But I wasn't kidding. This deal could bankrupt us.

"How are we supposed to do that?" someone said. "Sam's never going to agree to let us shop assets in advance. He already said he wouldn't let us presell the properties."

I had known Sam for twenty years and seen him in action. I knew that he wanted the highest payday possible. Now that we were so close, he wasn't going to quibble over details. Whatever he had said earlier in the process was a matter of tactics, not principle. A request like ours was essential for us and would land well within his zone of fairness.

"Go and tell him," I said. "If he wants us in this, he's got to let us presell. What does he care if we presell anyway? Give the guy a little more money, and he'll go for it."

He went for it. On the next round of bids, Vornado topped us. But our right to presell changed everything. Harry Macklowe, a New York real estate magnate, offered to buy seven prime office skyscrapers in the city for $7 billion, which would cover nearly 18 percent of our offer price. Buyers came to us from all over the country, from Seattle to San Francisco to Chicago, all hungry for pieces of Sam's empire. They didn't share our view that the market had peaked or that a thousand-year flood was brewing. They saw the breakup of EOP as a rare chance to acquire trophy real estate.

We and Vornado went a couple more rounds until February 4, Super Bowl Sunday. Vornado had bid the same as us, but with a few sweeteners. Jon got the call that we needed to improve our offer in the opening minutes of the game. He grew up in suburban Chicago and is a lifelong Bears fan. They were playing the Indianapolis Colts and the Bears' Devin Hester had just returned the opening kick for a touchdown. He had to pry himself from the television to attend to business.

On Monday morning, Jon, Tony, John, and I decided to go up to $55.50 per share, around 24 percent higher than the market price when the bidding started. Our best and final offer remained all cash, valuing EOP at $39 billion including its debt. Vornado's offer was part cash and part stock. We knew Sam's purpose in selling EOP was to get out of real estate. The last thing he wanted was stock in another real estate firm. Jon submitted our offer that afternoon. Vornado folded. We had won.

There wasn't a moment to celebrate.

I had insisted on no daylight between closing and selling a significant portion of the portfolio. Every single member of the real estate team was packed into meeting rooms waiting for this moment. They had been there for days, lining up buyers and preparing documents. Now that the deal with Sam was closed, it was time to finalize the sale of billions of dollars' worth of property. No one was going home, and no one was sleeping until we were done.

These weren't small deals. Each one of them was big, and together they were shaking the market. We had closed the biggest acquisition in real estate history, and on the same day, we were trying to pull off a series of huge sales. The smell in the meeting rooms was overpowering. People hadn't showered for days. Messengers ran back and forth, up and down the elevators.

We closed our deal with Harry Macklowe. The timing meant that Harry bought these properties directly from EOP, without Blackstone ever actually owning them. We sold 11 million square feet in Seattle and Washington for $6.35 billion. Nearly $3 billion worth of space in Los Angeles and the same in San Francisco. Another $1 billion or so in each of Portland, Denver,

San Diego, and Atlanta. We had quickly recouped more than half of what we paid at a very big profit, relative to the value we'd attributed to those properties.

And then for two days, we rested. Everyone went home, cleaned up, and slept. But throughout those two days, my mind continued to churn.

————————

The week after we closed on EOP, I turned sixty. On my friends' birthdays, I call them and sing them "Happy Birthday." If they're not there, I leave my singing on their answering machine. My grandfather died in his forties, and I often thought I'd go early. As a teenager, I was in two near-fatal accidents in cars. In 1992, I got tuberculosis on a trip to the Middle East. Without modern medicine, it would have been fatal. In 1995, I developed phlebitis, which had killed my grandfather. In 2001, I had a 95 percent blocked artery in my heart, which was solved by inserting two stents to relieve the blockage. Every day since, I have taken an anticoagulant drug, Coumadin, that keeps me alive. Each birthday is a reminder of how glad I am still to be alive and in good health. It certainly beats the alternative.

Christine brought a great deal of joy into my life and loved organizing parties and holidays with family and friends. We decided we would mark my sixtieth in New York and make it one to remember. No cake, no toast, but a celebration with six hundred people we cared about. Christine loved dancing, so she hired Patti LaBelle and persuaded our favorite singer, Rod Stewart, to perform. My mother and father, my children, my brothers and their families, friends from high school, college, and New York all dressed up and came. It was a great night despite unfavorable media coverage, which created some controversy around the event.

As a gift, Christine put together a book of recollections from family and friends. My daughter, Zibby, recalled that in seventh grade, her school had assigned her the Communist Manifesto to read. I put aside my ideological reservations and we went through it together line by line. My son, Teddy, remembered me coming in to say goodnight, making sure the sheets were tucked in tight and shaking his entire bed for about thirty seconds. We called it the "milkshake." When Teddy played sports at school, he said his teams were often terrible, but I would still show up to watch them play, sitting down in a beach chair and talking non-stop on the phone.

As a parent, you strive for balance between doing enough at work to succeed and being there in person for your family, emotionally available for your kids. At the time, you never know if you're doing a good job. The reckoning comes years later. Looking back on the night of my sixtieth and the memories of those closest to me, I didn't think I'd done so badly.

———

When we came back to work, I gathered the real estate team back together in our main conference room. The cleaners had been to work, and the room smelled fresh for the first time in days. "You put in an absolutely unprecedented effort and achieved something no firm in history has ever achieved," I said. "A totally different scale. It's unbelievable what you have done. Congratulations!"

I paused to let them enjoy the moment.

"And now. We're going to do it again."

A hundred sets of eyes were staring at me.

"We need to offload half of what we have left. We'll make less money in the long run, but we'll be safer. We should aim at keeping only $10 billion worth of the best properties. At this point, we are already in the market. The market is red hot now, so let's keep feeding it. Because you know when the market's this heated, something bad's bound to happen."

Over the next few weeks, we sold the additional $10 billion. In two months, we had bought $40 billion and sold almost $30 billion, a total of $70 billion in real estate transactions in eight weeks. By the time we were done, we had managed to sell about 65 million square feet at a price of $461 per square foot. By contrast, the final cost to us of the 35 million square feet we kept was just $273 per square foot. We had acted at a scale and speed no one else in global real estate had ever done. We had reduced every bit of risk we could to protect and deliver for our investors.

LOAD THE BOAT

Around the time Sam called, we were going through another big change at Blackstone. Michael Klein, one of the heads of investment banking at Citibank, had called one Saturday morning in May 2006 with an idea. It was so exciting he wanted to tell me in person. I told him to come right over to my house at the beach. As we sat on my porch, finishing breakfast, Michael proposed that Blackstone go public.

Up to that point, no private equity firm had gone public. KKR had come closest that May, raising capital for an investment fund by issuing stock in that fund in the Netherlands. It was an innovative move. Firms like ours had traditionally raised money from institutional investors with the promise to return it after a few years. Now KKR had raised $5.4 billion from the public markets, capital they could invest but would never have to return. By going public in the Netherlands, they had also avoided some of the reporting required in the United States.

Every one of KKR's peers and competitors had studied the deal and wondered if some version of it might be right for them. Michael suggested that we go further: We shouldn't simply try to raise money for an investment fund. We should offer stock in Blackstone itself, the company that managed all these funds, as well as our businesses lines offering advisory, credit, and other investment services. This decision would be big, a transformation for the company that Pete and I had founded in 1985. A successful IPO would raise permanent capital to invest in the firm and expand our reach. If the markets turned, we would not have to worry about keeping the lights on. And it would allow our partners to sell their ownership stakes over time if that's what they wanted to do.

But there would be issues of control and ownership. We would have to open ourselves to public scrutiny. Up to now, we had enjoyed the flexibility and discretion afforded private companies. We were answerable only to ourselves and our limited partners. As a public company, if we missed earnings in a single quarter or our share price fell for any reason, we would be scrutinized, questioned, even attacked, no matter our long-term performance. We would be subject to the irrational pressures of the public markets, which can force companies into poor, short-term decision making. But if we pulled this IPO off, we would put ourselves ahead of our rivals.

I kept Michael's proposal to myself for a while as I mulled it over. Nikko had been wonderful partners for more than a decade, but in 1999, they had to sell their stake for regulatory reasons. We then sold a 7 percent stake in Blackstone to AIG, one of our most reliable investors, for a price that valued the entire firm at $2.25 billion. In 2006, Michael's calculations valued Blackstone at $35 billion. If that was true, the value of AIG's investment had risen by more than fifteen times in seven years.

When I told Tony, he was immediately supportive. He saw that we could use stock to make acquisitions and attract and retain the best people. We could reward our teams with stock in the firm rather than provide bonuses linked to their individual area of the business. This structure would reinforce our "one firm" culture. The money would give us financial and psychological comfort during the financial storm we both saw coming soon and allow us to reward Pete as he approached retirement.

The next person at the firm I spoke to about going public was our chief financial officer, Mike Puglisi. He said that we didn't have the internal systems in place to become a public company. Building them would require more work from people already stretched to their limits. If we were serious, he suggested we assemble a small team to work in secret away from our main office.

We had a lot of thinking to do about the right structure. As a private firm, we had fiduciary duties to our limited partners—the people who gave us their money to invest. These were sophisticated investors with clear strategies and long time horizons. But as a public firm, we would have an added duty to our shareholders. The limited partners were used to investing their money and waiting years while we put in the work. Public shareholders would track the value of their holding every second of every day. The interests of both wouldn't always be aligned.

Tony insisted we figure out the technicalities dispassionately and in private. He didn't want anyone getting distracted from their work by the prospect of an IPO windfall. Nor did he want to incite months of office politics and gossip. He suggested we invite Bob Friedman, our general counsel, to meet with us and Mike. I told them that I was still undecided. But if we did start to explore an IPO properly, I had three nonnegotiable terms that I believed would strike the right balance in our varying interests.

First, there could be no conflict between our duty to our limited partners and our public shareholders. Second, Pete and I had created billions of dollars of value out of our initial $400,000 investment, and I didn't want the world telling us how we should be running the company. We now had a firm that combined my entrepreneurial energy with Tony's gift for organization. Our culture was sacrosanct, and if going public risked disrupting it, we should not even consider it. Third, I knew I wanted to retain 100 percent control. In addition to ensuring my strategic vision for Blackstone as founder, I saw this as the surest way to keep the firm together and prevent it from fracturing into warring factions, the way Lehman had. If I kept the final word over people and compensation, I believed Blackstone would stay together and thrive. If we met these three terms, we could consider an IPO. Without them, we couldn't. I asked Tony, Bob, and Mike to try to figure this out in secret. If they had to reach out to people outside the firm, they should say we were investigating the idea for a portfolio company. Any leaks, I feared, would be fatal.

A few weeks later, Mike and Bob came to see Tony and me. They were smiling. To resolve the two issues of control, they found we could remain a limited partnership while issuing publicly traded units, the equivalent of stock. Outsiders wouldn't be given a vote on appointing the general partner or the board. That would be up to me. We would need to appoint independent outside directors for the audit committee. But otherwise I could keep the company united and running as I saw fit.

On the issue of prioritizing our commitment to our limited partners, the answer was even simpler: disclosure. We would tell prospective shareholders that our foremost duty was to investors in our funds. If we fulfilled that duty, the shareholders would do well. Since I would be the largest shareholder, they need not worry about my interests diverging from theirs. That alignment was more powerful than any complex legal promise. I had set some high hurdles for the IPO and was a little surprised that Mike and Bob had cleared them. It still felt like a long shot. But it seemed as if at least we should try.

I insisted we adopt the same approach we used for all of our investments. Start with an idea. Discuss it, criticize it, and question it. And only when we were as certain as we could possibly be, make a decision. There was a mountain of work. Our accountants would have to reorganize our financials to meet the regulatory standards for public companies. Our lawyers would have to restructure the entire company. We would have to draft materials for investors, get approval from the SEC, then hit the road with our sales offering. It would be a year at least.

We weren't the only ones looking at an IPO. If we were going to go public, we had to be the first. The first to hit the market would attract the most money. Everyone else would be fighting for leftovers.

I wanted us to keep running the firm as we always had, privately and quietly, while moving forward, developing the numbers and the legal structure of an IPO. Day to day, we were evaluating major deals in every sector—in private equity, real estate, alternative credit, and hedge funds. We had to retain our focus even while in the background we were reimagining our future. Mike dispatched a couple of members from his team to work with our accountants at Deloitte & Touche, while we had our lawyers working at Simpson Thacher out of sight of the rest of the firm.

Toward the end of 2006, Tony said we should start thinking about one of the hardest aspects of the process: figuring out the value of what each of us owned. Up to that point, Blackstone had been a confederation of some one hundred partnerships linked to our different lines of business. Some overlapped, some didn't; some had an expiration date, others didn't. All of the businesses were on different trajectories, most growing strongly, some flat, some occasionally shrinking. We had money either in or pledged to various funds that had yet to be invested. All of that had to be valued and assigned to the right owners. Everyone at the firm had to be considered, from me to the messengers, from senior managing directors who had been with us for twenty years to the latest class of associates, fresh out of college.

It was a monumental task, and Tony did it all, alone and in private. If anyone found out, he feared he would end up chewed

225

to pieces. His goal was to ensure that once we had gone public and everyone's stock had vested, we had a compensation system that was transparent and competitive, benchmarked against our peers. One that would ensure the long-term health of the business. He wanted to reward past and present partners and employees, yet leave enough in the pot for generations to come. It required a lot of analysis, but also a lot of judgment, understanding what people thought and felt and smoothing out any perceived differences. He had run a similar process before at DLJ, a firm with ten times the number of employees we had. But the complexity and novelty of our situation made this task ten times harder. It was the kind of multidimensional problem he excelled at solving.

In February 2007, as Tony was deep in his calculations and our lawyers and accountants were at work, another much smaller asset manager filed to go public. Fortress was a hedge fund that also did some principal investing. It managed just $30 billion in assets, around a third of what we were managing at the time. But its IPO proved successful. There was a strong appetite in the market. Fortress's success forced us to move even faster. I could imagine our rivals now all pushing toward the same goal, to be the first of us to file. I couldn't bear to be runner-up.

We informed the SEC of our intentions, and I called Morgan Stanley to discuss underwriting. We had been relying on Michael Klein's original, arm's-length estimate of our potential market value. Now I wanted another opinion. Morgan Stanley had old-fashioned corporate finance people and had done excellent work on a couple of our debt deals. They sent over two senior bankers, Ruth Porat, who later became Google's chief financial officer, and Ted Pick. Ruth and Ted both said the deal looked great and produced some thoughtful work to support their advice.

Everything was now in place: the legal and financial structures; the internal changes and compensation plan; and the underwriters—Morgan Stanley, Citibank, and Merrill Lynch. I had written a section for the prospectus myself, titled "We Intend to Be a Different Kind of Company." I described our intention to keep the culture of the firm as it was, with our long-term perspective, our partnership management structure, and widespread employee ownership. I also promised we would put $150 million of equity into a new Blackstone Charitable Foundation to oversee our corporate giving in the years to come. "Because of the nature of our business and the long-term focus we employ in managing them," I wrote, "our common units should only be purchased by investors who expect to remain unit holders for a number of years."

As the date of our public filing loomed, I went one evening to see *In the Heights*, Lin-Manuel Miranda's first musical, before he wrote *Hamilton*. It was spectacular, I'm sure, but my mind was elsewhere. The final draft of the Blackstone prospectus had arrived just as we were leaving and I was so eager that I tried reading it in the dark of the theater. Finally I took it out into the lobby. It was 221 pages of numbers, charts, and clear, persuasive language. When I finished, I thought to myself, *What a marvelous company. I'd buy stock in a minute.*

Before we revealed our plans to the firm, I needed to talk to Pete. We had been working together for the better part of thirty-five years. We had conceived Blackstone during those long breakfasts at the Mayfair Hotel. We had endured the agony of raising our first fund, and deal by deal, we had built the firm together. Pete had been active in our M&A work from the beginning, and he was always there if I needed advice. In recent years, he had pulled back. He was writing books about his favorite cause, cutting the federal deficit, and spending an increasing amount of time in Washington where he was creating an institute dedicated to international economics. I hadn't included him in our IPO plans yet because I had always handled the financial aspects of the firm, and Pete often had trouble keeping secrets. I knew what he would say: "Really? Do you think that's a good idea?"

He listed the arguments against going public, the ones we had been wrestling with for months. The duty to shareholders and the exposure to public scrutiny. He added one more: I would now become a target, and I would hate the unpleasantness of being a public figure.

I told him he was right. Going public would give us permanent capital, stock to buy both assets and security. It would transform us into a global brand and bring us deals, new limited partners, and new opportunities. It would reinforce our "one-firm" culture even as it enabled us to develop new lines of business. Finally, because my antennas were telling me that the world was getting so crazy, we would do well to load up with cash sooner rather than later, I didn't feel we could wait any longer. If I had to become a public piñata to make this happen, so be it.

"We started this business together twenty-two years ago with almost nothing," I said. "And this is going to mean wealth for our families. It's a good economic event."

His math skills had always been good.

On March 21, 2007, the day before we filed, we held firmwide meetings to describe what we were doing. It was a lot to absorb. The news had not leaked and people were stunned. Once we pushed the button, the financial world began to light up.

————

The plan for our IPO was to raise $4 billion at a valuation of $35 billion. That changed with a single phone call. One evening, soon after we filed, I was sitting at home watching *Law & Order*, reading through investment committee memos, when Antony Leung called. We had hired Antony a few months earlier to be our partner in China. He had been chairman of Asia for JPMorgan and head of China and Hong Kong for Citigroup before becoming the equivalent of treasury secretary in Hong Kong. He had relationships rather than deal-making experience, but I had a feeling about him. We settled on the idea that he start an asset management business for us in China.

I had first visited China in 1990 with my family. It was a different country then, still feeling its way toward a market economy. The roads were choked with bicycles, not cars. In 1992, when Blackstone looked at a deal in China, I was amazed to learn that there was still no national money transfer system. You couldn't write a check in one place and cash it in another. We passed on the deal. I watched China's subsequent development with increasing interest over the next decade and a half, but as a firm, we had our hands full in the United States, Europe, and Japan. Antony, who joined us in early 2007, was our first real stake in the ground.

That evening, he told me that he had just come from the board meeting of ICBC, the Industrial and Commercial Bank of China, the most valuable bank in the world. Two former senior government officials had approached him and said the Chinese government was planning to create a sovereign wealth fund, a government-owned investment fund, and wanted Blackstone to be their first big investment. They liked what we did and what we stood for. They wanted to invest $3 billion in our $4 billion IPO. We were being adopted by the world's next great superpower and hadn't even made a pitch. I went in to see Tony the next morning at 8:30, and said, "I got a whopper for you."

If one of the main reasons to go public was to load the boat with capital, more capital had to be better. Tony didn't hesitate: "Take the money." We could increase the IPO to $7 billion and use the extra cash to pay down Pete and the other partners, then invest the rest in the firm. We proposed that in exchange for their $3 billion, the Chinese take nonvoting stock for just under 10 percent of the company and hold it for at least four years, at which point they could sell their stake in thirds over each of the next three years. This strategy would align them with our own and our fund investors' interests. The deal required the approval of China's State Council and premier, both of whom, to my astonishment, took just a few days to reply. In the United States or Europe, it could have taken months or longer. The speed with which official China acted showed me that this decision was more than just financial. This had profound political and diplomatic ramifications.

We were the Chinese government's first foreign equity investment since World War II. They had come in before their new state investment company was even operational.

———

I was about to get my first taste of the public scrutiny Pete had warned me about. In early June, Senators Chuck Grassley and Max Baucus introduced a bill that would change the tax laws for partnerships that went public after January 2007. People started calling it "The Blackstone Tax." If it came into effect, it would force us to reexamine all the risks of going public. At best, we would have to redo all the tax calculations we had been making for a year leading up our filing. At worst, we would have to yank the IPO. But after Tony and I talked it over with Wayne Berman, our longtime government relations adviser and then vice chairman of Ogilvy & Mather, we felt the bill was unlikely to pass. And even if it did, it would be a long while before it became law. It shouldn't hold us up.

A few days later, John Sweeney, the head of the AFL-CIO, wrote to the SEC demanding it hold off on our IPO until the union had investigated the treatment of employees at our portfolio companies. The SEC then chimed in themselves, saying that they were changing the accounting rules so our restructuring to go public would look more like we were buying a new company. That would lead to substantial new costs.

The SEC said that the way we were swapping our employees' interests in all the different Blackstone partnerships and entities into shares of a single firm looked as if we were buying them out. This wasn't a buyout. If we were buying them out, I'd know about it, as I'd have written the check. The owners were still the owners of the firm. What the SEC was doing made no sense to me, but they made it clear that they had the last word.

There was more. Senator Jim Webb of Virginia challenged the Chinese taking a stake. Although we had ticked every legal and regulatory box for foreign investments, he said the stake might pose a threat to national security. His challenge went nowhere.

As we fought these political wildfires, we still had to sell the Blackstone story to potential investors. The way this process typically works, which Wall Street refers to as a "road show," is that a team of senior managers goes out and pitches investors one by one or in small groups. We decided to do ours differently. We wanted to hit the world all at once. We hit the cities home to major investor accounts together—New York, Boston, and other cities—and then split up. Tony led the team for Europe and the Middle East. Mike Puglisi, our CFO, took Asia. I handled the largest accounts in the United States and Tom Hill and Jon Gray took the smaller ones.

At the first event I did, at the Pierre Hotel on Fifth Avenue in New York, we filled the ballroom as well as several overflow rooms where people could see me on video screens. Balloons everywhere added to the circus atmosphere. As I began my presentation, my cell phone rang. It was Zibby, my daughter, calling from the hospital. I had just become a grandfather of twins. It seemed like I had just been helping her with her elementary school homework by slithering across her bed to show her how glaciers moved and sending her postcards every day she was at summer camp. I left the stage to Tony and went straight to go see her. So much for a carefully choreographed launch.

The hoopla followed us to Boston and then to Chicago. Investors didn't seem to care about the issues in Washington. Within days, Morgan Stanley said there was more than enough demand to issue more stock.

As I was in Chicago riding to an event, one of Tony's team called to tell me that Tony had been taken to the hospital in Kuwait. He was in excruciating pain, but the doctors hadn't figured out what it was. I called David Blitzer, our senior partner in London, and told him to drop everything and fly to Kuwait. Rent a plane if necessary. Just make sure Tony was being taken care of. The road show could wait. I called Tony's number, and to my surprise, he picked up.

"I'll be fine," he said, phlegmatic as ever. "Don't worry."

"Tony, I'm sending Blitzer. I don't want you straining yourself for a road show."

"Steve, I don't need that. I'm telling you, I'm fine."

But he didn't sound fine. I phoned David again. "Just tie the guy down," I said. "I don't want him hurting himself."

David was on the first plane to Kuwait, but by the time he got there, Tony had checked himself out of the hospital. The doctors had diagnosed a large kidney stone, agonizingly painful but not life threatening. It still hadn't passed through his system, but Tony had been discharged with a box full of syringes filled with morphine so he could numb the pain while he waited. He was determined to press ahead.

With Blitz now in support, they finished their presentations in Kuwait, then moved on to Saudi Arabia and Dubai. Tony refused the morphine, preferring to gut through the pain. It was torture for him, but over the course of those three days, he never missed a meeting. In Dubai, he checked himself back into the hospital, and then when he was ready, he chartered a plane to fly him and his team back to London.

Just as I was about to relax, I got another call. There was a problem with Tony's plane. One of its engines had failed over Iranian airspace, but the pilot hadn't filed for permission to fly over Iran. His manual told him to make an emergency landing at the nearest airstrip, but he didn't like the idea of putting down in the middle of the night somewhere in Iran with a plane of Americans who had been flying through Iranian airspace without permission. The other option was to press on to Athens on one engine and hope they could make it. Tony, lying on a cot in the back of the plane still in awful pain, urged him to try.

Now I had visions of my colleagues and friends crashing or making an emergency landing in Iran, which was led at the time by Mahmoud Ahmadinejad, who hated the United States and Israel. He believed that the United States planned the 9/11 attacks as a pretext for the war on terror and that the Holocaust was a myth. We all agreed that the pilot should fly on to Athens. The plane just made it on the single engine. Tony and team took another charter to London and completed a full day of meetings before finally flying back to New York. Upon his return, Tony admitted in his understated way that even he had been rattled. "That was a tough trip," he said.

———

By the middle of June, we had done only half the presentations we had planned, but the IPO was oversubscribed by fifteen times. We priced the offering at $31, the top of our expected range, and increased the number of shares we put out to market. On June 24 we sold 133.3 million shares and raised more than $7 billion, including the investment from China. It was the second largest IPO of the decade after Google.

The night we priced the deal, I went home to an empty apartment. Christine was traveling in Africa with her daughter, Meg, and her nephews and nieces. I was drained. I took a hot shower; changed into jeans, a polo shirt, and slippers; and slumped down in a chair with my dinner on a tray. I turned on the television, and to my horror, there I was. The channel had been left on CNBC. I was too tired even to change it, and just sat there, mesmerized, staring at myself, wondering if I was ever going to escape this IPO madness.

The *New York Times* wrote that the stock had "an almost Google-like mystique," and observed that all the challenges that would have derailed many market debuts hadn't affected us. "The Blackstone juggernaut kept going," the journalist wrote. The morning of our first day as a public company, I could have gone down to the stock exchange to ring the opening bell but asked Pete and Tony to do it without me. Instead, I went to the office and sat in my conference room alone.

It was strange to feel this way at what should be a high point in any entrepreneur's life. In the early 1990s, we had seen the opportunity to buy real estate when prices were at historic lows but been restricted by our lack of funds and our investors' anxiety. Their irrational fears had held us back, and we had missed opportunities while we raised the money. We weren't going to have the same problem now. We had plenty of capital in our investment funds locked up for years, and the money we raised through the IPO meant we could keep investing in our business to ensure we had the people and resources to pursue the most attractive opportunities wherever and whenever they arose.

That day, there wasn't the usual hum of activity around the office. The corridors were empty, the whole place hushed. I turned the TV to CNBC to watch the market open. "Good morning. Today we're bringing you all-day coverage of the Blackstone IPO." I stared at it for an hour, semicomatose. There I was again, inescapable. I couldn't even remember doing the interviews they were showing. I shut it off. It was nuts, an absolute blur. I thought I had understood what I was getting myself into. But I had no idea.

———

Soon after we went public, we received a call from Bennett Goodman, co-founder of GSO Capital Partners. Ever since Tony had joined Blackstone in 2001, he had been interested in expanding our relatively small credit business. For several years, we had tried to recruit Bennett's group from DLJ but were turned down. But after the IPO, Bennett called to say he was ready to merge GSO with Blackstone. He and his partners were stunned by how rapidly we were growing, as well as the breadth of our relationships. They thought they might be able to supercharge GSO's growth by teaming up with us, and as it turns out, they were right. By merging, we created one of the largest credit platforms in the alternative asset management business, and GSO ultimately grew more than fifteen times in the decade following the IPO.

SPRINTING
DOWNFIELD

BE A FRIEND
TO THE SITUATION

By the time we became a public company, the market's nerves were beginning to fray. In February 2007, Freddie Mac announced that it was no longer buying subprime loans, the mortgages given to less creditworthy borrowers who had pumped up the housing market. Mortgage lenders that specialized in subprime lending were increasingly in trouble. Their problems would eventually infect the entire credit market.

Several weeks later, I got a call from Jimmy Cayne, the CEO of Bear Stearns. He needed help. Two of his hedge funds were in trouble, and he wanted an outside opinion. I sent over a couple of our people who understood these funds. They returned with troubling news.

The first fund had bought only securities collateralized by subprime mortgages. These weren't publicly traded, so it was hard to determine their value. As people started defaulting on their mortgages in increasing numbers, you could assume these securities would plummet in price and no one would buy them. Yet under the terms of the fund, investors could withdraw their money once a month.

You couldn't make this up: an opaque and fast-depreciating fund that was still promising monthly liquidity to investors. The second fund was the same as the first one, but with leverage: if the first fund was broke, the second was astonishingly broke.

I called Jimmy and told him the funds were going to blow up and there wouldn't be any equity for investors. I advised him to take the hit and write the investors a check to cover their losses. This concession was not necessary from a legal perspective, but it would be less expensive than the hit to Bear Stearns's reputation from the failure of these two ill-conceived funds.

"I love you, Steve," said Jimmy. "But what the hell are you talking about? I'm not writing any checks. This game is for grown-ups. We've got a prospectus. People take risks. Sometimes you win, sometimes you lose."

I told him that such logic did not apply to a firm as big as Bear Stearns, with so much else at stake. He had its broader reputation to think about. His best brokers had recommended this product, under the supervision of Bear Stearns's president. If the funds collapsed, the firm's sales force would be damaged. If investors felt mistreated, he had to make it up to them or risk the failure contaminating the entire company and the livelihoods of thousands of employees.

"I don't have to write a check to anybody," he said. "This is the way markets work."

"I don't know about markets," I said. "But there are times when you just have to stand up and write a check. You have to show customers that you own this, because if you don't, they're not going to trust you ever again." I had felt the pain of this dilemma after our experience with Edgcomb, I had made sure we paid back the banks that lent to us. It would have cost us a lot more to earn back their trust on later deals if we had not made them whole right then.

At Blackstone, our adrenaline was still pumping after the EOP deal and the IPO. Stock prices continued to rise, with most investors still locked into their position of psychological comfort, refusing to absorb the changes, draw conclusions, and act based on the negative data in the credit markets. But as we saw the coming dislocation in markets getting closer, we got ready. Many people make the mistake of thinking the moments when markets collapse are the moments of highest risk. They are the opposite.

Entering the crisis, Blackstone had $4 billion in cash from the IPO and a $1.5 billion revolving credit line to draw on if we needed it. As a fundamental operating tenet, Tony and I had insisted on having no net debt. It was part of our aversion to risk. We had more than $20 billion in committed funds locked up for ten years, so we could ride out a storm without worrying about a run by our clients on their money. Thanks to our strong capital position, we were open for business, but our disciplined investment process kept us out of another major deal that would eventually become a financial disaster.

Between the late 1990s and early 2000s, we had begun taking a harder look at the US energy sector when we saw two forces changing the industry. The first was steady deregulation, which was driving more and more of the energy industry into the hands of smaller, private firms. The second was the collapse of Enron, which forced many companies to sell assets, from drilling rights to refineries to pipelines, at low prices under financial duress.

We had started modestly and spent years building up our knowledge, experience, and relationships so that we could maximize our rewards and minimize our risks over the course of multiple turns in the cycle.

In 2004, we had partnered with three other private equity firms, Hellman and Friedman, Kohlberg Kravis and Roberts, and Texas Pacific Group (TPG), to buy Texas Genco, a set of power plants in Texas. A year later, we sold the company and split a gain of around $5 billion on our equity. It was one of the most profitable private equity investments ever made. The source of our profit was the rising price of electricity, which regulators had pegged to the price of natural gas. Texas Genco produced electricity mostly from much cheaper sources, coal and nuclear, so as electricity prices went up along with the price of gas, so did its profits in greater proportion. KKR and TPG went back to that trough in 2007 for a much bigger deal, offering $44 billion for TXU, another Texas power company. I asked David Foley, the head of our energy fund, why we were missing out.

I had recruited David out of business school. He had had no background in energy when he launched our first fund, but he had immersed himself in the industry. He talked the investment committee through the math of the TXU deal and explained why it made no sense. Energy, like real estate, is an industry dictated by cycles. As an investor, you have to understand that the troughs can be deep and long, and you cannot get carried away when the markets peak. The buyers of TXU were borrowing over 90 percent of the $44 billion purchase price, which left them little margin for error. They were betting that the price of gas, and thus the regulated price of electricity, would remain high. In that scenario, they would have years of strong profits, on the difference between the high price of electricity charged to consumers and the low cost of producing it from their coal-fired power plants. But if gas prices fell, so too would the price of electricity for consumers. TXU's owners would be stuck selling electricity for dwindling profits and struggling to service their debts. David was emphatic that we shouldn't put in a bid.

It took a little while to play out, but by 2014, TXU was bankrupt, producing electricity from coal as the price of natural gas and electricity collapsed. Investors had been caught buying at the top of a cycle and paid a heavy price.

242

It was just as we were passing on most of the deals in the marketplace that Steve Bollenbach, the CEO of Hilton, called us. A few months earlier, we had looked at his company and made an offer, which Steve had rejected. But now he was ready. He wanted to retire, and a sale would be the capstone on his career, both financially and personally. And perhaps like Sam Zell, he saw that if he hesitated now, he might have to wait years before the market rebounded.

We had been buying and selling hotels since 1993, from chains like La Quinta and Extended Stay in the United States to the Savoy Group in London. We knew when to buy them and how to operate them. We also understood labor relations, a big part of owning hotels. Hilton had interesting domestic and international businesses. For years, the two had been run separately. They had recently been reunited, but the stitches holding them together were still fresh. The domestic business was headquartered in Beverly Hills. Its properties were aging, not having been renovated as frequently as they should have been. Costs were being duplicated across four separate divisions, and Hilton's margins were smaller than those at its competitors. Its managers seemed to have lost a step. Their corporate offices closed on Fridays at noon. And to top it all off, they kept an expensive fleet of corporate airplanes. We could see a lot of ways to increase value.

The international business, headquartered in London, was even more intriguing. Hilton International, we believed, was the Rip Van Winkle of the hotel business, fast asleep while the world boomed around it. It had not added any new properties in twenty years and had barely cracked the fast-emerging markets of China, India, and Brazil. Anyone could see that international business and tourist travel was growing as emerging economies became richer. Hilton was one of the most recognized brands in the world, up there with Coca-Cola. If it got this right, its runway looked endless. It already owned some of the best hotel properties in the world: the Waldorf-Astoria, the Hilton New York, the Hilton Park Lane in London, the Hilton Morumbi in São Paulo. Add all these individual properties up, and they were worth far more than the market cap of the whole firm. Combining Hilton's domestic and international businesses, though, had done little to wake either business from its slumber. They missed opportunities to grow, and the stock price had languished.

Based on our analysis, Hilton would cost $26 to $27 billion, after we'd just invested over $10 billion, net of all our sales, in EOP. But the way we looked at it, Hilton was already throwing off $1.7 billion a year in profit. If we could get that up to $2.7 billion through better management, organic growth, and selling noncore assets, we could offer more than our rivals and still make more money. But if EOP had been the hare, a deal done at breathtaking speed to maximize value in a white hot market, Hilton would be the tortoise, requiring years of diligent work.

One of our first steps was to recruit Chris Nassetta, then CEO of Host Hotels and a longtime friend of Jon Gray, which owned Marriott among other chains. Chris is a master of his craft. If anyone could improve Hilton, he could. His promise to join as CEO if Blackstone won boosted our confidence. There were still risks, of course: another major terrorist attack like 9/11 freezing travel; an international virus like severe acute respiratory syndrome (SARS). But if the whole world had to stop traveling, we would all have bigger problems.

Even contemplating Hilton after EOP felt like finishing one Olympic final, then lining up for another. But you don't get to choose the timing of these moments. You just have to be ready.

We offered a 32 percent premium over Hilton's stock price, and Bollenbach accepted, barely two weeks after we went public. We invested $6.5 billion in equity from Blackstone funds and co-investors and borrowed $21 billion from more than twenty lenders. We now had to chew our fingernails until we closed.

Bear Stearns led our group of lenders for the Hilton deal. While we waited to close, the hedge funds I had discussed with Jimmy Cayne imploded. Bear lent the two funds $1.6 billion to keep them going, but by late July, there was nothing more to be done. The funds were forced into bankruptcy.

On August 9, the French bank BNP Paris halted redemptions from three of its funds, which were invested heavily in subprime American mortgages. They said there was no liquidity left in the market. That same day, Countrywide, America's largest originator of mortgages, filed its quarterly report with the SEC, citing "unprecedented market conditions." Within days, it was drawing down its credit lines and two weeks later accepted a $2 billion investment from Bank of America to keep the lights on.

Around this time, I got a call from Jimmy Lee. He told me I couldn't tell anyone, but for three days, JPMorgan hadn't been able to roll over its commercial paper. These are the loans that corporate America lives on, the most liquid kind of debt, used to run their operations. It's the closest debt gets to cash. And it wasn't just JPMorgan. Bank of America and Citi couldn't roll theirs over either. Jimmy told me they had sorted it out by offering extra protections to the other banks and institutions that lent to them. But if the biggest banks in the country had to hustle to get short-term loans to pay their bills, this problem had gone way beyond subprime mortgages.

We closed Hilton on October 24, almost twenty years to the day since we had closed that first Blackstone fund on the eve of Black Monday. We had once again come in just in time. The same day, Merrill Lynch announced a quarterly loss of $2.3 billion. Citi later said it was writing down $17 billion of mortgage holdings. By the first week of November, the CEOs of both firms, Stan O'Neal at Merrill and Chuck Prince at Citi, had resigned. The entire financial system was entering cardiac arrest.

—————

Starting in late 2007, I received an unusual crash course in the foundations of the financial crisis by attending a series of lunches at the Federal Reserve Bank of New York on Liberty Street. Hosted by Tim Geithner, then head of the New York Fed, they often included Ben Bernanke, chairman of the Federal Reserve; Hank Paulson, secretary of the treasury; the CEOs and chairmen of New York's biggest banks; Larry Fink of Black-Rock; and me.

For all I knew about finance, what I learned at these lunches astounded me. I knew that Fannie Mae and Freddy Mac, the two government-sponsored mortgage giants, bought and securitized half the residential mortgages in the country, to the tune of around $5 trillion. What I didn't know was that they were nearing bankruptcy. It was a given to everyone else in the room, but it made my jaw drop.

There were two chronic problems in the system. First were subprimes. For years now, the market for mortgages had become more liquid, thanks to securitization. Since the 1980s and thanks to people like Larry Fink, mortgages had been packaged and bought and sold like other securities, such as stocks and bonds. Successive administrations had been pressuring banks to make more loans to people who could not previously afford to buy their own homes. Many politicians considered home ownership the first step toward fulfilling the American dream. This combination of financial innovation and political pressure led to new kinds of mortgages requiring low to zero down payments, or ultralow interest rates for the first few years. Poor regulatory oversight led to unscrupulous lenders that took advantage of borrowers by offering loans without insisting on the proper documentation, such as proof of income or assets. The increase in the number of buyers pushed up the price of homes, causing the market to overheat. In the mid-1990s, subprime mortgages had made up 2 percent of the entire US mortgage book. By 2007, they were 16 percent. You didn't have to be a genius to see that if the economy tipped into recession or home prices fell for any other reason, a housing market fueled by subprime lending would collapse.

The second chronic problem had been created by regulators. Technically, the problem was a regulation, FAS 157, that had been intended to ensure so-called fair value accounting. The problem was that it was neither fair, nor did it lead to the proper accounting of value. One of the most important lessons from the collapse of Enron in 2001 and then the telecoms giant WorldCom in 2002 was that companies could obfuscate what they owned and what they owed. They could use accounting tricks to pump up the value of assets and hide liabilities. The solution, said a group of influential academics, was more transparency. If everyone knew everything all the time, we wouldn't have scandals like Enron. Marking assets and their liabilities to their market prices every day was considered the cure-all to corporate chicanery.

What made sense in theory, though, made no sense in reality. Imagine owning a stock. You buy it for your retirement, which is still twenty years off. You buy ten shares at $100 each. The price of the stock rises to $120, then falls back to $80. But you don't care, because you have a twenty-year horizon and you consider the stock a good long-term investment. All it means is that the numbers on your quarterly statement change.

But what if every time the stock rose or fell, you received a check for the difference in any increase or had to write a check to cover any shortfall? And furthermore, you had to inform every single one of your creditors, from your mortgage lender to the company that lent you money to buy a car, and they reassessed your creditworthiness based on this new value? You would be working on a twenty-year horizon, but they would be evaluating you on what happened today, holding you accountable for the latest shifts in the market.

In the late 1930s, the US government, scarred by the Great Depression, prohibited mark-to-market accounting. They saw that in any normal year, almost any asset class, including stocks and bonds, will go up or down by 10 to 15 percent. In a boom or crisis year, it could be even more. It would be terrible for the health of the economy if companies acted like Chicken Little, constantly rebalancing their assets or liabilities based on that day's movements in the markets instead of coolly managing for the long term.

During the second half of the twentieth century, it was typical for a bank to borrow twenty-five times its equity to lend money to customers. If it could lend at a higher interest rate than the one at which it borrowed, it could make a profit. Since successful banks tended to be good at lending, choosing customers who would pay back what they borrowed, regulators didn't require them to hold a lot of emergency cash. If there were an emergency, though, the answer would not be to demand they unload all their assets in a fire sale to raise cash.

I had started my career in finance in 1972 and watched in 1975 as the Federal Reserve and the Comptroller's Office managed twin crises in real estate and shipping loans. They didn't force the owners of troubled loans to mark them to market. Instead they gave them time for the loans to recover or to be charged off quarter by quarter over several years. That's how real life works. If you're faced with a problem, you don't panic and declare immediate catastrophe. You call for quiet and give everyone time.

FAS 157 required the opposite. In the name of transparency, it made the balance sheets of financial institutions look insanely volatile. Portfolios of assets that had been built up to be held over long durations now had to be priced when their values were collapsing. Institutions were required to hold more cash at the moment when cash was scarce. The combination of irresponsible subprime lending and FAS 157 was leading to the market's hysteria and driving the banks to insolvency.

In early 2008, I had dinner with John Mack, the CEO of Morgan Stanley. He was miserable, having just reported a quarterly loss of $7 billion. How had he managed to lose so much money? He hadn't, he said. It was all on paper. He had portfolios of subprime securities dating back four years. The underlying mortgages on the securities for 2004 were defaulting at a rate of around 4 percent, for 2005–2006 at 6 percent, and for 2007 around 8 percent. But the market for these securities, even with default rates below 10 percent, had evaporated. No one would buy them. Fewer than one in ten Americans were defaulting on the mortgages backing these securities, yet they were considered untouchable. Under Sarbanes-Oxley, the financial reform act introduced in 2002 to protect investors after the accounting scandals at Enron and WorldCom, you couldn't take the risk of misrepresenting the value of any assets. So John had brought in BlackRock to value its portfolio. They estimated the loss to be somewhere between $5 and $9 billion. He simply split the difference, reporting a vastly larger loss than the value of the securities that were actually defaulting. And suddenly everyone was panicking about the health of Morgan Stanley.

At Lehman Brothers, my old employer, the problems were piling up even more. Its CEO, Dick Fuld, and I had come up together in the early 1970s and both became partners in 1978. Dick had been a C student at college, where he spent most of his time skiing and partying. He then earned his MBA at New York University. Dick would joke that the only reason Lehman appointed him CEO in 1994 was that all of the smart guys had left while he had stuck around. We weren't close, but we saw each other at different public events and had dinner with our wives perhaps once a year.

Sadly, people inside Lehman rarely saw the warm, self-effacing side of him. Dick was an autocratic leader, feared more than loved. And by 2008, he had put his company in a tough spot. That spring, my real estate team saw that Lehman's real estate portfolio was in a mess. They were holding a large block of bad mortgages alongside some good residential assets, such as Archstone, a major investor in apartment buildings. They owned a lot of commercial real estate they had bought but failed to sell before the crisis bit. Now the debt on those commercial properties was putting pressure on them. In a healthy market, the total portfolio might have been worth $30 billion. But the buyers had fled and values were impossible to estimate. We offered $10 billion to take it off Lehman's hands. We could be more patient about selling the assets over time. Dick turned us down. He preferred to stagger on than to take the hit to his equity.

Shortly afterward, on March 16, JPMorgan, under government orders, agreed to buy Bear Stearns. Now all eyes were on Lehman, wondering if it would be next. Dick was looking for a buyer as the deepening crisis in mortgages made his task ever more difficult. And despite the way he joked about his improbable ascent at Lehman, he had a strong, sentimental attachment to the firm. He struggled to accept how little it was now worth. In early August, Dick told me that out of his $675 billion of assets, around $25 billion was linked to bad real estate loans. The remaining $650 billion was healthy and making plenty of money for the firm. So why not separate the two? I suggested. Call the $650 billion "Old Lehman" and let it carry on, uncontaminated by the real estate book. Then move the $25 billion pool of assets into a new firm, Lehman Real Estate, and give it enough capital to survive the cycle. It might take five years, but real estate would come back. It always does. Shareholders would still own 100 percent of the assets in both firms, but their risks and rewards would be decoupled to take account of what was happening to real estate. The government would likely have no objection if this split lifted some of the uncertainty Lehman was inflicting on the markets.

Dick liked the idea and asked if Blackstone would buy a couple of billion dollars' worth of Old Lehman if he executed the split. With the appropriate diligence, I said yes. But our discussions were proceeding slowly. Worry paralyzed Dick. His quarter was due to end on September 30, when he would be required to mark down his real estate assets to their current value. In the end, his agonizing meant we ran out of time to complete the diligence, file a proxy, and get the SEC to accept the split we'd discussed. I felt terrible for him. He had been out there trying to sell his company and haggling over price when price wasn't the issue. Short sellers were punishing Lehman's stock. If Dick had been able to create two separate securities—one for real estate, one for the rest of Lehman—he could have saved the firm. The financial meltdown would have continued, but good Lehman would have been cordoned off. Instead, Lehman became the largest bankruptcy in US history, and Dick an emblem of all that went wrong.

Lehman went bust on Monday, September 15. The next day, money market funds, normally viewed as a very low-risk investment and virtually equivalent to cash, dropped in value for the first time in recent memory. Every dollar invested in one of these funds fell to 97 cents. On Wednesday, September 17, the yield on Treasury bonds turned negative. People were so panicked they were now buying government securities knowing they would take a loss. It just seemed safer than any alternative.

Thanks to the IPO and vigorous fundraising leading up to the crisis, Blackstone was in a strong financial position. But the week Lehman went down, I called down all of our bank credit lines. Before I hunkered down for what was bound to be a nuclear winter, I wanted all the cash we could lay our hands on. There would be a lot of people in trouble and trying to sell. I was determined that we would be ready to buy.

———

At 3:30 p.m. Wednesday, September 17, Christine called.

"How has your day been, dear?" And as usual, she asked, "What do you feel like having for dinner?"

"My day has been terrible," I said.

"Oh, I'm sorry . . . why?"

"Well, everything's collapsing. Treasuries have a negative yield. Mutual funds have broken the buck. Companies are drawing down their bank lines. The whole financial system is going to collapse."

"That's awful," she said. "What are you going to do about it?"

"What am I going to do about it? I'm drawing down my bank lines."

"No, I mean what are you going to do to stop the whole thing?"

"Sweetie, I don't have the ability to stop it."

"Do you think Hank knows all of this?"

"Yes, I'm sure he knows."

"How do you know he knows?"

"Because if I know about it, he knows about it. He's the treasury secretary."

"But what if he doesn't actually know? And he does nothing and the system collapses?"

"It's not possible that he doesn't know," I said.

"But what if he doesn't and you could have done something, like warn him? I think you have to call Hank."

"Sweetie, I'm sure Hank's in meetings. It's a crisis. He's not reachable."

"What's the harm of trying to call him?"

"But it's a ridiculous call."

"But you should call him."

By now I'm realizing that I'm never going to get off this call unless I agree to phone Hank.

"Okay," I said. "I'll call him."

"Oh, by the way," Christine added. "When you call him, you ought to have some solutions to help him. Also, we're having your favorite—curry!"

I called.

———

"I'm sorry, Mr. Schwarzman," said Hank's assistant. "Secretary Paulson's in a meeting." That was hardly a surprise.

"Here's my number," I said. "Please tell him I called."

An hour later, quite unexpectedly, he called back. When Hank had been chairman and CEO of Goldman Sachs, Blackstone had been a major client and sometimes a competitor of his. I had always found him intelligent, logical, determined, tough, and fair with a deep understanding of finance. He was a very good listener as well as having excellent sales abilities. Most important, he was highly ethical, someone to trust.

"Hank," I said, "how's your day?"

"Not good," he said. "Whaddya got?"

Throughout the crisis, Hank and his team were in constant communication with senior financial executives across Wall Street like me in an effort to develop real-time knowledge of what was happening. We were closer to the markets than he was by virtue of the companies we ran. I knew he would appreciate honest, straightforward observations and advice.

I told him companies were drawing down their bank lines, and at the rate things were going, the banks were going to fail. There was a good chance they wouldn't be able to open for business on Monday morning.

"How can you be so sure of that?" he asked.

"Because this panic is gaining such momentum that it's all going to be over.

"You need to stop the panic," I said. I described the situation like an old Western movie, where the cowboys had just come into town after a cattle drive. The cowboys are drunk, shooting their guns in the streets. The sheriff was the only one who could stop them. Hank was the sheriff. He had to put on his hat, pick up his shotgun, walk out into the street, and shoot straight into the air. That's how you stop a panic, I told him. You freeze the mob in their tracks.

"And how do I do that?" said Hank.

"First, you need to eliminate the ability to short financial stocks," I said. People might say it's bad policy, but it would signal to people that the rules of the game are no longer reliable. Every hedge fund and short seller trying to make money by driving down bank stocks would worry what the Treasury was going to do next.

"Okay," said Hank. "I like that. What else?"

"Credit default swaps," I said. People were putting pressure on financial institutions by effectively buying insurance in the hope that banks would default on their obligations and collapse. Hank should make these credit default swaps nonactionable.

"That's a great idea," he said, "but I don't have the legal ability to do that. What else?"

I had learned that since Lehman filed for bankruptcy earlier in the week, investors were frantically trying to move their brokerage accounts over to the one bank everyone thought would survive: JPMorgan. They were closing their accounts at Morgan Stanley and Goldman Sachs, pushing these institutions toward failure, while JPMorgan was struggling to process all the requests. I suggested that Hank stop allowing people to transfer their accounts.

Again, he did not have the authority. "Anything else?" he said.

More than anything else, I told him, the market needed to be reassured that the system wasn't going to collapse. The only way to stop the panic was for someone to show up with so much money, such brute force, that it shocked the market into submission. That someone had to be the US government. That would stop all the dysfunctional behavior. And Hank needed to do this tomorrow.

"If you don't announce tomorrow, it'll be too late. The banking system will collapse and you won't be able to open the banks on Monday," I said. This was on Wednesday at around 4:30 p.m.

"I don't trust the system anymore." I said. "In the last few days I've witnessed the downfall of Lehman and Bank of America saving Merrill Lynch through a last-minute merger. AIG would have gone under yesterday had it not been for your intervention, and Fannie and Freddie had to be bailed out in August. Nothing is sacred. Everyone believes the same thing. You've got a financial system that won't be able to survive this level of mistrust. You need this large pool of capital to give people confidence that the system won't collapse. It's all happening so fast that every hour you wait, the more money you're going to need. You have to announce it tomorrow, the earlier the better."

"Are you going to be around for the next hour or so?"

"Sure. The world's ending. Where else do I have to go?"

I later learned that Hank was already working to persuade the SEC to put a moratorium on short selling. But as for the rest, the Treasury needed congressional approval to intervene at the speed and scale now required. For months as the crisis deepened, Hank had considered asking for that approval but feared that a Democrat-controlled Congress would refuse to hand so much power to the Republican-controlled executive. On the night Lehman failed, there was no longer any choice: Hank and his team had to act. They decided to ask for what they needed.

On Friday, President Bush announced from the Rose Garden that the treasury secretary had asked Congress to appropriate emergency funding of $700 billion to stem the crisis. The legislation was called the Troubled Asset Relief Program, or TARP. I wished it were bigger, but $700 billion was pretty big. It would probably be enough to stop the madness. That same day, the SEC also banned short selling.

That should focus people's attention, I thought. The shorts and others busy exploiting the chaos now had to ask themselves whether they wanted to be in a game where the government was playing against them, where the government would put anything on the table in order to protect the system. Once Congress passed the TARP, we would be on the road to survival.

———

Ten days later, on September 29, I was in Zurich, Switzerland. I had just checked into my hotel and turned the television on to watch the House vote on the TARP legislation. I saw the votes coming in, 228 to 205 against the program I thought could save the country. Not enough Democrats voted for it, and the Republicans killed it. The panic was going to start all over again.

I sat there wondering how this could have happened. At Congress's request, Hank's team had prepared a three-page outline of the TARP legislation soon after it was announced, with the expectation that it would be fleshed out into a much fuller document. Their critics, though, portrayed it as an inadequate, entitled approach to securing and spending $700 billion of taxpayer money. As Hank wrote in his memoir, *On the Brink*, "We were pilloried for the proposal—not least because it was so short, and hence appeared to critics as if it had been done offhandedly. In fact, we'd kept it short to give Congress plenty of room to operate."

The eventual hundred-plus page of TARP legislation arrived in a challenging political environment. We were only five weeks from the presidential and congressional elections. Politicians were staking out their territory. The vote to reject it reflected ideological rather than national interests.

I was so freaked out I called Wayne Berman, our government relations advisor. As an insider's insider, I hoped he might have some thoughts on what could be done to save the situation.

"Wayne, we must get the TARP passed," I said. "It's the survival of the system. We can't let it get bogged down in some horrible political mess." I suggested we assemble all living US presidents—Jimmy Carter, Bill Clinton, and George H. W. Bush—to deliver a national address on television urging Congress to pass the TARP legislation. Wayne said he would work on it. I fell asleep that night thinking that everybody involved with the crisis at Treasury and the Fed must be so exhausted and sleepless that they could use help. They had a million things on their minds: short- and long-range fiscal and economic consequences and implications, political posturing and egos, campaign exigencies. But I only had one objective: to stop the system from returning to a state of panic.

The next day Wayne and I continued to focus on the presidential broadcast idea. I thought it was the only thing that might have the gravitas to persuade the nation. But after taking soundings, Wayne assured me we could stand down. "They're going to solve it," he said. "It's going to get done."

After intensive work by Hank and his team and Ben Bernanke, the chair of the Federal Reserve, working closely with Congress, the TARP finally passed on October 3. A sharp drop in the stock market after the first rejection of the deal had also helped to focus minds. This turned out to be the last time in recent history that Congress acted on a bipartisan basis to pass a consequential and controversial piece of legislation.

But when I read the redrafted legislation, I identified what I considered a serious flaw. Without Christine's urging this time, I made another call to Hank.

"Congratulations on finally getting TARP done," I said. "There's only one problem."

"What's that?" he said.

"You'll never be able to buy a troubled security."

"What do you mean?"

"Everybody owns these subprime packages, full of house mortgages. In the old days, we all used to know what a house was worth on a given street because there was a kind of blue book. But when there are five houses for sale on the same street, nobody knows what a house is worth, so nobody knows how to value any of these pools of subprime securities. You will literally have to go out to every street and see how many houses are for sale, because if a house used to be $200,000 and there are five houses for sale on the street, you can buy them for much less, maybe $140,000 or lower. But if you don't even know how many houses are for sale, you won't know how to price them and what to pay. And the sellers won't know. So there's no ability to transact and the banks aren't lending anyhow. So if no one can value these securities, they will just be illiquid and you'll never buy a troubled security."

"So what's your suggestion?" said Hank.

"Take the $700 billion and put it into the banks as either equity or preferred stock with warrants. That will give the banks stability." With stability, banks would be able to attract many times what the Treasury gave them in terms of new deposits. Those deposits could be used to make profitable loans to restart the economy. The government would make money on the equity investment and banks would have what they needed to weather the crisis and start investing. Leveraged 12:1, the banks' equity would mean $8 or $9 trillion—a huge amount of firepower.

Hank, Ben, and Tim Geithner, president of the New York Federal Reserve, were a few steps ahead of me. They had already discussed the idea of injecting equity into the banks and even proposed it to President Bush, but they were concerned about creating any unintentional pressure to nationalize the banks. What they eventually developed was an innovative, and ultimately profitable, way to recapitalize seven hundred US banks, including both healthy and weak ones. Hank's conversations with people like me, in the marketplace, were a way for him to think through such a complex issue.

"One more thing," I said. "It's terrible that people are calling TARP a 'bailout.'" Hank and Treasury never used the term themselves, but it was being widely used by politicians and the media. "You're not bailing anybody out. You're lending them money, which is going to be repaid. It's just a bridge loan where the taxpayers are going to get all their money back, with interest and probably with a big profit when the banks recover. Describing it as a bailout is going to create a PR nightmare. It's going to be completely misunderstood."

Hank agreed, but it was clear that his focus was required elsewhere. He was in the eye of the storm, besieged by demands from Congress, the Fed, the regulators, the media, and even other countries. It was unimaginably difficult.

————

A week or so later, I was still in Europe. I had just landed at night in Toulon, France, and gotten into a car when my phone rang. It was Jim Wilkinson, Hank's chief of staff.

"Hank asked me to call and say thank you. Most people who talk to us basically do things that are good for them. Whenever you talk to us, you only care about what's good for the system. You've given us some of the best advice that we've gotten."

"Thanks, Jim," I said. "I appreciate it." I shut my flip phone and settled back in my seat. It was about 8:00 p.m. and pitch black out. I was alone with the driver. *What an amazing thing*, I thought. *I have been helpful here.* It felt extremely good. Nobody knew what to do as we risked heading into something worse than the Great Depression. Thanks to Christine's persistence, I had volunteered to be part of the solution, and Hank had taken the time to listen. Later he told me that my "sense of urgency and conviction, along with that of other well-respected market participants, helped confirm our judgments and impending actions." I was very proud that I had been able to help the country and still am.

————

As the smoke cleared in late 2008, my instincts told me that the worst had passed. But there was still a huge amount of work to be done to restore the US economy. Months before the crisis hit, I had promised my friend Paul Achleitner, then CFO of Allianz, to make a speech at Munich Technical University, where his wife, Ann-Kristin, was a professor. I arrived in Munich on October 15 to an auditorium packed with students and press; they were crammed into the rows and sitting on the steps. They had one question for the American financier standing before them: Would we survive?

"The financial crisis is over," I said. "You all think it's going on, but the decisions have been taken to end it." Other countries were getting ready to follow the US example and recapitalize their banks. The financial system was safe. "I realize this is a bold prediction five weeks after the collapse of Lehman Brothers," I admitted. "And it is true that markets are in a terrible condition. But you should not worry. I'm not worried about it and I have the advantage of knowing what's going on. So you should all feel very secure." I got a big round of applause and hundreds of thanks as I left the auditorium. But as I sat back in the car taking me to the airport, I felt nauseated. I had now said it publicly. I had better be right.

TURN CRISIS INTO
OPPORTUNITY

Despite what we had done at Blackstone to prepare for the global financial crisis, we weren't spared its aftermath. Our share price fell from $31 at the time of our IPO to a low of $3.55 in February 2009. For the last quarter of 2008, we wrote down the value of our private equity portfolio by 20 percent and our real estate portfolio by 30 percent. In my 2008 letter to Blackstone shareholders, I made it clear that Blackstone was different from most other financial services firms: "We are long-term investors and we are patient. That means we can hold existing investments until markets are higher and more liquid and can exit at full value rather than being forced to sell into a rapidly deleveraging market. And that allows us to be more aggressive in a depressed environment when we can deploy capital to the maximum benefit of our investors at the right time." We had $27 billion in dry powder to invest and could see opportunities to buy in every sector. But the markets could not see beyond the next few weeks and months of gloom.

Investors were selling assets for reasons that had nothing to do with fundamental values. They needed cash or had to meet margin calls. I got a call one day from one of our investors asking us not to draw down more money to make new investments, no matter how large and attractive they were. I realized that he wasn't asking me to violate my fiduciary duty because there weren't excellent investment opportunities; he was asking me to hold back because he needed to conserve cash. I told him that it was our fiduciary duty to invest the money all of the investors had committed. His short-term liquidity problems could not dictate our investment strategy.

Even with TARP now going ahead, the largest banks were still under enormous strain. JPMorgan cut our revolving line of credit by half. I could not believe it. We had worked together so successfully for so long on tens of billions of dollars' worth of transactions. Jimmy Lee said he knew nothing about it. So I called Jamie Dimon, the CEO.

"Things are tough," said Jamie. "We're still leaving you with credit."

I reminded him of our long relationship. "We're part of you guys. And we're a terrific credit. We've got $4 billion in cash."

"Yeah, I know," said Jamie. "If you weren't a good credit, we'd pull it all."

Citi was a different story. We deposited $800 million with them shortly after TARP passed, gave them some underwriting work and let them into one of our private equity deals. In our view, there was no way Citi could fail. Governments and corporations used its Global Transactions Service to pay their employees and move money. Without Citi, money would stop moving around the world.

Shortly after we made our deposit, Vikram Pandit, Citi's CEO, came to see me. Citi was under huge pressure, and Vikram joked that perhaps we should switch jobs. Running Blackstone looked a whole lot easier than running Citi. But in seriousness, he said that he was grateful for our show of support and asked if there was anything he could do. I told him what JPMorgan had done and asked if Citi would take its place. Vikram didn't hesitate. We had supported him in a moment of difficulty, and he was more than just happy to help. Life is long, and helping people when they need it often comes back to you in ways you least expect it. You never forget the friends who came to your aid in tough situations.

By fall 2008, with our earnings down, we had a decision to make about our dividend. In planning our IPO, the underwriters insisted that offering a dividend during our first two years as a public company would help us attract more investors. It turned out to be unnecessary because we were oversubscribed fifteen times, but we had made the promise.

Now, in the thick of the financial crisis, our earnings alone wouldn't cover the payments to our shareholders. We could either cut the dividend or borrow to pay it in full. I didn't want to borrow. It seemed like bad corporate finance to borrow to pay a dividend in a volatile market with a volatile stock. If we cut it, our investors wouldn't like it, but we would argue that it was in the best long-term interests of the company. Since I was the biggest shareholder, no one would suffer from the cut more than me, so no one could accuse me of self-dealing. Give us time and the stock would recover, and everyone would be happy.

I raised the matter at the next board meeting. I predicted that the Chinese, who had invested $3 billion on the eve of the IPO and could not start selling down their position for another two years, would not be happy. But I argued that it was more important now to preserve capital than to pay the dividend we had promised.

Dick Jenrette, who had recently joined the board as a public member, was the first to disagree. He reminded us of the significance of this investment to the Chinese. This investment wasn't just one among many. It was the first major investment by their nascent sovereign wealth fund outside China. The value of their shares had already fallen. If we cut the dividend as well, it would make the people who had trusted us look even worse. We would go from being an embarrassment to a severe disappointment. "If you make people really angry," said Dick, "that doesn't just go away like it never happened. If I were you, I'd suck it up and pay everybody the same dividend for the next quarter."

"That's just like burning $50 million," I said. "Just burning it."

"I understand," said Dick. "But if you don't, you're making a mistake."

Jay Light, my old professor who was then dean of the Harvard Business School, and another board member, agreed with Dick. The Chinese were already embarrassed at home by the drop in the value of their investment. Cut the dividend, and it would be even worse for them. In addition to buying our stock, the Chinese had invested in our funds. Over time, there could be much more to come, billions perhaps of future investments and partnerships. To jeopardize our long-term relationship for the sake of cash flow in one difficult quarter didn't make sense.

A year earlier, I had advised Jimmy Cayne to write a check to make the investors in Bear Stearns's hedge funds whole again. Now Dick and Jay were giving me a version of the same advice. Painful as it can be, sometimes it pays to write the check.

When we thought about becoming a public company, we knew we would have to balance serving our shareholders and our investors. Jay and Dick were financially astute, with sage advice on our short- and long-term considerations. I valued them for disagreeing with me.

"This isn't easy," I said. "But if both of you really feel that way, we'll pay it. I don't like the decision, but okay: $50 million for goodwill." As the largest shareholder at Blackstone, I understood that the long-term interests of the firm would not be served by cutting the dividend given the costs of damaging a valuable commercial relationship. It would take several more years, but as we did more and more business in China and my philanthropic activity grew there, I realized that dividend turned out to be one of the best checks we ever wrote.

In late 2008, I traveled to Beijing for a meeting of the board of the Tsinghua School of Economics and Management, on which I served. The Chinese had invested vast amounts of money in US companies in the preceding years and held over $1 trillion in Fannie Mae and Freddie Mac securities alone, a huge bet on the US housing market. US borrowers had grown used to Chinese money, and the Chinese were hooked on the ease and availability of US investments. Now, Fannie Mae and Freddie Mac had been seized by the federal government. The Chinese had no idea if Washington was going to make good on its obligations.

China had also lost around $1.5 billion on its Blackstone stock since the IPO. We weren't China's biggest investment in the United States, but we were one of its most visible. I could argue that Blackstone was in excellent health, but in that market environment, nothing could increase the share price. The Chinese were unhappy, and I knew it when I boarded my flight to Beijing.

During a break in the Tsinghua board meetings, former premier Zhu Rongji called me over. Zhu comes from that remarkable generation of Chinese politicians whose lives straddled several eras of postrevolutionary China. He grew up in a family of intellectuals and landowners and became a civil servant. But when he criticized Mao Zedong's economic politics, the Communist Party expelled him. During the Cultural Revolution, Zhu was sent to a farm for disgraced government workers, where he did manual labor for five years. When Mao died and was succeeded by Deng Xiaoping, Zhou's career recovered.

His ascent through academia and politics coincided with a time of rapid growth for China. He was the first dean of Tsinghua's School of Economics and Management, then mayor of Shanghai, and eventually China's fifth premier, the equivalent of prime minister, working just below the president. He became instrumental in developing Deng's vision of "socialism with Chinese characteristics," which meant a market economy overseen by the Communist Party.

Zhu is a tall, angular man, known for his energy and impatience. Larry Summers, the former treasury secretary and president of Harvard, once estimated Zhu's IQ at 200. As mayor and premier, Zhu had all kinds of nicknames alluding to his determination: One-Chop Zhu, Zhu the Boss, even Madman Zhu, for his willingness to crash through political structures and bureaucratic rules to get things done. Even five years after stepping down as premier, he still exuded the authority of his office.

As we spoke, he waved over Lou Jiwei, his protégé, who had made the Chinese investment in Blackstone and subsequently became minister of finance.

"Come over here," said Zhu. "See Schwarzman, Lou Jiwei, the guy who lost your money." He was only half-joking. We were going to have to work to regain his confidence.

———

In December, I ran into Ben Bernanke at a holiday party given at the German ambassador's residence in Washington. We stepped away from the crowd to talk. He asked me what I was seeing. I told him that many financial institutions were deleveraging because of the mark-to-market accounting rules issued by the SEC in September 2006. They were flooding the markets with good assets because of the plummeting value of their bad ones, but there were no buyers, so the price of everything was collapsing.

Ben was weighing whether the Federal Reserve should step in and start buying these unwanted assets. I told him it was the only way to restore confidence in the financial system. By spring 2009, the Fed was buying bank debt, mortgage debt, and Treasury notes, sending cash pouring through the financial markets.

The Fed's actions, though, needed governmental support, and I worried that the new president was not doing enough to talk up the economy and inspire confidence. On the evening of Sunday, March 8, 2009, I bumped into Rahm Emanuel, President Obama's first chief of staff, at an event at the Kennedy Center. During the intermission, we stepped into a private room near our seats. I suggested to Rahm that the president needed to sound a bit more positive. The stock market had fallen 25 percent since his inauguration in January, yet he was focused on health care. He was undermining what little business confidence there was left in the economy.

Rahm was polite at first, but soon he was yelling at me: "Steve, you're everything we hate: rich, Republican businessman." I was shocked. All I wanted to do was help the system survive. We argued for twenty-five minutes. Christine popped her head around the door twice, telling me I had to come and meet the president, but I waved her off and kept at it until I had to leave to shake the president's hand and watch the second half of the show.

The next morning, Rahm called to apologize. Our discussion had gotten more heated than he intended. He had so much going on with the new administration, he did not want to be listening to show tunes on a Sunday night. I thanked him and said I understood. He told me that morning he had arranged for all the top administration officials, including the president, to go on TV or give speeches about "green shoots" in the economy. That week saw the bottom of the stock market decline in the United States.

At Blackstone, we had our own challenges. Our young people, in particular, were scared. Every year, we have off-sites for each of our lines of business, and Tony was invited to cheer them up, to tell them everything would be fine. But that's not Tony's style. Instead, he told them how lucky they were to have this historical meltdown to learn from right at the beginning of their careers. If they were smart, they would learn from it and apply the lessons over their entire professional lives. Success breeds arrogance and complacency, he said. You only learn from your mistakes and when the worst happens.

Around the time of my conversation with Rahm, I was walking to the Waldorf Astoria in New York with my friend and colleague, Ken Whitney. Ken was disconsolate. He told me that the real estate team had just calculated the current value of all their holdings, and the results were grim. On Hilton alone, we had to write down the value of our investment by 70 percent as the company's revenues and earnings collapsed. I told Ken not to worry. These low-asset valuations were just marks. They would come back. We invest based on a thesis. If we still believed it, we just had to keep working and be patient. If the financial system collapsed, we would all be finished. As long as it survived, so would we.

After a while, we no longer felt like the entire economy was in free fall. We adjusted and got back to work. Across the firm, we went back to basics. We asked ourselves, What are the businesses we want to be in? We pulled back from new initiatives, which would struggle to attract funding anyway, and focused on our core. As a firm, we wanted a fortress balance sheet, immune to the volatility of the markets.

That fall, though, I was back in Tsinghua, with Blackstone's stock no higher than the year before.

"Schwarzman, how's Blackstone stock now?" asked Zhu Rong-ji, though he knew the answer. "How low can it go? Ha ha ha!"

But with patience and hard work, we were beginning to see the decisions we made before and during the crisis panning out well. Our advisory and restructuring businesses boomed as so many companies needed help. Our investment teams didn't have a huge precrisis mistake consuming all of their attention. Even if the rest of the world was traumatized, we were as open to growth and opportunity as ever before.

In the United Kingdom, one of our youngest partners, Joe Baratta, had teamed up with a walk-on-water entrepreneur, Nick Varney, and they were building Europe's largest theme park business. When Joe first presented the deal for Varney's collection of twenty aquariums and three "dungeons"—gruesome attractions in London, York, and Amsterdam—none of us in New York liked it. I had visited the London dungeon with my two children, who enjoyed the stories of murderers, torturers, and executioners, and I remembered the long lines waiting to get in. But I couldn't see the business ever achieving significant scale. It seemed like a lot of work for limited reward. Merlin, Nick's company, had already gone through two private equity owners before us.

Joe, though, was convinced by Nick's talent and ambition. The theme parks business was full of dissatisfied owners. Lego wanted to get rid of its theme parks to raise money for a corporate restructuring. Other small parks were owned by families or private equity groups and sovereign wealth funds that had no idea of what to do with them. Despite my doubts, at Joe's urging, we had paid £102 million for Merlin in 2005. It was a small deal, and our expectations in New York were modest.

But within a few months, Joe and Nick made their first move. They paid €370 million in cash and stock to buy four Legoland parks in the United Kingdom, Denmark, Germany, and California. The following year, they bought Gardaland, the largest theme park in Italy, for €500 million. And in spring 2007, they capped it off with the £1.2 billion acquisition of the Tussaud's Group, which included six of the famous wax museums and three theme parks, including Alton Towers, the biggest in the United Kingdom.

Nick improved the marketing, added new attractions, and multiplied earnings. Working together, Joe and Nick took a tiny company with $50 million in equity and built it into the second largest theme parks business in the world after Disney. It was an explosive meeting of our capital and a great entrepreneur, and Merlin grew during a time of widespread recession. By the time we sold our final shares in the company in 2015, we had created thousands of jobs, entertained millions of families, and made our investors more than six times their money.

Almost from the moment we bought Hilton in 2007, our critics said we had bought a trophy asset at the top of the market. But we pressed ahead with our original plan to expand and improve the business. In 2008 and 2009, we franchised fifty thousand new rooms a year in markets such as Asia, Italy, and Turkey, which raised cash flow. We moved the headquarters of the business from Beverly Hills to a less expensive site in Virginia. And we survived a dramatic drop in travel thanks to the financing that Jon and his team had arranged at acquisition. Even through a dire economy, we could still cover our debt payments.

But in spring 2010, we made extra sure by renegotiating with our lenders. Many had struggled to sell the debt they had issued for Hilton in 2007, so we used some of the capital we'd reserved to buy some of it ourselves at a discount. By the end of our discussions, we were able to substantially reduce our debt, and although we were still a long way from turning a profit on the deal, we had significantly cut its risk and given ourselves more room to maneuver. As people began traveling again, Hilton's cash flows surpassed their 2008 peak, and the value of our investment soared well above what we had paid. Our operational improvements and geographic and brand expansion paid off as well. We implemented a variety of energy-efficiency initiatives and improved the employee experience. We transformed the company, with over 600,000 employees, including over 17,000 US veterans and spouses, and doubled the number of rooms in the Hilton portfolio. Hilton was named the #1 Best Place to Work in the United States in 2019 by Fortune, making it the first hospitality company ever to achieve this ranking. Our investors ultimately made over $14 billion on Hilton, making it the most profitable private equity investment in history.

Back again at Tsinghua in 2010, I saw Zhu coming over to deliver his annual ribbing. "Schwarzman. How should I think about Blackstone stock? Can it come back? What do you think?"

Third time around, I was ready. "Mr. Premier, the company is doing very well. You shouldn't worry about the stock."

"Schwarzman, why not worry?"

"Because we're like farmers," I said. Zhu had spent time on farms growing up with his family and later as a political exile. "When we buy companies and real estate, it's like planting crops. You put seeds in the ground, you water, and the seeds start growing, but you can't see the crop yet. Then they grow very high, and it will be a great crop, and you will be very, very happy."

"Lou Jiwei, Lou Jiwei, come here," he said, laughing. "We have a farmer. Farmer Blackstone." From then on, I was always Farmer Blackstone. We kept paying dividends, our stock recovered, and the Chinese gave us increasingly large sums of money to invest on their behalf. And Zhu's welcomes became warmer.

"Farmer Blackstone, good to see you. A lot of crops coming up. We're very glad you're a good farmer. Can't wait to see you next year!"

273

In 2012, we closed our sixth private equity fund: $15.1 billion in commitments. It was short of the $20.4 billion fund we had raised in 2007, but still the sixth biggest fund ever raised, a sign that we had made it through the worst, and our investors still believed in what we did.

————

Following the financial crisis, the market for single-family homes in the United States, the largest private asset class in the world, was broken. Borrowers were defaulting and banks were foreclosing, flooding the market with properties. But it would take a series of bold, innovative actions to invest successfully in what was for many a terrible situation.

Historians of the financial crisis will tell you that in the insanity of the housing market, two connected sets of government actions stand out. The first was politically encouraging home ownership before the crisis, even by people who couldn't afford it. Lending standards fell, mortgages were pushed on uninformed and unsophisticated borrowers who could never realistically hope to pay them back, and the price of houses skyrocketed. Banks were willing accomplices in this profit machine. As we saw when the crisis hit, many subprime borrowers couldn't afford their monthly payments. The value of their homes fell, and either they or their lenders were forced to sell.

In the aftermath of the crisis, the government initiated its second set of disastrous actions by clamping down on banks and requiring them to tighten their lending standards. Banks that hadn't soured on mortgage lending altogether now required significantly higher down payments and higher credit scores from borrowers. What might have seemed like the proper, cautious response to fix an overheated market actually choked off any hopes of recovery. In both the housing boom that preceded the crisis and the bust that followed, the government's policies exacerbated the situation. When the market was going too fast, they slammed on the gas. When it was grinding to a halt, they hit the brakes. The poor American consumer suffered whiplash in the passenger seat.

Across the United States, house prices fell sharply. In the worst-hit areas, like Southern California, Phoenix, Atlanta, and Florida, new home construction all but stopped. Millions of Americans were now looking to rent instead of buy their homes.

Historically, mom-and-pop operations dominated the business of buying, fixing, and renting out houses in America. Of the 13 million rental homes, most belonged to individuals or small real estate businesses. Many landlords were absentee and didn't maintain their properties to the standard of a professionally run apartment complex. Our real estate team saw an opportunity to consolidate and professionalize the sector.

Were we the right people to try this? Blackstone did huge, multibillion-dollar real estate deals, the biggest in the industry, for hotel chains, office complexes, and warehouses. Why would we consider the small-time buy-to-let business? Our banks weren't convinced and wouldn't lend to us. Sam Zell, who knows more about real estate than anyone else, told us, "No way." But Jon Gray and his team were insistent. The basic math of the opportunity seemed straightforward—and unprecedented. Here was the biggest asset class in the world, in our home market, trading at historic lows, and the whole world was frozen. It was the right point in the cycle and exactly the kind of moment for investors like us. I'd seen something similar in the early 1990s, when we had made our first investments with Joe Robert: a real estate market distorted by fear, an irrational herd mentality, and borrowers and lenders all trying to scramble free from the latest collapse. The opportunity this time was much bigger. Worthy of our best efforts. We came at it with more knowledge and more experience, and armed with all the cash we had raised shortly before the crisis. We believed there were bargains to be had, and if we struggled to rent the houses we bought, at least we would turn a profit when house prices returned to normal.

In spring 2012, we paid $100,000 for our first home, in Phoenix, the same month US house prices bottomed out. We started buying in the West and moved east, city by city, from Seattle to Las Vegas, to Chicago, down to Orlando. Local courthouses published lists for their upcoming foreclosure auctions, and our acquisition teams went street by street to look at the homes for sale. They couldn't go inside, so they drove by, looking at neighborhoods and studying school districts. They would decide how many homes they wanted to buy and show up on the courthouse steps for the auction with a cashier's check. The deals would close in a couple of days. Within a few months, we were buying $125 million worth of homes every week.

The next step was renovation. We put to work over ten thousand builders, painters, electricians, carpenters, plumbers, HVAC installers, and landscapers, many of whom had been left unemployed by the recession. We spent around twenty-five thousand dollars fixing up each home. The final piece was a sales and service organization to rent out and maintain the homes.

We called the company Invitation Homes, which ended up owning over fifty thousand homes, making it the largest residential property owner in the United States and a huge employer at a critical time for the US economy. Our public pension fund investors liked the faith we showed in the resilience of the US economy at a moment when others were scared. We went into neighborhoods where homes were abandoned and lawns overgrown. Once we fixed up the houses and leased them out to families, we saw these neighborhoods come back to life, their social fabric restored.

Looking back, our initial observation seems to have been a simple one: When people are being stopped, for no good reason, from buying what they need, the system has to adjust. When it adjusts, the price of the commodity will rise. People needed houses, but after the crash, irrational regulators and fearful bankers got in their way. It was just a question of buying in the right way at the right time in the cycle.

———

After the crisis, we also had opportunities to deploy the dry powder we had worked so hard to accumulate and protect major investments in an otherwise capital-scarce environment. These opportunities soon began popping up in many different sectors, but perhaps most significantly in energy.

We had been slowly building our expertise in this field by running deals through our investment process. One of the major theses we'd developed as a result was that most public energy companies were chronically overvalued. Analyzed piece by piece, adding up the value of their refineries, pipelines, and gas stations, for example, it was clear that they were almost always priced well over the sum of their parts. The opportunity, then, was to buy or build pieces of the energy industry's infrastructure and sell them at full market prices.

In 2012, we had the chance to invest in an especially large piece of this infrastructure, a facility in Louisiana to prepare natural gas for export from the United States. The story of the Sabine Pass facility has all the elements of an energy industry classic, a visionary and daring entrepreneur trying to build a large, complex industrial plant amid rapid technological change, fickle politics, and volatile global markets.

Back in 2008, Charif Souki, an investment banker turned restaurateur turned energy entrepreneur, began work on a plant to receive natural gas shipments at the mouth of the Sabine Pass River, on the border of Texas and Louisiana, close to the Gulf of Mexico. Whereas oil is simple to transport in the vast hulls of container ships, gas is more difficult. It has to be chilled into a liquid for transportation and then turned back into gas at its destination. It is an expensive process, but the United States was short of natural gas at the time, and prices were soaring.

As Charif was building his new import facility, though, natural gas began pouring out of the ground in the United States, a result of the development of fracking. His plant was redundant. At that moment, he had a great entrepreneurial insight: What if he converted Sabine Pass from an import to an export facility, to send all that excess American gas out to the world?

It sounds simple enough, but there was more to it than just sending the gas flowing the other way. Cheniere Energy, Charif's business, was valued at $600 million and needed $8 billion to make the conversion from an import to an export facility. Banks were uncomfortable lending Charif more money because there had been times when he had struggled to make the payments on his debts. Second, his project depended on government approval of the facility and his right to export American fossil fuels. Third, this was going to be an enormous construction project, riddled with potential risks. If he couldn't be sure of doing it right, he shouldn't even start. When the opportunity reached the investment committee, we had a lot of concerns. We don't care if a deal is the best oil and gas deal out there. It has to stand up against the entire universe of investments we can make, from health care to real estate, media to technology.

We planned to commit $2 billion of equity and raise the remaining $6 billion we needed in debt. This was a big check for us and our limited partners, so we wanted to be sure we had the debt financing in place before we wrote it. Fortunately, banks were willing to lend to us on a project this large because of our reputation for always paying back our creditors.

We brought similar clout to the regulatory process. Our name enhanced the credibility of the project for federal regulators. But still, we had it written into the contract that if regulators stalled the project for any reason, we could pull out. We didn't want our investors' capital taken hostage by a never-ending regulatory approval process.

Another concern was Charif himself. Founder entrepreneurs can have strong ideas and personalities to match, so we drafted a clear set of expectations and targets to minimize the risk of any future disagreements. As long as the project stayed on track, he stayed in charge. We insisted that Cheniere sign off-take agreements with energy firms, in which they promised to buy a certain amount of gas from our facility over fixed periods of up to twenty years. These agreements provided guaranteed revenue regardless of changes in the price of gas. You might lose some upside if gas prices went up, but you protected your downside, which was essential in a project that was going to consume so much capital.

Finally, we had to minimize the risk in construction, which would be long, complex, and expensive. So we agreed to pay an extra fee to Bechtel, our construction firm, to accept a lump sum payment and promise turnkey delivery. If the plant didn't work as promised, Bechtel would have to pay penalties. We also hired a former Bechtel engineer to act as our embedded observer during construction.

Once we had analyzed all the risks, we told David Foley, the partner running the deal for us, "Go get it—and go get it now." Over President's weekend, David left his family and flew to Aspen where Charif was skiing. Their teams spent three days in the basement of the Little Nell hotel working out terms. Within days of announcing the deal, several other bids came in. But this deal was ours, and it would make its mark on an entire industry.

———

That same year, 2012, Tony had an idea for a new business line after talking with a few limited partners—a new strategy that straddled all of our asset classes and delivered a steady annual yield of around 12 percent, lower than we typically delivered. I gathered the heads of our various businesses to put together a proposal based on that idea for the New Jersey state pension fund. The fund's managers wanted us to look at investing in assets that regulators were forcing banks to sell in the wake of the crisis. It was a curious request, but as an entrepreneur, I've learned that finance is a simple business. When somebody asks you for something new, the odds that he or she is the only person on the planet at that point of time who would find that of interest is zero. When you get one of those inquiries, it's potentially a huge opportunity. Those who are asking don't know that. They are just looking at their own needs. But if those needs make sense and you create the right product to fit those needs, you can roll it out more broadly and your competitors will be left wondering how you figured it out.

As each of our businesses presented its ideas, each one seemed better than the last. By the time the third group made their pitch, I was stunned. I had never seen deals like this presented at the firm before. Deals that used to go to Goldman Sachs were now coming to us. They involved everything from container ships and the land under cell towers to mines and esoteric lending products. The challenge would be finding a place for them all in our existing funds.

Back in the early days of Blackstone, my friend Steve Fenster (with the two left wingtips) had arranged a meeting for me with an up-and-coming entrepreneur named Mike Bloomberg. Mike was looking for money for his young financial data company. I knew it was going to be a big success, but it wasn't the right fit for us at the time. We had promised our investors we would return their money in five to seven years. Mike said he would never sell his company. He wanted a partner for life, and we were his first choice. It was a huge miss, which I never forgot. Our $100 million investment would have ultimately grown to over $8 billion. I had always hoped that one day, we would have the flexibility at Blackstone to invest in entrepreneurs like Mike and in opportunities that didn't fit the traditional private equity model. Tactical Opportunities, as we would call our new fund, was my long-sought answer.

We applied our usual three tests for a new line of business. It must have the potential to be hugely rewarding for investors. It must add to Blackstone's intellectual capital. And it must have a 10 in charge of it.

There was no doubt about the economic potential of all these new opportunities. As for intellectual capital, Tac Opps was a great chance for all of us to learn and think in new ways to identify new patterns from the unusual opportunities popping up in the postcrisis landscape. We staffed the new fund's investment committee with the heads of each of our major asset classes, as well as Tony and me. We wanted to draw on all of our collective expertise to take these strange, popcorn stand deals and give them a thorough analysis.

To lead the fund, we chose David Blitzer, who had just returned home to New York from London. This was all so novel that we needed someone experienced who could make the unusual asks and pitch the unusual deals within the firm itself and to outsiders. David had successfully built Blackstone's European business. Ultimately, he turned Tac Opps into a $27-billion-plus business.

Five years after the crisis, we were accelerating away from our rivals, raising more money and doing more deals. Although we hardly emerged from the crisis unscathed (for example, we took a significant loss on our equity investment in Deutsche Telekom), we were able to move ahead in new and exciting directions while much of our competition was still busy cleaning up after old, top-of-the-cycle deals.

At the 2009 Kennedy Center Honors. FROM LEFT TO RIGHT: my brother
Mark, First Lady Michelle Obama, my mother, my stepdaughter Megan,
Christine, me, and President Barack Obama.

Receiving the Légion d'honneur from French President Nicolas Sarkozy
at the Élysée Palace in Paris, 2011.

At Tsinghua University in Beijing for the Schwarzman College
groundbreaking ceremony, 2013.

With Chinese Vice Premier Madam Liu Yandong, a friend and
invaluable supporter of Schwarzman Scholars, 2013.

Back in start-up mode, building Schwarzman College
from the ground up, 2014.

With my close friend Jimmy Lee, vice-chairman of J.P. Morgan, 2014. Jimmy
and I worked closely together from the earliest days of
Blackstone and our careers developed side by side.

At the future site of the Schwarzman Center at Yale University, 2015.
Mike Marsland/Yale University

Catching up with Jack Ma, co-founder and executive chairman of
Alibaba Group at the Economic Club of New York, 2015. Jack would
tell me "You and I are the same animals."

Speaking at the annual Milken Institute Global Conference in Beverly Hills, California, 2016. *Patrick T. Fallon/Bloomberg via Getty Images*

On the cover of *Forbes* magazine, 2016. *© 2016 Forbes. All rights reserved. Used under license.*

Schwarzman College at Tsinghua University, 2016. We wanted Schwarzman College to combine the very best of Chinese and Western architecture and design.

Interior courtyard of Schwarzman College.

With former PepsiCo CEO Indra Nooyi and President Trump at the
White House for the first President's Strategic & Policy Forum meeting, 2017.
Kevin Lamarque/Reuters

With President Trump and
Chinese President Xi at
Mar-a-Lago in Palm Beach,
Florida, 2017.

With Japanese Prime Minister Shinzō Abe during United Nations General Assembly Week in New York, 2017.

Walking through the College with Schwarzman Scholars from the Class of 2017.

Having lunch with students in the Schwarzman College courtyard, 2017.

With executive director Amy Stursberg and the Schwarzman Scholars Women's Soccer team, 2018.

Handing out diplomas at Schwarzman Scholars Class of 2018 Commencement.

Taking a selfie with the third cohort of Schwarzman Scholars. FRONT ROW, LEFT TO RIGHT: Imane el Morabit (taking selfie), me, executive director Amy Stursberg, and executive dean David Pan.

Christine and me at the Vatican with Pope Francis, 2018.

Arriving at the White House State Dinner for French President Emmanuel Macron with Christine, 2018. *Lawrence Jackson/The New York Times/Redux.*

Christine and me with the New York Catholic high school graduates we sponsored in 2018.

Arriving at the 2018 Met Gala with Christine. We were honorary co-chairs of the Gala after sponsoring the *Heavenly Bodies: Fashion and the Catholic Imagination* exhibit at the Metropolitan Museum of Art, the most visited exhibition in the history of the museum. *Neilson Barnard/ Getty Images Entertainment* via *Getty Images*

Michael Chae, Tony James, me, and Jon Gray
at Blackstone Investor Day 2018.

Receiving the Order of the Aztec Eagle from Mexican
President Enrique Peña Nieto in recognition of my work
during the US Mexico trade talks, 2018.

With White House Industries of the Future Group in the Oval Office. FRONT ROW, LEFT TO RIGHT: me, President Trump, and former U.S. Secretary of State Henry Kissinger. BACK ROW, LEFT TO RIGHT: White House Deputy Chief of Staff for Policy Coordination Chris Liddell, Oracle CEO Safra Catz, IBM CEO Ginni Rometty, Senior Advisor to the President Jared Kushner, Qualcomm CEO Steven Mollenkopf, Google CEO Sundar Pichai, Microsoft CEO Satya Nadella, MIT President Rafael Reif, Advisor to the President Ivanka Trump, Carnegie Mellon University President Farnam Jahanian, and Deputy U.S. Chief Technology Officer Michael Kratsios. *Official White House Photo by Joyce N. Boghosian*

Me, MIT President Rafael Reif, and CNBC anchor Becky Quick at the launch event for the Schwarzman College of Computing, 2019.

Hosting some of my USA Track & Field grantees, several of whom are Olympic medalists, for lunch at Blackstone, 2019.

With Chinese Vice President Wang Qishan in Beijing, 2019.

With Chinese Vice Premier Liu He in Beijing, 2019.

Financial Times coverage of my gift to the University of Oxford, 2019.
I was very surprised to find the picture and story on the front page—
a testament to the importance of the gift to the UK. *Andrew Jack,
Financial Times, June 19, 2019. Used under license from the Financial Times.
All rights reserved.*

ENGAGE

For many years, building Blackstone took all of my focus. Running the company often felt like an endless series of stress tests involving competitors, employees and former employees, the media, volatile macro and political forces, and sometimes, just plain bad luck.

But one of the great things about the entrepreneurial experience is that over time, if everything works out, life does get easier. As your business matures, the quality of the people around you gets better and your systems become more consistent. You put the right risk controls in place. You create an institution with successors who care. Your reputation improves and starts doing some of the work for you. The virtuous cycle spins faster, and in the case of Blackstone, clients and investors give us more money in larger amounts than they ever did before.

As the crisis receded, I had time to look around and see what else I might do with the resources, networks, and know-how at my disposal. As a boy, I had watched my grandfather, Jacob Schwarzman, gathering prosthetics and wheelchairs, clothes, books, and toys to send each month to children in Israel. I had seen my father extending credit to newly arrived immigrants when they came to his store. Buy what you need, he would tell them, and pay me when you can. He wrote regular checks to Boys Town in Jerusalem, the way his father had, to educate children in need. And like many middle-class Jewish families, we would save ten cents a week to plant a tree in Israel. Giving was a part of life, a habit that my good fortune has allowed me to continue. I gave money to institutions I cared about and to individuals who needed it. Sometimes they were friends, sometimes strangers I learned about from the news—people experiencing hardship through no fault of their own.

As chairman of the Kennedy Center, I had applied the skills and relationships I already had to raise more money, lift standards, and expand the range of performances. We had increased the profile of the center in the artistic hubs of New York and Los Angeles through our awards ceremonies that honored America's greatest creative talent. My time at the Kennedy Center in Washington also deepened my understanding of politics and politicians.

Over time, my many experiences have provided a filter for me in evaluating my philanthropic activities in political and nonprofit activities internationally. For example, I have always been aware of the profound influence that education has had on my life. Without moving to the high-quality Abington school system in Pennsylvania, I would never have been able to qualify for Yale or Harvard Business School, which subsequently opened many important possibilities for me. It's because of this that I am passionate about providing the same type of life-changing opportunities to as many people as possible. In the same way, my experience in the army helped me understand the many sacrifices that servicemen and servicewomen make to protect ordinary citizens, convincing me they must be recognized. My meeting with Averell Harriman convinced me of the huge impact that political engagement can have in improving the prospects for individuals, as well as for global peace and prosperity.

In 2008, I gave $100 million to the New York Public Library to support the renovation of its main building on Forty-Second Street and Fifth Avenue and several of its local branches. I hoped my gift would fund the creation of beautiful, calm spaces in the heart of the city. More important, it would also expand the library's literacy programs and offer Internet access in communities where it was lacking.

Shortly before Thanksgiving 2009, Christine and I visited one of the New York schools supported by the Inner-City Scholarship Fund. Christine is Catholic and had introduced me to the remarkable system of Catholic-run schools in which 90 percent of students are minorities, 70 percent live at or below the poverty line, and 98 percent go on to college. These schools provide an excellent academic foundation and the social and moral grounding for fulfilling lives. But as we walked around the school, Susan George, executive director of the Inner-City Scholarship Fund, told me that a lot of the students were dropping out: their parents had lost their jobs and could no longer afford even the tuition. It was the same in Catholic schools all over the city.

I told Susan that the schools should contact every family who had decided to withdraw a child and tell them they didn't need to do so. I would cover the difference between whatever they could afford and the full tuition. I couldn't imagine a child having to suffer like that. These kids and their parents weren't slackers. They had taken a hit they didn't see coming. It wasn't their fault. This would be my Christmas present to them.

I made a similar decision in 2013 when I started supporting the USA Track & Field Foundation with annual grants for the most promising athletes who were training for the World Championships and Olympic Games. I wanted to ensure that young, elite American track and field athletes had the time and resources necessary to train and compete without the worry of financial burden. Without financial help, these athletes might need two to three jobs to support themselves, which is impossible to maintain while training twice a day. Most of them would be forced to drop out of the sport. It's been amazing to see what these young men and women are capable of accomplishing without that burden. In the 2016 Rio de Janeiro Olympics, my grantees won four gold, three silver, and two bronze medals. I am now the largest individual donor to the USATF Foundation and am proud to help athletes with talents vastly superior to mine realize their potential.

Also in 2013, I attended a meeting of the Business Roundtable where First Lady Michelle Obama spoke about the unique support needs of US service members, veterans, and their families. She highlighted the obstacles that military veterans and their families face that result in high levels of unemployment and also mentioned the severe consequences, including twenty suicides a day. She asked every company in attendance to participate in her national initiative to reduce veterans' unemployment. As I made my way home from Washington that evening, I couldn't help but reflect on everything she had said. We owed our servicemen and servicewomen more—at the very least an easier transition back into civilian life. Before I arrived home, I dictated a note to the First Lady committing Blackstone and its portfolio companies to hiring fifty thousand veterans and their families over the next five years. Although this was the type of thing I would normally discuss with my management committee first, I was convinced that this was the moral thing to do and knew Blackstone would stand behind my promise. We ended up making the fifty thousand hires in just four years, so in 2017, we committed to hiring an additional fifty thousand. It was a great example of the significant impact Blackstone can have as a result of its scale and reach.

As time passed and I became involved in more causes, the more I began to wonder what I could accomplish if I went beyond writing checks. What if I applied my entrepreneurial energy and the skills I had acquired building Blackstone to philanthropic challenges of similar ambition?

In 2005, the Kennedy Center hosted a China festival. I sat next to China's minister of culture on opening night, watching a troupe of dancers and gymnasts form a human pyramid, one on top of another, climbing higher and higher, to the sound of an orchestra. Each time the pyramid rose, a dancer sprinted across the stage and vaulted over it. We all wondered how long this could go on.

The next dancer circled the stage and took his run-up, gathered speed . . . and went crashing into the pyramid. Bodies flew all over the stage. If this were ballet or ice skating, the performers would just pick themselves up and move on as if nothing had happened. Not in China. The music stopped and everybody went back to their place. They rebuilt the pyramid, the dancer took his spot, and we all covered our eyes. He ran and made it over. Barely.

I looked at the minister of culture. His expression was impassive. I asked him why he seemed so unruffled by the whole thing. "In China, we aspire for greatness," he told me. "If it does not happen the first time, we simply continue until we achieve greatness."

The full strategic nature of China's decision to invest in Blackstone's IPO in 2007 had become clearer to me when I visited the country soon afterward to thank our investors for their support. As I made my way from meeting to meeting, a camera crew from Chinese state television followed me around. The Chinese government had made a huge deal of its investment in Blackstone. To my surprise, I was a minor celebrity. When I made a speech, the audience spilled over into the aisles. Everything I said and did was covered on the news. But I still had a lot to learn.

Fortunately, sitting on the advisory board of the Tsinghua School of Economics and Management gave me access to excellent teachers. Tsinghua University had evolved from an act of American largesse. In 1901, China agreed to pay the United States reparations for its help suppressing the anti-Western Boxer Rebellion. President Theodore Roosevelt insisted China keep most of the money and pay for scholarships for Chinese students to study in the United States. A preparatory school was established for them, Tsinghua College, which became today's university, by most counts the best in China.

Tsinghua's graduates include the current president, Xi Jinping; his predecessor, Hu Jintao; and many members of the powerful State Council. Since 2015, it has been ranked by *U.S. News & World Report* as the best engineering and computer science school in the world, higher than MIT. The School of Economics and Management was founded in 1984, inspired by the best American business schools. It was one of the first Chinese institutions to develop deep relationships with American business and has become a regular stop for leaders from Wall Street to Silicon Valley. Its board leaders come from China and around the rest of the world.

Since 1980, China's GDP has grown from 11 percent of that of the United States to 67 percent in 2019.* Though it remains less on a per capita basis—ten thousand dollars GDP per capita in 2019 versus sixty-five thousand dollars in the United States†— China's GDP per capita has increased thirty-three times since 1980, compared to an increase of just five times for US GDP per capita over the same period. Its exports have grown from 6 percent of those of the United States, to more than 100 percent. It has gone from having an economy smaller than Holland's to

---

*GDP, current prices in US dollars; International Monetary Fund. World Economic Outlook database; April 2019.

† GDP per capita, current prices in US dollars; International Monetary Fund. World Economic Outlook database; April 2019.

adding the equivalent of the Dutch economy every year. Since 2007, when China made its first investment in Blackstone, China has caught up with or overtaken the United States in many of the major indicators of economic growth and innovation. It is a larger manufacturer, exporter, saver, and consumer of energy. It is a bigger market for everything from luxury goods to smartphones. From 2007 to 2015, nearly 40 percent of all the growth in the global economy occurred in China. Its growth rate in 2019, even as it slows, is still more than double that of the United States.

Lee Kuan Yew, Singapore's late prime minister and one of the most astute observers of China, was asked shortly before his death in March 2015 if he thought China would eventually displace the United States as the dominant power in Asia. He was unequivocal: "Of course. Why not? How could they not aspire to be number one in Asia and in time the world?" And when it happens, he added, it would be on China's terms, not on the West's. China's emergence is the defining geopolitical fact of our time.

Graham Allison, a Harvard historian, has warned that this process of rebalancing power from West to East contains a trap. As the United States steps back and China steps up, both powers, and their dependents, will feel unbalanced, out of sync with decades of history, creating a moment when the slightest misunderstanding, resentment, or offense could topple everyone into the trap of war. It happened in the fifth century B.C. when Athens' rise threatened Sparta. Hence Allison's name for it, the Thucydides trap, after the Greek historian who wrote the defining history of the Peloponnesian War. It happened in the twentieth century, when Germany threatened the established European order and provoked two world wars. It could happen again if China and the United States cannot find a cooperative, trusting way to manage the shift in political power that must follow the shift in economic power that has already taken place.

As Tsinghua marked its centenary, its president, Chen Jining, asked to come and see me in Paris, where Christine and I had been living for eight months. I knew he was soliciting money. But I had begun thinking about what else I might do with the resources and networks I could bring to bear.

I had no personal history or emotional connection with the university. It was thousands of miles from home in a country and culture that I was still just getting to know. So as I prepared for President Chen's visit to Paris, I searched widely for inspiration. Whatever idea I came up with, I knew it would be up to me, and a small team around me, to create the momentum it would need to become reality.

When he was twenty-three years old, Cecil Rhodes was yet to build his fortune mining in Africa. But he wrote that the "chief good in life" was "to render myself useful to my country." When he died in 1902, his will laid out plans for a scholarship program that would bring together young men from the British Empire, its former colonies, and Germany to study at a British university, to give "breadth to their views, for their instruction in life and manners and [to instill] into their minds, the advantages to the Colonies as well as to the United Kingdom of the retention of the unity of the Empire." His vision eventually became the Rhodes Scholarship program at Oxford. Rhodes was a controversial figure, a brutal employer, and someone who helped prepare the way for apartheid in South Africa. However, his scholarship remains one of the most prestigious in the world, a rare chance for some of the most accomplished young men and women from different countries to live and study together at an influential moment in their lives.

What if, I suggested to President Chen, we created something similar in China? A program to encourage the best and brightest from all over the world to study together at Tsinghua. They could travel and intern at ministries and Chinese companies. They could study under Chinese and Western professors who would help them find the links between cultures. Each cohort of scholars would be enriched by the experience. Then, as they rose to positions of influence in different countries, they would understand each other and their ambitions. They would act out of friendship and reason, not with the kind of suspicions and mistrust that cause countries to stumble into the Thucydides trap. President Chen listened. He agreed, but added: "This could be expensive." I pledged the first $100 million and assured him we could raise the rest. With that, Schwarzman Scholars was born.

There was just one problem. I wasn't an educator and hadn't sat in a classroom since 1972. I knew nothing about building a college from the ground up, let alone a college in China.

Jay Light, the former dean of Harvard Business School who was also on the Blackstone board, introduced us to Professor Bill Kirby, the former head of the Chinese department and dean of the Faculty of Arts and Sciences at Harvard. Nitin Nohria, the dean of Harvard Business School, suggested we speak to Professor Warren McFarlan, a longtime member of the HBS faculty who had taught at Tsinghua and knew everyone there. Together, Bill and Warren invited an academic advisory board to join us on our adventure.

They helped us answer many of the questions we were asking ourselves: What was the right range of ages for our students? The right mix of disciplines? How do we provide career advice for when they graduate? What would it cost to fund a single scholar: housing, teaching, and flying one person back and forth to Beijing? That still left the student life issues. If you think supporting higher education is just about writing a check in return for an honorary cap and gown, you have no idea.

As we developed the program, I thought back to my own

291

higher education, often toiling away in classes with little reward, and my first few months on Wall Street, with no training or mentor. That experience taught me that the prestige of that first job didn't matter nearly as much as the opportunities I lost to develop my skills. I had eventually found what I needed at Lehman, and that was the basis for my ability to perform at the highest level as I got older.

So I began to imagine a program that accelerated that process—one purposefully designed to give young people a great academic experience, help them forge lifelong relationships with their peers, get advice from mentors, and engage in the practical experience of work. First, we had to decide the length of the program. Should it be one year or two? I put myself in the shoes of our ideal applicants, many of whom would be like the young analysts we hire at Blackstone. Two years felt far too long in the life of an ambitious twenty-three-year-old. If we wanted the most capable young people in the world, we would have to give them a great experience without taking too much time away from their pursuit of other ambitions. One year would be perfect.

Next, we had to decide if we wanted our students to be taught by Tsinghua's Chinese faculty, an international faculty, or a mix of both. I attended several classes at Tsinghua to observe the teaching. While the language went over my head, I found that even in the smaller classes, Chinese professors did most of the talking. In large lectures, they did all of it. The classes were longer than you would find in a Western university, and the students I imagined as Schwarzman Scholars would be bored quickly.

But I did not want a fully international faculty either. Our students would be coming from the greatest universities in the United States, Europe, and the rest of the world. There was no point in sending them to Beijing to get the same academic experience they could have at home. So we settled on a blend: half foreign faculty, half Chinese, sometimes both teaching the same class. Two cultures in one classroom.

The third big piece of the academic program was getting to know China in depth. This would have three elements: mentorship from prominent Chinese leaders in business, nonprofit, or government work, whatever was relevant to each scholar; travel around China to understand the country outside Beijing; and practical experience of working at Chinese organizations to see how they functioned.

It was tough initially persuading the Chinese of the merits of our plan. They didn't do blended classes, apprenticeships, or what we called "deep dives"—our program of immersive travel to the different parts of China. But our supporters at the top of the university got it. As we battled bureaucratic resistance, President Xi's own ambitions became a tailwind. He wanted China's leading universities to rise in global rankings and set a goal of having two in the top ten in the world within two decades. He proposed they integrate the latest pedagogy from the best Western universities.

Amy Stursberg, head of the Blackstone Foundation and eventual executive director of Schwarzman Scholars, and I became missionaries for Tsinghua. We went into full start-up mode. The first priority for any team of entrepreneurs is to build momentum, that sense of inevitable success, around their vision. So we went to meet the heads of every major university in the United States and Europe: Oxford, Cambridge, the London School of Economics, and Imperial College in the United Kingdom; the Ivy League universities in the United States, Stanford, and Chicago; and 250 other universities around the world. We encouraged them to send their best students to our program. No chancellor, president, or director of fellowships of a major university was spared the case for Schwarzman Scholars.

None of this would be cheap, and we realized that my initial gift of $100 million would not be nearly enough. It was like building a house. Somehow everything was going to take twice as long and cost twice as much than we anticipated. To meet the rising costs, I had to start selling. When Pete and I raised our first buyout fund in 1986, we went one for seventeen with potential investors. Since then, everything had gotten a lot easier as Blackstone built a record of great performance. I had gotten used to showing up to prescreened investors knowing there was a 90 to 100 percent chance I would close them.

With Schwarzman Scholars, though, it didn't matter if China was the most exciting country in the world, supplying 40 percent of the world's growth. Or that we had the backing of its most powerful people. I was back to selling an idea—one that was unproven, unprecedented, and, in many people's eyes, impossible.

Everywhere I went, from the Business Roundtable to weddings, from Davos to parties in New York, I talked up the program. If I thought the person I was talking to had the slightest interest in China or education, I pitched my idea. Anyone who had the money to write a check was vulnerable. I was fast wearing out my welcome almost everywhere.

We wrote nearly two thousand letters over five years, tailored to each potential donor, explaining why this would be a fantastic use of their money. If they showed the slightest interest, more letters and more discussions followed. I kept those who turned me down on our mailing list. When Mike Bloomberg gave me a check, he said he did it out of the fear that I would never stop asking.

On December 12, 2012, I was invited to speak at the *New York Times* Dealbook conference. In the green room I saw one of my fellow panelists, Ray Dalio, the founder of Bridgewater, the world's largest hedge fund. He was sitting in the far corner, and I went over to introduce myself. We didn't have long before we had to be onstage, so I went straight into my pitch. I proposed that Ray should be a founding partner of Schwarzman Scholars for $25 million. He looked at me painfully and told me he had been active in China since 1984. The country fascinated him immensely and he had even sent his son to a Chinese high school for a year. But as much as he loved China, he thought the project I had in mind was unachievable. He was convinced I had no idea what I was taking on.

But I kept pressing until he gave in. He pledged $10 million and the balance of $15 million if we were successful in getting the project up and running. "Let's stay in touch. Let me know how it goes," he said before we stepped onstage. He seemed pretty certain that he wouldn't have to write me another check.

Of course we didn't need Ray to tell us what a tough challenge we had taken on. We had already begun discovering that for ourselves. Here we were in Manhattan trying to create an institution and program from scratch halfway around the world, in a country we still knew little about. The twelve-hour time difference between New York and Beijing meant that we had to spend our nights working on Scholars, then return to our day jobs when the sun came up. We quickly lost count of the number of consultants who promised to solve our problems, and failed. I knew that if we weren't great out of the gate, our program would never have the prestige it needed to succeed. But no one except our small team thought we could ever make it happen, and even we had our moments of doubt as every task, small or large, took five times longer than it should.

When our fundraising got bogged down, we started offering potential donors the opportunity to sponsor parts of the building and then students, as if they were professors, with their own endowments. Two and a half million dollars would fund a student a year for fifteen years. After fifteen years, we would resell the same right to another donor and raise another $2.5 million for the endowment. We found people were eager to endow scholarships for students from their own country or their alma mater.

Many corporations already had philanthropic engagements in China. But we found ways for them to be involved with ours. Indra Nooyi, then chief executive of Pepsi, sponsored two individual scholarships, one to be named the Pepsi Fellow and the other the Henry Paulson Fellow. No one, with the possible exception of Henry Kissinger and Hank Greenberg, had done more for US-China relations than Hank. The honor delighted him. Entrepreneurs often succeed based on the company they keep. The more prominent the donors and corporations, like Disney and JPMorgan, that signed up to support us, the more attractive we became to others.

In some cases, my appeal for Schwarzman Scholars led to new friendships. I was in Tokyo to see Masayoshi Son, the founder of SoftBank and the richest person in Japan, about a business issue. As our conversation drifted, inevitably I told him about Schwarzman Scholars. As a salesman, I had thought through my approach beforehand. Japan, I said, historically had a terrible relationship with China. For decades, Japan had been the far stronger economy. But now China was getting richer, and Japan's population was shrinking. Perhaps it was time to fix the relationship.

Masa was worth around $15 billion at the time. He was in his late fifties, and assuming he worked another decade or so, his net worth would likely double. With a fortune that size, I told him, he needed a plan to give more of it away. A gift of $25 million for Schwarzman Scholars seemed a good place to start. He countered with an offer to endow four Japanese students at a cost of $2.5 million each. From that initial $10 million, he has since increased his gift to $25 million, and we have become great friends.

The Chinese were a different challenge. Before the college was built and the students on site, Chinese donors would not give us anything. They don't trust ideas. I could promise a building and great students, but until they saw them, they weren't going to write us a check. So we decided to wait until Schwarzman College opened in 2016 and our first class was enrolled. And as soon as they did, the perception of what we were doing changed completely. Our first wave of Chinese donors had made their fortunes in real estate. Next came the major conglomerates, then technology firms, and, finally, individual entrepreneurs specializing in artificial intelligence, all wanting to be associated with our mission. Now we have the largest endowment of its kind in China, over $580 million, consisting of foreign and Chinese money.

The institution, the program, and the network we have built today was born out of my desperation and sheer will to make Schwarzman Scholars a reality and my refusal to accept anything but success.

I learned from the project the importance of relationships in China. If you want to get anything done, the strength of your relationships means everything. We could have done what we did only with strong relationships with the Chinese. When we started, we worked with Chen Jining, Tsinghua's dynamic young president. He was courageous and flexible, and he also knew that if our project went wrong, his career would suffer and his political enemies would hold it against him.

In 2015, Chen was promoted to minister of environmental protection and subsequently became mayor of Beijing. Qiu Yong succeeded him as the new president of the university. Before he was sworn in, I visited Tsinghua to see my friend, Madame Chen Xu, the party secretary who oversees the university. Usually I met her in her private office. But this time, I was shown into a large meeting room and invited to sit in the chair to Madame Chen's right, the place of honor for any visitor. She was sending a clear message to the new president, who sat to her left: Schwarzman Scholars had Tsinghua's unqualified support. We would need it, and fortunately for us, Qiu gave it. He became a great supporter of the Schwarzman Scholars and someone I communicate with weekly.

Back in 2012, once we decided to move ahead with Schwarzman Scholars, Chen took me on a bus tour of the Tsinghua campus. He showed me three plots of land where we might build a home for our new program. Rhodes Scholars lived in Oxford's various colleges but had a center, Rhodes House, where they could study and socialize. I thought our scholars should live together and take classes together under one roof to make the most of their time in Beijing. I wanted them to meet each other in hallways and common rooms, to bump into each other on the stairs and have lunch together. Our program shouldn't just be about what they learned. It had to be about the relationships they built while learning. I wanted to put as much care into the design of our building as I had into the design of Blackstone's offices.

We started by inviting ten architects to compete for the project. Their proposals were depressing. Most were for the kind of glass boxes found anywhere from Dallas to Dubai. One firm suggested we surround our main building with replica rocket ships, to suggest we were taking off into a new world. Eventually I turned to Bob Stern, then dean of Yale's School of Architecture, and told him that if we were going to bring people from all over the world to China, our building needed to feel like China. It should remind visitors of China's past and present and its enduring civilization.

After tossing out the glass box idea, I asked Bob to design a modern interpretation of a traditional Chinese courtyard house, and he returned with something magnificent. The entrance would lead from the bustling street on campus into a protected courtyard, the Chinese version of a classic college quad. Bob's building wrapped itself around those in it. A sunken courtyard drew light into the classrooms and auditoriums, and there were meeting points and social areas scattered around the building to encourage the kinds of casual interactions so important to the experience. It was old and new, East and West, a unique setting for our program.

While the building was under construction, we built a model dorm room for visitors to see what daily life would be like for our students. Before we let anyone visit, I tried out the bed, the reading chair, and the desk we picked to make sure everything was right. When Schwarzman College was completed, *Architectural Digest* named it one of the nine best academic buildings in the world, the only one in Asia on the list.

But getting it built was another fight. The university had strong views on the feng shui of Bob's design. Then we had to go hand-to-hand with Chinese contractors, who had lost touch with the old world craftsmanship of China's traditional buildings. We wanted wooden floors to last two hundred years, but were told we could only get artificial wood, which we would have to replace in twelve years. We wanted wood paneling on the walls but were told the only option was plastic made to look like wood. Instead of brick, our contractors offered us brick veneer.

I could not imagine taking such cheap shortcuts and suspected that all these excuses were schemes to force us into using certain favored vendors. So we got to work finding a furniture maker who would make us wood floors and wood paneling. For the wooden front doors of Schwarzman College, we hired the company that had restored the doors in the Great Hall of the People. And for the brick walls, we had our local builders instructed in classic brickwork.

Initially we left our Chinese contractors in charge of the project. But as time passed and the obstacles and excuses piled up, we began to suspect that no one was in any hurry to finish. When we installed an American observer on the ground, it became clear that we were going to have our first class of Schwarzman Scholars arriving to take up residence in a half-completed building. So with a year to go, I toured the site and asked our team to compile a list of everything that needed to be done to open Schwarzman College on time and to the standards I expected. It wasn't just about fake wood and brick. The site was not even lit properly at night, and workers could have been hurt. I insisted that be fixed within forty-eight hours.

The next morning, we lined up our project manager and our subcontractors, and I told them how disappointing they had been. I could sense my translator hesitating to repeat what I was saying. But I could tell from the builders' stunned looks that they understood my fury. This project had support at the highest levels in China. I told them I would be back every six weeks until the completion of the building to check on its progress. If there were any more delays or failures, the consequences for those responsible did not bear thinking about. I would leave them to face the full wrath of their government. The work accelerated.

Building Schwarzman College, I learned that the Chinese respect power but are continually testing it. They want to know who has it and who can bring it to bear. As we realized our vision, we witnessed power descending from the president, to the vice premier, to the minister of education, to the party secretary, and to the president of the university. If you have all of that, you *are* China and no one can get in your way or refuse you. When our construction team failed us, I had to wield that power to get them back on track. When all was said and done, I must have made thirty trips to China, and my team double that number, to ensure we got all the details right.

———————

Every entrepreneur needs luck, and I got some at an event at the White House in late 2012. When President Obama asked me, "Steve, how're you doing? What're you working on? What's interesting?" I told him about the Scholars program, which seemed to intrigue him, and he said if there was anything he could do to help, to let him know.

So as we approached our formal launch in China, I contacted the White House and asked if the president would draft a formal message of support. True to his word, he did. What we didn't count on was the Chinese side. The night before the formal announcement of our program, our team was already exhausted tying up the final details before the event. The White House had sent President Obama's letter of support to the US embassy in Beijing. I knew that for an event in the Great Hall of the People supported by the president of the United States, President Xi would want to issue his own statement. I wanted his endorsement because it would resonate at every level in China. It would become the official position on what we had created and be of enormous help to us in the future. But when we approached his office, they insisted they had to see the original of President Obama's letter. Anyone, they told us, could mock up a letter and make it look like it came from the White House. They would not accept an email or photocopy.

The US ambassador and his two deputies were away. The person left to handle our request was not senior enough to ignore protocol, which dictated that a presidential letter could be viewed or read aloud but not released. The Americans wouldn't let it out of the embassy, and the Chinese wouldn't come over to see it. We were stuck.

Help came from a member of our advisory board, Steve Orlins, a former investment banker and then president of the National Committee on United States–China Relations. He went to the embassy and somehow wrangled something to show to President Xi's office. Overnight, the status of our announcement ceremony went up. It was originally to be hosted by the minister for education. Now, the newly appointed vice premier, Madam Liu Yandong, decided to preside, making our event her first public appearance in her new role.

We entered the Great Hall together to find it packed with hundreds of people as far as I could see. Onstage was a huge billboard with the words "Schwarzman Scholars" in giant gold letters above a painting of our future building.

The minister of education read out loud President Xi's letter of support: "We encourage increased mutual understanding among the students of the world's nations, plant the roots of global vision, and encourage the muse of innovation, setting a far-reaching ambition to contribute wisdom and power for peace and for the development of humanity. I wish the Schwarzman Scholars program at Tsinghua University every possible success."

President Obama wrote: "Throughout history educational exchanges have transformed students and moved nations forward in deeper understanding and mutual respect. By promoting learning and building bridges through scholarship and cultural immersion in China, the Schwarzman Scholars program takes its place in this proud legacy."

It was staggering to see the majesty of China and the United States in support of a program bearing my name. We had created this program out of nothing because President Chen was coming to see me and I wanted to offer him something out of the ordinary. The whole experience of that day—all the work, creativity, and persistence that had gone into making it happen— overwhelmed me.

————

We received over three thousand applications for 110 slots for our inaugural class. We had been scrupulous about our criteria for admission. Amy and I had spent an entire Sunday evening over Labor Day weekend defining what we meant by "leadership." We were looking for students who had taken risks, been creative, and brought others along with them. They had to be exceptional—10s in Blackstone-speak.

Ninety-seven percent of those we had accepted for that first class enrolled, a much higher yield than Harvard, Yale, or Stanford. After all our evangelizing at universities, that was no accident. I had attended every one of our global launch events to ensure we delivered a consistent message and a strong brand. In Singapore, I was just about to go onstage when Rob Garris, our head of admissions, pointed out that I wasn't wearing one of our new distinctive purple Schwarzman Scholars ties, designed by my wife, Christine. Rob passed me a spare tie, and there in the middle of the reception I changed ties before stepping up to speak.

We interviewed three hundred candidates in London, New York, Beijing, and Bangkok. In London and New York, I met all of the candidates, shook their hand when they arrived for their interviews, and wished them luck. If I learned that an accepted candidate was wavering about taking up our offer, I called that person myself to get him or her off the fence. There were only two reasons I would accept a no: if the candidate was unwell or had been offered a Rhodes scholarship. Otherwise, I stayed on the phone until the candidate accepted, even if it took hours.

Besides their class work, internships, and travel, our first class of scholars threw themselves into Tsinghua life. I would be sitting at home in New York watching TV and my phone would ping to tell me of another extraordinary feat. Despite being only 110 out of 44,000 regular Tsinghua students, they had been crowned university champions in track and field, women's soccer, and men's basketball. One of our students won gold in the 2017 Beijing fencing championships. In the eleven months after the first class arrived on campus, they had built a vibrant college life out of nothing. They wrote their own pledge, created a student government, published a literary journal, and organized a Schwarzman College ball. Surely it wouldn't be long before someone organized a visit from a ballet troupe, the way I had at Yale.

When Ray Dalio saw that we had achieved what he thought impossible, he wrote that second check for $15 million. The auditorium at Schwarzman College now carries his name.

Our Chinese donors told me that they were used to the idea of the Chinese traveling abroad to learn, but were so proud that Schwarzman Scholars was reversing that and bringing the best foreign students to China. To them, it was a sign of China's restoration to the place it had occupied for thousands of years.

———

I am now quite certain that China is no longer an elective course for future generations; rather, it is core curriculum, and Schwarzman Scholars is the best version of that curriculum we could devise.

ANSWER WHEN YOUR
COUNTRY CALLS

O n December 15, 2012, I was in a meeting when my assistant
came in with a note saying the president was on the line.
"The president of what?" I asked her. She scribbled on the note:
"US." When POTUS calls, you answer. I stepped into my office
and picked up the phone.

It was the day after the school shootings in Sandy Hook, Con-
necticut, and President Obama was clearly deeply distressed.
After fifteen minutes of discussing the shooting and its consequences, he told me why he was calling. Budget talks with the
Republicans were bogged down over typical differences about
raising taxes or cutting spending.

"I could really use your help," said the president.

If Democrats and Republicans failed to reach an agreement
by January 1, they would trigger a set of automatic decreases in
spending and increases in taxes embedded in previous budget
agreements that would take the country over the so-called fiscal
cliff.

"Are you saying you want to hire me to be your investment
banker with no compensation?" I said. He laughed, gave me his
private number, and said I could call any time of day or night—
though preferably not after 11:00 p.m. I admired him for reach-

ing out to people outside Washington who might help break the logjam.

For the next week and a half, I went to work. I knew the leaders on the Republican side well, and we debated various options. I talked to the president most days during this period. Once he called to check in when I was having a Christmas celebration dinner at a friend's house. I had to step away during dessert, dodging my hostess who was eager to know what I was up to.

We got to what I thought was a fair offer from the Republican side—$1 trillion over ten years, $100 billion, or $10 billion a year, shy of the tax increases the Democrats wanted. The president wouldn't accept it. I pleaded with him. Ten billion a year was a rounding error in the federal government's $4 trillion annual budget. The Republicans had started these negotiations refusing to raise taxes at all, and now they were proposing $1 trillion of additional revenue by raising taxes, closing loopholes, and ending deductions. There was room here for a deal, but not much, and the window would likely slam shut if the Democrats continued to balk.

You might know about deal making, the president told me, but he knew politics—a fair point from a man fresh from winning his second presidential term. He did not want to start this second term spending precious political capital by pushing a deal he knew he couldn't get his own party to support. I told him I could imagine him and John Boehner, the Republican Speaker of the House, in the Oval Office together, raising their arms in triumph and all the dissenters scattering like roaches, the way they always do when the lights come on. The country would love them for it. And as for political capital? It's like hair, I said. Cut it, it grows back, provided you do the right things. The president was gracious. He acknowledged that I had done all I could and thanked me for my effort. The negotiations rumbled on until the early hours of January 1, after a long haggle led by Vice President Joe Biden and Senator Mitch McConnell, the Republican leader in the Senate. The deal was far from perfect, but it prevented the country from falling off that cliff.

Politicians across the spectrum are just people looking for answers. If you can help, you should. In the early 1990s, I was invited to a dinner at the White House. I was between marriages so I took a date, a magazine writer from New York. During the party, I approached President George H. W. Bush, whom I had met years before when he visited his son George W. at Yale. We stepped aside and talked intently for ten minutes. When I walked back to my date, she asked what on earth we had been talking about. Simple, I told her: I had some ideas for him about the ailing US economy, his biggest problem at the time. World leaders are no different from anyone else. If you talk about what's on their mind and have something to offer, they will listen, Democrats, Republicans, princes, or prime ministers.

———

In November 2016, my engagement in politics took me to the twenty-sixth floor of Trump Tower to meet with the most improbable president-elect in recent US history. For years, I had run into Donald Trump socially in New York and Florida. Now he had won an election that few predicted he could, and he was looking for people to fill his administration. His office and the rooms around it were heavily protected by Secret Service agents. He was in the bubble now, and the transformation felt surreal. There was little time to talk, but he called again a week later, this time asking if I might consider joining his team. I thanked him and told him I was very happy with my life as it was; I didn't want to disrupt it. He told me he thought I'd say that, but also that he needed to hear directly from America's business leaders as he tried to accelerate the economy. "I need a group of people who can tell me the truth," he told me. "Do you think you could put that group together and be in charge of it?"

He wanted a small group, twenty-five people at most. Republican or Democrat, he didn't care. This was about talent and knowledge, not politics. The group need not approve of everything the president did or said, but by participating they could be friends to the situation, friends to our country. The US growth rate had been stuck around 1.8 percent per year since the Great Recession. There was a need to create jobs, stimulate productivity, and restore America's economic health. This group could help boost confidence after an election that had provoked extraordinary levels of uncertainty and unrest. If the president-elect was sincere about this, then so was I. When you take up any challenge laid down in Washington, you can never be certain of the outcome. But whether you succeed or fail, if the goal is to help your country, it is almost always worth doing.

After a week, I had an initial roster for the president's Strategic and Policy Forum, including Jack Welch, the former CEO of GE; Jamie Dimon of JPMorgan Chase; Larry Fink of Black-Rock; Mary Barra of General Motors; Toby Cosgrove of the Cleveland Clinic; Bob Iger of Walt Disney; Doug McMillon of Walmart; Jim McNerney of Boeing; Ginni Rometty of IBM; Elon Musk of Tesla; Indra Nooyi of Pepsi; Bayo Ogunlesi of Global Infrastructure Partners; Paul Atkins of Patomak Global Partners; Dan Yergin of Cambridge Energy Research Associates; Rich Lesser of the Boston Consulting Group; Kevin Warsh of Stanford University and the Hoover Institution; and Mark Weinberger of Ernst & Young. It was an all-star team, covering a broad span of the US economy.

When I presented the list to the president, he had only two requests. One: I remove a foreign policy expert I had included to get a more global perspective. He said he could get foreign policy advice elsewhere. Two: I ask Bill Gates and Tim Cook to join. I told him they'd refuse, Bill because he has his hands full with the Gates Foundation and Tim because he was so busy running Apple. The president asked me to invite them anyway. Bill wrote me back a nice note, saying he would be available for crucial meetings or for direct input but he simply doesn't join groups. Tim answered along the same gracious lines.

We had the first of several meetings in February. The president and his senior staff sat in. The noise around his administration was deafening. It was easy to be distracted by the politics and personalities. So I asked each member of the group to bring the problem areas that most affected them and how they might handle them as a CEO. I spoke to all of them beforehand to preview what they wanted to discuss and insisted that we didn't spend time at these meetings arguing over the source or nature of the problems. I wanted to frame the issues for a productive discussion. The members of our forum were serious, direct people who were good at being heard. Between meetings, we followed up based on feedback from the administration and Congress. The president seemed to appreciate the unfiltered flow of information. We were starting to gain traction.

But in August 2017, I saw up close how politics and business, despite our best efforts, can collide. Two groups of protesters, neo-Nazis and Antifa, met and fought in Charlottesville, Virginia, with a tragic outcome. The president blamed both sides. His opponents, and even many of his supporters, erupted, offended by what they perceived as moral equivalence. The president was unable to calm the situation, and as the fury intensified, the members of the Forum came under pressure. Even if we were acting with the best, nonpartisan, and patriotic intentions, associating with this president was intolerable to many.

As an investor, I was used to crises. From investment banking at Lehman Brothers, to setting up Blackstone and seeing it through its many stages of growth and changes, I had learned not only to manage through crises, but also to create them for ourselves and our clients in order to provoke a change in the status quo that creates opportunity. But corporate executives are the opposite. They are conditioned to expect and maintain order. They get uncomfortable easily, particularly when there is negative publicity or pressure from customers. They hated being in the middle of very public dramas, especially one as inflamed as this. If we were going to break up the Forum, though, I wanted us to do so as a group, not as individuals peeling off one by one. Sensing the unease, I arranged a teleconference for the group. There were three options: keep the Forum, suspend it, or disband it.

The majority wanted to disband. I circulated a press release I had drafted in advance. A couple of our members asked if they could think on it and offer suggestions. I refused. The moment this went out to a broader group of advisers, it would leak, I was sure of it. If we wanted to make an announcement, this was how we would do it. I also insisted we inform the president. If we planned to disband, it was basic courtesy to tell him.

Not long after I told the White House staff, though, the president preempted us. Before we could make any announcement, he announced that he was disbanding the Forum. My biggest regret from the episode is that this smart, committed group representing the best of American business could have done so much to help the administration and the country. But sparks in a combustible political atmosphere can lead to widespread collateral damage. We all wanted to befriend the situation, to have a voice at the table in the discussion of how to improve life for all Americans, but our engagement in that capacity was no longer possible.

Despite my disappointment, I felt duty bound to continue to try to be of service to our country. From the moment Donald Trump was elected president, I had been getting calls from people who did not know what to make of him. They had listened to him during the campaign and were nervous about what he might do. Long before he ran for president, he was convinced that American manufacturing had been gutted by free trade. American jobs had gone to wherever labor was cheapest, whether to Mexico or Asia. Trade deficits and economic decline in the Rust Belt were symptoms of this underlying disease. Renegotiate our free trade agreements, he thought, and you could bring back American jobs and "Make America Great Again," as he had promised during his campaign. Whether you agreed with him or not, there was no doubt that his ideas and tactical approaches were going to jolt the economic status quo. But how was he going to do it?

The president chose to operate in a way that was profoundly different from his predecessors. He worked with a tight inner circle rather than through the traditional diplomatic and bureaucratic channels. Even our closest allies were unsure how to communicate with him. The heads of state or senior ministers of more than twenty countries reached out to me to understand the Trump administration.

With the President's support, I became involved in trade talks between the United States and China, and the United States, Canada, and Mexico for a simple reason: I knew the people on all sides and they trusted me. Aside from the president, I have known Steve Mnuchin, the treasury secretary, for years. We have apartments in the same building in New York and are close, personal friends. I have known Wilbur Ross, the commerce secretary, for just as long.

I had forged strong relationships in China through Blackstone and later Schwarzman Scholars. I had met then party secretary Xi Jinping, the current president of China, in 2007, and knew many of the members of the Standing Committee and the State Council. I met the Mexican president, Enrique Peña Nieto, in 2015, and he had endowed two Schwarzman Scholarships for students from Mexico. His finance minister, Luis Videgaray Caso, often called me or came by to talk whenever he was in New York. And on the Canadian side, I had known the foreign minister, Chrystia Freeland, since she was a journalist for the *Financial Times*. She had covered Blackstone, and I had always found her to be smart and well intentioned.

A couple of days after the president's inauguration, at Chrystia's invitation, I went to Calgary to speak at a retreat held by Prime Minister Justin Trudeau for his cabinet. Like the Mexicans, the Canadians were unsettled by the president's rhetoric and nervous about US plans for NAFTA—the North American Free Trade Agreement. I met with the prime minister and his staff privately for an hour, then the prime minister interviewed me for a couple hours, and I took questions from cabinet members regarding the US position. I assured them that based on my understanding, although there would be changes, the president's main priority was faster growth in the United States. The US-Canada relationship remained sound. My assurance became headline news in Canada.

NAFTA is the biggest trade agreement in the world, but it has different implications for the three countries involved. Canada's economy is 10 percent the size of the US economy, but deeply intertwined with the United States economically, politically, and culturally. Mexico is an emerging economy where growth is highly concentrated in areas close to the US border. Canada and the United States have a fairly equal trading relationship, in which the value of imports and exports between our countries is roughly equivalent. But the United States runs a large trade deficit with Mexico, importing many more goods than we export.

Neither the Mexicans nor the Canadians wanted NAFTA to collapse. Both countries treasure their special relationship with the United States. Without it, their economies would fall into recession. But the specifics of each relationship were quite different.

Based on my discussions with the administration, Washington's main issue with Canada centered on its heavily subsidized dairy farmers, who flooded the United States with cheap product to the detriment of dairy farmers in the Midwest. In addition, there were other inequities, such as Canada's "cultural exemption," which prevented US companies from buying Canadian media properties even though Canadians could buy media assets in the United States.

But as I learned, the White House's real issues were with Mexico, which became increasingly obvious during the negotiations. The United States was serious about addressing the large trade deficit between the two countries. One key issue was that many American companies had built factories in Mexico close to the US border in order to take advantage of skilled but much less expensive labor. This was especially relevant for automobile manufacturing, where cars built in Mexico by US companies for the US market are counted as imports from Mexico.

The complexity of international trade throws up endless Dr. Strangelove–like absurdities: car parts that go back and forth between Mexico and the United States multiple times as they are prepared for final assembly; duty-free shoppers who load up on alcohol on one side of the United States–Canada border before returning home to the other side; television signals in Minneapolis that are hijacked and rebroadcast in Ontario. Defining rules for all of this economic activity would be enough to keep scores of lawyers busy for a lifetime. Add in a very determined and unorthodox US president, and it was a perfect recipe for confusion. So with a complex set of issues and priorities for the United States, I tried to do what we do in Blackstone's investment committees: study the problem in detail, then pull back and look for the handful of variables that could determine the key points for any deal. Where would the zone of fairness be?

Luis and Chrystia called and emailed frequently to try their ideas on me before they raised them directly with the administration. However, by summer 2018, our three countries had reached an impasse. The president had fired trade salvos at China and Europe, and even within the White House, there was concern that the administration was taking on too much.

At the president's request, I met with him to offer my advice on the situation. We met in the private quarters of the White House. When the president arrived, I told him that the way I saw it, the United States was now fighting a multifront trade war with Asia, Europe, and the Americas. America's flanks were exposed, and as important as America is, we are only 23 percent of the global economy; give the remaining 77 percent time, and they would figure out a way to band together and make us miserable.

As I considered how to advance the president's agenda, I advised that the United States should begin closing some deals, starting with NAFTA, the biggest deal of all, right on our borders. Whatever may have been said or done over the past few months, our neighbors would always be our neighbors. Agreeing to a deal would show the rest of the world that the United States was serious about renegotiating trade deals, not just blowing them up. With the midterm elections approaching, it would also be useful to have a deal as proof of the president's campaign promises to voters, particularly in possible swing states in the Midwest.

The negotiations began moving again when the government

decided it had to treat the Mexicans and Canadians differently on certain key issues. A single set of terms could not be applied to such different economic relationships. This led to a preliminary deal with Mexico in August 2018, covering auto manufacturing. It raised the percentage of parts in a car that had to be made in North America and required higher labor standards for workers. It also put a sixteen-year limit on the deal, with reviews every six years. That left the Canadians, who tried to put pressure on the White House by building alliances all over Washington, from Congress to the Departments of Defense and State.

As the countries closed in on a deal, I helped the administration frame the concerns and objections of the various parties. Under NAFTA, if one country felt another was flooding goods into its market, it could appeal to an impartial panel. The process was known as Chapter 19. The Canadians refused to let it go. I asked a member of the Canadian negotiating team why they were taking such a hard stance. It wasn't just business, I learned. It was political. Canada is a major exporter of softwood lumber, the wood commonly used in construction and furniture making. The United States had accused Canada of dumping softwood into the United States at the expense of US producers. But the Chapter 19 panel had ruled repeatedly in favor of Canada. That alone, though, was not the issue. Much of Canada's softwood lumber comes from British Columbia. If the current government caved on Chapter 19, they would lose British Columbia in the next elections, and if they lost British Columbia, the Liberal Party would lose power. To give ground on Chapter 19 would be political suicide for Prime Minister Trudeau. When the Canadians informed the administration of that reality, the US view on what it would take to reach an agreement changed.

The final week of September, when the world's leaders came to New York for the United Nations General Assembly, the prime minister asked me to organize a meeting with US business leaders. Trade talks had once again stalled. The prime minister said Canada could not offer any more concessions and wanted to close out the talks. But the president refused a private meeting with the prime minister at the General Assembly. The White House had gone quiet. Prime Minister Trudeau thought a meeting with US CEOs might foster a better understanding of US business priorities and provide him with new ideas on how to progress negotiations. We held the meeting in my conference room at Blackstone.

Afterward, I spoke to the prime minister in private. I knew the US priorities and positions on all the issues based on my frequent conversations with senior officials in the administration. I gave him my view on what it would take to successfully negotiate a deal and told him that the Americans wanted the Canadians to put their terms on paper. The prime minister said he was worried the Americans would leak them and use them against him. I told him that I did deals for a living and the moment had come for him to stop agonizing. If he refused to meet the US demands of a deal, Canada would almost certainly go into a recession, and no politician wins reelection in a recession. If he did a deal, at least he'd have a chance at political survival. Write down the outline, I urged. Empty your pockets on dairy. Make any last concessions you can and draw the line at Chapter 19 and the cultural exemption, the laws protecting Canadian media from foreign ownership, if you have to. Move the lingering secondary issues to the bottom of the page and state simply what you are or are not prepared to do about them. Send the document to the administration and walk away.

I told him I was seeing the president that evening at 5:30 and that any deal needed to be signed by midnight on Sunday, which all parties understood.

The prime minister looked at me from the couch. He said it would be tough, but he would do it. When I met with the president that evening, he reaffirmed that in my discussions with the Canadians, I had accurately reflected terms that the United States would accept. I called the Canadians to let them know. It took another forty-eight hours of waiting and pleading from all sides before finally, at 10:00 a.m. on Friday, the Americans received the Canadians' written offer. Over the weekend, the details were worked out between the two countries, and on Monday, October 1, 2018, the president announced a revised NAFTA, the United States–Mexico–Canada Agreement, or USMCA.

China was an equally tough situation. The United States's basic tariff arrangements with China were drafted decades ago, when China needed to protect its nascent free-market economy and America was the undisputed global economic superpower. But the world had changed, and the president and his advisers believed China was now rich enough not to need protectionist trade policies. It no longer seemed right that US exports to China were charged three times more in tariffs and taxes than Chinese imports into the United States. China had also made clear its ambition to overtake the United States as the world's leader in technology. If this were to be a fair fight, the administration believed that now was the time for the United States to call out China for intellectual property theft, a source of contention for many years. Moreover, there was broad concern in the business community that China's approach to US intellectual property laws was unacceptable.

In January 2017, I met President Xi Jinping at Davos, at a luncheon arranged by Klaus Schwab, the founder of the World

Economic Forum. There were thirty-four of us there besides Schwab—seventeen from the Chinese government and seventeen prominent non-Chinese. At lunch, President Xi asked me to talk about newly elected President Trump and his views on China and how he had defeated Hillary Clinton. I explained to him the facts President Trump was dealing with, the economic dislocations suffered by many working and middle-class Americans because of globalization. A study by the Federal Reserve had found that nearly half the country was living paycheck to paycheck, unable to write an emergency check for $400. For the first time in American history, millions of people feared they would end up poorer than their parents. Among them were many of the president's voters in the Midwest. The trade deficit made China an easy target, and the strong criticism of China was only likely to get worse.

President Xi told me that if that were the case, he would be prepared to do a major economic reset with the United States. Given he knew that I spoke with the president on a wide variety of issues, including trade, he asked me to tell President Trump that we had spoken and to pass along what he had said. In front of the entire group, he also welcomed my participation on behalf of the administration in these talks, a sign of the trust I enjoyed with the Chinese. I found myself in a practical test of the mission of Schwarzman Scholars, with an opportunity to help the United States avoid the Thucydides Trap as the dynamics of global power shifted East.

I called President Trump and told him about my conversation with President Xi. He asked me to invite Xi to Mar-a-Lago in Palm Beach, Florida. Jared Kushner, the president's senior adviser, and China's ambassador to Washington, Cui Tiankai, set it up. That meeting at Mar-a-Lago in April 2017 opened a period of intense dialogue between our two countries.

In July 2017, I co-chaired with Jack Ma of Alibaba a meeting at the Commerce Department in Washington, DC, for US and Chinese CEOs. Afterward I went to see Vice Premier Wang Yang, the leader of China's delegation, to talk about the practical implications of discussions between our two countries. At the request of Wilbur Ross, the commerce secretary, I asked if China would consider cutting its steel capacity by 15 to 20 percent. To my astonishment, Vice Premier Wang said yes. Wilbur was delighted. But President Trump wanted nothing of the deal. China had far too much steel capacity as it was. They would have closed their excess plants anyway. It wasn't a big enough concession to warrant his support.

In the meantime, the White House was ratcheting up its rhetoric, threatening higher tariffs and investigations into Chinese trade practices. China's concerns about a trade war began to grow. Given that the president trusted me, he asked that I continue to be involved by being candid with the Chinese as to the US position.

I made eight trips to China in 2018 alone on behalf of the administration, trying to assure China's most senior officials that the president was not looking for a trade war. The United States did not want to constrain China's growth, but rather wanted to update the trading relationship to make it fairer and more reflective of our two countries' current economic positions. After each trip, I made sure to brief the relevant parties in the US government on my conversations, hopeful that my efforts would help the United States achieve the deal it sought.

But what America viewed as a request for China to modernize its economy and bring it in line with the standards required by international law, China viewed as a demand to become more like America. And China didn't want to be more like America. The Chinese are highly practical and willing to change. They understood how irritated America gets when China violates its trading agreements. But they didn't want to be told that they had to give up everything that works in China, everything that had enabled their country to grow so rapidly for so long. What they wanted to hear was what exactly the United States wanted them to concede, and in what sequence. They were trying to understand the zone of fairness for any potential trade deal.

In April 2018, I was one of a few non-Chinese CEOs to attend the Boao Forum for Asia in Hainan, where President Xi announced he was ready to make major changes to China's economy. He wanted to broaden market access to the auto and financial industries, attract more foreign investment, strengthen protection for intellectual property, and move China faster from an export-driven economy to one with higher domestic demand for imports. I couldn't believe that he was saying what America had wanted him to say. Afterward, at his request, I spoke to Vice Premier Liu He, President Xi's top economic adviser. He wanted to know what else China should be putting on the table. He was open to fresh and positive talks with America.

Following my return, I shared with the administration my thoughts on what the Chinese would need to do to meet US needs for a trade agreement, as well as the US proposals I thought the Chinese might accept. It was nothing official, just the views of a concerned individual who understood the issues on both sides. But later that month, another issue arose when the United States revoked export licenses for ZTE, China's second largest telecommunications equipment manufacturer. The Department of Commerce had already punished ZTE for doing business with Iran and North Korea, and US intelligence had said it was concerned ZTE phones were installed with hardware to spy on US citizens. Without the right to export American components for their phones, though, ZTE could not survive. Within a month, it ceased operations. It took another month and pleading from the Chinese, who were desperate to save the huge employer of Chinese citizens, for the United States to restore ZTE's export licenses.

In June, Vice Premier Liu He came to Washington for trade talks that ultimately collapsed. For the next two months, the Chinese went off the air, exhausted and confused. By the end of the summer, views on China in the United States had become increasingly hostile. The Chinese could not understand why the business leaders they thought were friends were now turning on them. I knew I would be in Beijing in early September for convocation of the third class of Schwarzman Scholars and thought I might also use that trip to have a few government meetings and try to gain a better understanding of what the Chinese were thinking.

In August, before my trip, I was visited by a few Chinese officials in New York. They asked me for my views on what the United States needed on everything from technology, to trade, to cybersecurity, to selected military issues. I explained the US position and predicted that the differences between the United States and China would only get worse. They recorded our conversation and went back to China.

On the morning of September 6, I met Xi's vice president, Wang Qishan, in Beijing in a large, formal meeting room, Ziguang Ge, "The Hall of Purple Light," located in the leadership compound, Zhongnanhai. He was dressed casually, and we were alone—except for the ten people in the back taking notes. He told me he had read the reports of my conversation with his representatives in New York.

"You scared them to death," he said, referring to the Chinese officials who had visited my office a few weeks prior. Vice President Wang mainly wanted to understand why US perceptions of China had changed so drastically. So for the next two hours I gave him my views, and we ended up discussing a broad range of topics.

Later that afternoon, I met with Vice Premier Liu He. We spoke in detail about the challenges facing our two countries and focused our conversation on finding a way to restart formal trade talks. The vice premier had several specific issues he wanted relayed to President Trump. Our discussion led me to believe there might be another opening, and when I relayed this to the president, he asked me to set up a meeting with Liu He in Washington.

Everything was set. Liu He would visit Washington in late September. But three days before the scheduled talks, President Trump announced new tariffs on $200 billion worth of Chinese goods. The Chinese pulled out. It was another huge blow. The Chinese lost face and told me they didn't know what to do or whom to trust anymore.

I ran into Vice President Wang again at a dinner for the Tsinghua School of Economics and Management board in mid-October. We didn't have a scheduled one-on-one meeting, but he happened to be the honored guest at the SEM board dinner with Chinese state leaders. We managed to speak for about twenty minutes. I told him I felt there might be an opportunity for Presidents Trump and Xi to meet at the G20 meetings in Buenos Aires at the end of November to get trade talks back on track. The two leaders had a genuine rapport, and this was a chance for them to meet without the formality of a bilateral summit. I told Vice President Wang that within the US administration, there were divergent views on China. He should not assume the Americans would come to a meeting with President Xi prepared with a list of demands. I thought that President Xi should come with his own list, offer five or six substantive proposals, and control the meeting. If our president felt the proposals were compelling and significant enough, he would engage. It was as simple as that.

This wasn't the Chinese way, Vice President Wang said, but he liked the idea. Both sides would have a chance to achieve their objectives. This was the way to a deal.

I've learned that when dealing with the Chinese they need time to consider and socialize an idea. The Chinese now had five weeks to act on what I suggested. President Xi did come to Buenos Aires with a short list of well-received proposals and smartly gave the president a major domestic win by promising to crack down on the export of fentanyl, one of the drugs at the root of America's opioid crisis. The Buenos Aires meeting succeeded in deescalating the tension between the United States and China and led to the restart of direct talks.

Negotiations recommenced quickly after the meeting in Argentina, resulting in a series of visits, calls, and videoconferences between Vice Premier Liu He, US Trade Representative Robert Lighthizer, and US Treasury Secretary Steven Mnuchin. Expectations built on both sides that these discussions would lead to a successful conclusion. However, in May 2019, the Chinese changed their preliminary views on a number of important points and negotiations were suspended. Both the US and China began taking an increasingly nationalistic stance toward each other and tensions flared once again, as did the potential for a serious and enduring trade war.

Fortunately, President Trump and President Xi met again at G20 in late June 2019, this time in Osaka, Japan. There they were able to re-establish talks, which will hopefully result in a trade agreement in the future.

These trade discussions were some of the most complicated negotiations I have ever experienced. Only time will tell how they resolve themselves.

SPIN THE
VIRTUOUS CYCLE

When Pete and I founded Blackstone, we believed that alternative asset managers would become essential to the investment strategies of institutional investors. But we also built an advisory business as a complement to our investment activities, so we could withstand the ups and downs of the market cycle. We designed our culture and organization for the long term. We wanted Blackstone to be an enduring financial institution. The better our performance, the more money our investors gave us to manage. And the more we had to manage, the more we could innovate. We could do bigger deals, add new lines of business, and attract the right talent to manage them.

Our growth had several significant consequences. The first was that we got to see deals that no one else did, because only we could execute at a certain scale. In 2015, GE decided to wind down GE Capital, its finance business, which had been a major source of profits for many years but had run into trouble during the financial crisis. The company was eager to get out of finance and back to its core industrial businesses. But first it needed to signal to the market that it was serious about selling a business that had been so integral to its success for so long. It decided that the way to do that was to first sell its real estate portfolio, a sprawling collection of 26 properties in the United States; 229

properties in 14 other countries, mostly in France, the United Kingdom, and Spain; as well as most of its mortgage business. It wanted to complete the transaction quickly and cleanly and move on to the much more substantial work of finding bidders for the rest of GE Capital. They made one phone call.

Analyzing a real estate portfolio as complex as GE's in such a short time frame was brutal, but ultimately we gave GE what its leaders wanted: a single transaction, worth $23 billion, to clear the books. In return, we got a great portfolio at a better price than if we had had to buy all the assets piecemeal in competition with others. Seeing deals like this was one of the unanticipated advantages of emerging so strong from the crisis.

In the equity markets, being big can hurt your performance. If you want to buy $1 million of an S&P 500 stock, you can do so without moving the price. If you want to buy $1 billion worth, the market will push up the price before you can complete your purchase. In our world, we found the opposite happening: as our funds grew and our rivals struggled, our size became a major source of advantage. We found buyers and sellers eager to work with us, and us alone. We moved away from participating in many competitive auctions with other private equity firms into situations where we could focus more specifically on the value to both sides and less on rival bidders.

Thomson Reuters was formed in 2007 when Thomson, a Canadian media conglomerate, acquired the Reuters news service. Its financial and risk division sold news, data, analytical tools, and services to help banks and other corporations trade financial products. But it struggled to compete with its rival, Bloomberg. We first looked at the possibility of buying the financial and risk business in 2013. At that time, it was intriguing but not quite right for us. It reappeared on Blackstone's radar in 2016. Martin Brand, a partner in private equity, had traded foreign exchange derivatives early in his career. He had used products from Thomson Reuters, and the possibility of an acquisition fascinated him.

He and his team saw that the markets misunderstood the business, tagging it as a poor man's Bloomberg. In fact, it was more like a colossus hiding in plain sight, a market leader in trading government bonds and foreign exchange and providing financial data to companies, banks, and investors. But there was plenty of room for improvement. Costs were too high, the bureaucracy pervasive, and sales and marketing in need of an overhaul. There was also an opportunity to carve out certain pieces of the business, notably Tradeweb, an electronic platform for trading foreign exchange and derivatives, that we thought might be worth more on a stand-alone basis.

We knew that the managers of the financial and risk division shared our belief that they could operate more successfully as a private company. But Reuters had been a major acquisition for Thomson in 2007. Though it hadn't gone as well as they hoped, the company and its board were not desperate to sell. The price had to be right and the terms compelling.

It took six months for both sides to complete the diligence process and draw up the outline of a $20 billion deal. We kept the deal exclusive and avoided a public auction process.

Our reputation and size gave us substantial credibility with the Thomson Reuters board. We decided to offer 85 percent of the present value of the financial and risk business in return for a 55 percent stake. Thomson Reuters would get cash for almost the entire business yet keep nearly half of it to share in its future growth. We and our co-investors, the Canada Pension Plan Investment Board and GIC, Singapore's sovereign wealth fund, would become the new majority shareholders, with Blackstone maintaining operational control. This arrangement would be a strategic partnership, not an outright sale, thereby avoiding the need for a shareholder vote.

The Thomson Reuters board liked it. But they gave us one piece of homework: to square the deal with Reuters News, the news-gathering and journalistic heart of the Reuters business. In 1941, during World War II, Reuters had drafted a set of "Trust Principles" to ensure that its journalism remained independent and immune to propaganda. The first of the five principles states that "Reuters shall at no time fall into the hands of any one interest, group, or faction." In 1984, when Reuters became a publicly listed company, a special board of directors was created, made up of judges, diplomats, politicians, journalists, and businesspeople, to protect and enforce the Trust Principles. The merged Thomson Reuters had retained this board. But while the principles were still relevant to Reuters News, they did not seem suited for the separate financial and risk division, which we were acquiring.

We came up with an arrangement where the financial and risk division would pay more than $300 million a year to Reuters News for the next thirty years to carry its services on its terminals. News would have the promise of decades of financial stability, a rarity in the modern media business. In return, financial and risk, which we were renaming Refinitiv, would have operational independence.

We finally announced the deal in early 2018. In April 2019, we took Tradeweb public as a stand-alone company on the Nasdaq. Its value shot up to $8 billion by the end of the first day of trading. It unlocked significant value and was also an extraordinary validation of our investment, and we still have the rest of the Refinitiv business to work with and improve.

———

The year 2018 brought another major development for the firm: the succession of Tony James. When Tony joined Blackstone in 2002, he told me that he would retire when he neared seventy. In 2016, he turned sixty-five and was as involved as ever in every aspect of Blackstone, developing new initiatives and always teaching the younger people at the firm. His contribution has been incalculable. But true to his word, he began talking about succession. I would remain chairman and CEO. Tony would stay on as executive vice chairman, as present as ever. But we would need a new president and chief operating officer to run the day-to-day business of Blackstone.

Asset management firms are so dependent on people and personalities that succession often becomes their Achilles' heel. One generation stays on too long, the next generation gets tired of waiting, and firms lose momentum. Regaining that momentum is always much harder than sustaining it. So if leaders don't want their organization to tire, they have to start working on succession when their drive, their intellect, and their competitiveness are yet to peak.

Starting in 2013, Tony had begun to involve Jon Gray in the management discussions involving the entire firm. Jon had grown up in Chicago, where his father ran a small auto parts maker and his mother a catering company. He went to public school and was an enthusiastic basketball player—so enthusiastic, in fact, that during one season in high school, he sat on the bench while his team went 1–23. It was a lesson in commitment, humility, and having a sense of humor. He had joined us from the University of Pennsylvania in 1992, where he had received one bachelor's degree in English and one in finance from Wharton. During his final year, he received his offer to join Blackstone and also met his future wife, Mindy, in a class on romantic poetry. He has been with both of us ever since.

Jon's character and values, forged out of his middle-class, midwestern upbringing, were obvious to us early in his career. Once, when he was still a junior analyst, he had waded into a fierce argument between senior partners over the fees we had to pay our lawyers and brokers on a particular deal. He asked, "Why are we trying to beat these guys up? We work with them all the time, and chances are we're going to work with them a lot more in years to come. Why not treat them well?" That Wall Street had always worked this way in the past didn't mean it had to continue. Jon was thinking long term, about his own relationships and the reputation of the firm.

He loved the personalities in real estate and that we were buying buildings we could see and touch. He had a great mentor in John Schreiber. When Jon took over the real estate business in 2005, it had $5 billion under management. Over the next few years, he increased it through a series of deals that transformed the entire industry: EOP in 2007, followed by Hilton, then Invitation Homes. In 2015, his team acquired Stuyvesant Town in New York, an eighty-five-acre parcel of residential housing, in a deal that required complex negotiations with bondholders, tenants, and New York City. It was an important deal for the city and state. By voluntarily including terms that allowed affordable housing to remain for half of the ten thousand units for the long term, we supported the city's efforts to preserve affordable housing.

Once Jon feels confident in a thesis, he articulates it clearly, sets an objective, and sprints ahead. He decided, for example, that online shopping would spark a boom in demand for warehouses, and over several years he made Blackstone the second biggest owner of warehouses in the world. By 2018, Jon's real estate team had returned $83 billion to investors, and managed $136 billion investor capital plus over $250 billion worth of buildings and real estate businesses. It is now the largest business at Blackstone. Jon's extraordinary record as an investor, with virtually no losses, is the foundation for his rise at Blackstone. But it's only part of the reason we chose him to lead the firm.

Jon has been on the Blackstone management committee for a long time, so I have watched him think through many complex issues at the firm. Jon is always emotionally balanced, eager to learn new facts, and confident in his own judgment. During the recession, he came to me with a proposal to put more equity into Hilton. Given the length and depth of the downturn, he felt it would be prudent to put in an extra $800 million. He was nicely insistent about it. He was being protective about the deal and the firm, thinking long term. I looked at the numbers and felt we had put in enough. The travel market would soon recover, and we had enough cash to service our debt. Investing more equity would lower our rate of return, and I did not feel it was necessary. Although we disagreed, we did what he proposed. I respected him for balancing the various interests. That's exactly how you want someone to be thinking in a seat of power.

Watching him work through crises, I noticed that the harder the problem, the calmer he seemed to be. He would buck the consensus and invest when others were scared. If there was a hard conversation to be had, he would have it. Under pressure, he always asked for the ball. Every day, he walked the mile to work from his apartment and kept his team cheerful and motivated through even the toughest dips in the market. His integrity and unassuming charm made him well liked on all sides of a highly charged and competitive industry.

Once we had decided he would succeed Tony, we began involving him in the most sensitive areas of the firm, from strategic issues relating to our different business lines to compensation and other personnel matters. Sitting beside Tony, he saw how much everyone at the firm was paid and why. Under Tony's guidance, he learned what it would take to manage the firm, applying our talent and intellectual capital to future opportunities.

By February 2018, when we announced the change in the leadership of Blackstone, Jon had been sharing the steering wheel with Tony for over a year. Tony had taken it upon himself to clean up any lingering management issues, so that Jon could start with a clean slate. We had seeded the idea that Jon's succession was the most natural thing in the world. With a lot of nudging and attention to personal feelings, no one got ruffled. The succession felt organic and inevitable, a rarity in our industry.

When a new leader is appointed at any organization, a lot of those below then move into new positions. And Jon wasn't the only leader from that generation of young analysts who had grown into the firm's heirs and culture carriers. When we needed a new head of our private equity business several years earlier, we asked our partners who it should be. Most suggested themselves, but the second choice on nearly every list was the same: Joe Baratta.

Joe had joined Blackstone in 1997 but brought himself most vividly to my attention in 2004. He asked to see me when I was visiting London, and I could tell that he wanted to be made a partner. I went to his office, which was so small a visitor could barely push his chair back before hitting the wall. He was thirty-four years old, too young in my mind for promotion, but I let him talk anyway. He described the deals he had done and compared his body of work to those of his peers. "I love the firm," he told me, and "you know, I've helped build a business from nowhere."

I had gone to see Joe as a courtesy with no intention of promoting him, as it was sure to provoke controversy among his older colleagues. But as he spoke, objectively and clearly but with obvious passion, I started to change my mind. He was selling me on his own promotion.

Listening to him reminded me of my own struggles at Lehman, where my own promotion to partner was held back a year when it should have been accelerated. I remembered how it felt to be denied, and how at that point in my career, the title of partner seemed so important. When we founded Blackstone, I had promised that we would be different. We would let talent flourish.

Joe persuaded me, and his deals have been at the heart of every one of our private equity funds since. Joe grew up in California watching his father build and manage a small chain of gyms, so he empathizes instinctively with the operators at the companies we acquire. But he also inspires the trust of our professional investors and the respect of our most hardened competitors. He is a natural teacher and mentor, the person everyone, from senior partners to analysts, turns to for help.

In 2019, fifteen years after that conversation in his cramped office, Joe raised the largest private equity fund in the world, Blackstone Capital Partners VIII, with $26 billion in committed capital, a record for our industry. It was more than thirty times the size of our first private equity fund, the fund Pete and I pounded the pavement relentlessly to raise in 1987. And I didn't need to make a single presentation to investors. Joe and our fantastic team did it all. It was a proud moment for me.

With Jon moving up, we appointed two people to run global real estate: Ken Caplan to oversee investing and Kathleen McCarthy to manage fundraising and operations of our biggest business. Ken had been with us since 1997 and worked alongside Jon on many of our largest real estate deals. Kathleen had joined us from Goldman Sachs in 2010 and proved herself as a manager, colleague, and someone ready to take on the toughest challenges.

Whenever we promote people to senior roles at Blackstone, I congratulate them in person and we talk about their new responsibilities. My conversation with Kathleen was typical of those I have with many people across the firm. She began by asking me about how we maintain the spirit of entrepreneurship at Blackstone. The trick, I told her, was finding fantastic people and giving them the chance to be the best at what they do. We keep our edge by reinventing everything we do to make it better. We also talked about the emotions that surround succession. When people are promoted, there are a lot of feelings to consider. Those promoted might feel a sense of pride in their own success but also anxiety about their new responsibilities. Others will have thought they would get promoted and didn't. Some will feel excited about having a new boss; others will feel unmoored and frightened of change. The effects of those feelings will show up in unusual ways and at strange times, and being aware of them, understanding and managing them, is essential to the success of any leader. This was one of those management lessons you learn only from experience.

I also remind those promoted to senior roles of the message I give to our analysts every year on their first day of work at Blackstone. You are not alone here, so don't wear the weight of the world. Every tough decision has been made at Blackstone by someone. What may seem new to you, won't be new to the institution. Just ask for help. We make decisions as a team, and we own the outcome as a team. That applies just as much to the people running our biggest businesses as it does to our most junior staff.

Finally, I reminded Kathleen that she had been promoted because she was terrific at what she did. We all knew she had the talent to be successful, to grow as a person and as a professional. And she had my complete confidence. It is so important that people understand how much you appreciate them and that you make them feel good about themselves. That self-confidence is the basis for great performance.

To be a good manager requires being emotionally open and direct about everything, good and bad. When we are thinking about our next class of partners at Blackstone, I interview everyone being considered and we talk about what they have achieved, how we feel about it, and we ask each other questions. Once the decisions are made, I call everyone who has been made partner, and those who haven't. I tell each of them how I feel about them—about their abilities, their potential, and what I think we can build together at Blackstone. That openness creates cohesion in the business. I can't imagine building an organization any other way.

In 2018 we also transitioned the leadership for two of our other businesses: GSO and Blackstone Alternative Asset Management (BAAM). Dwight Scott was appointed head of GSO Capital Partners, and John McCormick head of BAAM to help manage the enormous growth of each of those businesses. Across the board, we now have young executives in charge of major businesses, with impressive track records and decades of great work ahead of them.

――――――

Over time, we have also taken care to professionalize the firm and ensure that our exceptional growth never runs afoul of regulations or harms our reputation. We were very fortunate to bring in John Finley from our longtime law firm, Simpson Thacher & Bartlett, to serve as our general counsel. He is deeply involved in our daily decision making and has one of the most important legal skills of all: great judgment. Michael Chae joined Blackstone early in his career and was one of our top private equity partners, in charge of Asia, before becoming our chief financial officer. His intimate knowledge of the business allows him to ensure we have strong financial planning and controls. We also hired David Calhoun, former CEO of Nielsen Holdings and vice chairman of General Electric, to lead our portfolio operations group and drive value creation in our companies.

Every public company needs to ensure its external facing activities are just as strong as internal ones. For shareholder relations, Tony recruited a former partner from DLJ, Joan Solotar. Joan has also assumed leadership of our private wealth solutions business for retail investors. Finally, Christine Anderson oversees our public relations, branding, marketing, and internal communications functions. She's the primary spokesperson for the firm and ensures that the press and public understand our work, our motivations, and our contributions to society.

The members of our management committee have been at Blackstone for eighteen years on average, and the average tenure of our senior managing directors is ten years. Such longevity is rare in the financial industry. These long-serving leaders haven't just built our business, they have built our culture and they are going to be its most reliable guardians in the future.

A MISSION
TO BE THE BEST

I have no doubt that without Yale, my life would never have turned out the way it did. I have long been in touch with Yale's presidents, past and present, looking for ways to give back to one of the most consequential institutions to my life, and in 2014 I found the right opportunity. I first spoke with Yale president Rick Levin about renovating Commons in 1997. Commons was the cavernous building at the heart of the campus, where I had eaten every day as a freshman. I have clear memories of its damp, cold air, and the sound of hundreds of young men eating, the clatter of their plates and cutlery echoing in the giant space.

In 2014, Levin's successor, Peter Salovey, conveyed the urgent need for a stronger center to campus life. Student life had atomized, and there were increasing instances of heavy drinking and accompanying bad decisions in the fraternities. Three student government organizations had written to Peter begging for a "campus-wide center that bridges the boundaries between undergraduate, graduate and professional school students" and that "encourages vibrant, significant and inclusive social interaction at Yale."

I've always felt that Commons could be much more than a dining room. It was located at the very heart of Yale. What if we could make it a place that was open close to twenty-four hours a day, with meeting rooms and spaces for students to do everything: study, socialize, rehearse, and meet? Even better, what if we could modernize the facilities and add a performing arts component with entertainment venues to provide students with an alternative to fraternity and other off-campus socialization? I would have loved a place like that when I was an undergraduate.

In the renovation of Commons, I saw a real opportunity to transform Yale's campus and create an entirely new model for a hybrid student union and cultural/performing arts center. When it opens in 2020, the Schwarzman Center at Yale University will completely change the standard for student life and cultural activity at Yale. With five state-of-the-art performance venues, the facility will enable Yale students to be exposed to a range of cultural activities that has never been possible before, enriching their experience in ways that can spark new dialogue, new ways of thinking, and creative possibilities.

My work with Yale helped convince me that even the oldest institutions can benefit from a fresh pair of eyes that reimagine what education could or should look like as times change.

I had the good fortune of meeting Rafael Reif, the seventeenth president of MIT, in 2016 in Davos when I was in the process of establishing Schwarzman Scholars.

"I don't know much about MIT," I told him. It had been three decades since that early trip to MIT with Pete, when the school's endowment team had stood us up, and I hadn't had a reason to revisit that trip since.

"You're not supposed to. We like to fly under the radar," he said.

"Well, I like to live above the radar."

Despite that difference, we became great friends. Rafael was born in Venezuela, earned his doctorate in electrical engineering at Stanford, and spent most of his career at MIT. He has a wide-ranging intellect and is a natural leader. Over our many ensuing conversations, I was taken by his ability to see where we are going in technological, economic, political, and profoundly human terms. I was also struck by the urgency of his message regarding the breadth of implications that advances in artificial intelligence (AI) and other new computing technologies would have on human development and American competitiveness.

We talked about the rise of China and the role that America's great research universities had always played in driving innovation that was critical to economic prosperity and national security. Since MIT was founded in 1861, its faculty, researchers, and alumni have won ninety-three Nobel Prizes and twenty-five Turing Awards, given for contributions to the field of computing. They have long been global leaders in scientific innovation—everything from air defense and missile guidance systems to sequencing the human genome. The few blocks around MIT, a concentration of public and private labs, start-ups, and corporate research centers, are known as the most innovative square mile in the world.

Yet Rafael told me that while 40 percent of MIT's students took courses in computer science, only 7 percent of MIT's faculty specialized in the subject. The situation was the same, or worse, across the American university landscape. Everyone understood the need for greater investment in computer science, but hardly anyone was doing much about it. The US talent pool in the fields of science, technology, engineering, and math was outstanding but did not have adequate resources to maximize their full potential.

I suggested to Rafael that if we were to make America more competitive, we should start by trying to solve this basic problem of matching supply to demand. His first proposal, to expand computer science at MIT, was practical but seemed insufficient in terms of impact. I asked him to think bigger. About a month later, he came back. MIT would create a new college, its first since 1951, dedicated to the study of artificial intelligence and computing and connected to every other school at the university. The university would double the number of its computer scientists by creating fifty new faculty positions, half in computer science, half joint appointments with the other schools at MIT. This new college would enable every professor, researcher, and student to learn, practice, and speak the language of AI, regardless of whether they were students of engineering, urban studies, political science, or philosophy. They would become, as Rafael put it, the "bilinguals of the future," fluent in both AI and their own academic discipline, scientific or not.

Innovation wasn't the only goal of the college; we also wanted to educate students on the responsible development and application of AI and computing technologies. The college would offer new curricula and research opportunities, as well as convene forums to engage national leaders from business, government, academia, and journalism to examine the anticipated outcomes of advances in AI and machine learning and to shape policies around the ethics of AI. In doing this we created a structure to ensure that these groundbreaking technologies of the future are responsibly implemented in support of the greater good.

Together these changes would make MIT the world's first AI-enabled university. And it would prompt other institutions to take notice and form their own strategies for increasing investment in this area. The more universities that invested in the study and research of this technology, the better off the United States would be in terms of staying at the forefront of technological innovation and know-how, training the workforce of the future, and ensuring that the interests and well-being of the American people were secure.

Rafael proposed a budget of $1.1 billion, a staggering number, but appropriate to our ambitions. I pledged a significant anchor gift—my biggest philanthropic commitment to date and over three times what I gave to found Schwarzman Scholars—and asked MIT to match it. We announced the creation of the MIT Stephen A. Schwarzman College of Computing on October 15, 2018.

It didn't take long for MIT's plans to reverberate around the United States and the rest of the world. The response I received personally was extraordinary and reinforced that our concept was right on track and on time. People everywhere reached out to express their support. Many said that the topic of AI and American competitiveness had been on their mind, but they were unsure of what could or should be done. University presidents wanted to meet with me to discuss their respective AI capabilities and perspectives on related ethical considerations. I even started receiving calls from politicians on both sides of the aisle to discuss what funding a national agenda for AI could look like.

Eric Schmidt, the former CEO and executive chairman of Google, predicted that my gift would be one of the most important of our time, accelerating billions of dollars of additional commitments by others to the field of computer science. Sure enough, there have been several similar university initiatives announced since the creation of MIT's new college. These collective efforts have raised the visibility, momentum, and dialogue on the topic of AI even more, and my sincere hope is that this is just the beginning.

Jung-Shik Kim, the founder and chairman of Daeduck Electronics, a South Korean IT equipment manufacturing company, decided to give $50 million to Seoul National University, his alma mater, to advance AI research. Young Jae Kim, his son, wrote to me: "You may be surprised to note that, even on the other side of the globe, there are people who agree with your vision of new transforming technologies such as artificial intelligence and their impact on humanity and society."

While Rafael and I were concluding our discussions on the new college at MIT, I was also working on a gift to the University of Oxford, the largest single donation to the university since the Renaissance. I never attended Oxford, but had visited as a teenager. To this day, I remember being struck by its history and the contrast of the vivid green lawns against the golden sandstone of centuries-old colleges. Oxford has been at the heart of Western civilization for nearly a thousand years, so when Louise Richardson, vice-chancellor of the university, approached me about a new project to unite all the humanities departments currently spread across Oxford's campus into one common space, I was intrigued. I saw an opportunity to do something similar to what we were doing at Yale and MIT: create an environment that encourages cross-disciplinary research, scholarship, and insight, and position the humanities curriculum for the future.

After numerous conversations with Louise, we broadened the size and the ambition of the new Schwarzman Centre for the Humanities. The Centre would be located in a new building at the heart of the most important site at Oxford in 200 years—the historic Radcliffe Observatory Quarter—with state-of-the-art facilities for academics, exhibitions, and a new performing arts center. The facilities, including new resources for visitors and a broadcasting center, would also serve to open Oxford to local and global communities, expanding the reach of its learning and cultural programs.

Oxford has long been ranked number one in the world in the humanities. But as science and technology have accelerated, introducing the concept of machines which are designed to replicate human intelligence, there are many new moral, philosophical, and ethical questions to consider regarding what it means to be human and what values we want our technology to reflect. This is why we decided as part of this initiative that we had to include an institute dedicated to the study of ethics in artificial intelligence. As an unparalleled resource for western culture, Oxford was perfectly suited to lead in the research, evolution, and application of humanities disciplines and help guide the debate around some of society's most critical future challenges.

When we announced the gift in June 2019, the political environment in the United Kingdom was extremely uncertain, with no Brexit outcome in sight and conservative party leadership elections underway. It was difficult to anticipate how the announcement of the gift would land given the unpredictable news cycle. The day before the announcement, I spent hours doing embargoed interviews with reporter after reporter, explaining my motivation for the gift and underscoring the importance of Oxford using its expertise in the humanities to help governments, the media, and companies and organizations of all types to develop a framework for the responsible introduction of AI. It was exhausting, but the reporters were all very friendly and right away focused on the fact that the UK was unaccustomed to philanthropy at this scale.

Around 11:00 p.m. on the day before the announcement I received an email from my team. *The Financial Times* had just tweeted out their cover for the next day. I clicked on the link only to find a picture of my face set against the Oxford campus and the headline: *£150m gift is Oxford record.* The announcement had made the front page of the newspaper, above the fold.

The next day was a whirlwind. Every major UK media outlet featured the gift as front page news or in a prominent article. I also did TV interviews on several major news networks—the BBC, Bloomberg, CNBC, CNN, and Fox. During the course of the day I learned that my single gift was about half of the

£310 million given by all philanthropic individuals to arts and culture in England during 2017-18. No wonder the news was everywhere. The size of the gift had caught the country's attention and started conversations about the role of philanthropy in the UK as government funding for education and culture declines. Just as with MIT, I received notes from friends and acquaintances across the globe recognizing the importance of the gift. Many notes commented on the long-term impact of the gift and vote of confidence in the future of the UK, while others applauded the public reaffirmation of the humanities at a time when so much investment is devoted to technology and science.

I am encouraged to imagine what might be if the great minds at Oxford work with their counterparts at MIT, Tsinghua, Yale, and universities everywhere, to share knowledge and deliver multidisciplinary insights. In a world that is changing so quickly, it's quite possible this type of cross-institutional, global collaboration is the only way to ensure a safe and prosperous future for us all.

I have long believed that education is the passport to a better life. A good education has the power to affect whomever it touches for the better. We all have a duty to not only preserve the knowledge that is handed to us but also develop it in a way that improves its relevance and impact for future generations. I am hopeful that the contributions I have made, whether to higher education, the Catholic school system, my high school in Philadelphia, or track and field athletes, help generations for years to come aim high and embrace their own pursuits of excellence, whatever they may be.

EPILOGUE

I looked out of the car window as I left the hotel in Boston for MIT's campus. At 5:30 in the morning, it was pitch dark, but I could still see the snow falling against the cloudy winter sky. I smiled to myself and thought, *Well, at least it's not raining*. Rafael Reif and I were scheduled for a live interview with CNBC's "Squawk Box" at around 6:00 a.m. It was my first stop on the final day of MIT's three-day event to launch the new Stephen A. Schwarzman College of Computing. The entire day was being covered by CNBC and would be live-streamed to the world. It had been four months since the announcement of my gift to MIT in October 2018, but it seemed that global interest in what MIT was doing had only grown.

After the interview, I went to Kresge Auditorium where the day's festivities were about to begin. My wife, children, and their spouses had all made the trip to be with me to celebrate the new college. Over thirty famous technologists and public figures were set to be featured in a series of short talks and panels to explore the breadth of ideas that led to the founding of the college and the frontiers it aims to reach.

Massachusetts governor Charlie Baker opened the day by emphasizing the importance of responsible innovation for the good of society, Sir Tim Berners-Lee, the inventor of the World Wide Web, talked about the utopian promise of the early Internet, and the disappointments that followed, and Henry Kissinger, former US secretary of state, warned of the dangers of deploying AI in an uncontrolled manner. Speaker after speaker addressed the diverse, profound, and pervasive changes that are yet to come. Like most of the audience, I was astonished by the intellect and unlimited curiosity on display. I was also amazed at the sense of gratitude that almost every scientist expressed for what the new college was going to do for MIT and the world. There wasn't a minute of the day that the auditorium wasn't buzzing with a palpable energy and hope for what is yet to come. It was extraordinary.

To close that remarkable day at MIT, Rafael and I took the stage with Becky Quick, co-anchor of CNBC's "Squawk Box" and "On the Money," who moderated a discussion about our shared vision of computing for the future. We had a lot of fun, drawing several laughs from the audience as we told the story of how the new college came to be and what it will try to achieve. Our rapport onstage was in some ways the perfect reflection of the mission of the college—a nontechnologist and a scientist working together to deliver a bold solution to try to move the world forward.

As we left the stage to applause, Rafael leaned in: "Wow, I've never seen that before in my almost thirty years at MIT."

"What's that?" I said.

"A standing ovation."

It was certainly a very different ending from my first trip to MIT in 1987.

———

I don't feel a day over thirty-eight, the age I was when I started Blackstone and a year before my first trip to MIT. I sleep the same five hours I always have and am blessed with the same endless energy and unabated drive to engage in new experiences and tackle new challenges that I had when I was younger. I don't want to slow down or retire. Losing my parents has only sharpened my desire to create new things and accomplish more. But I'm very lucky to have two wonderful children, my stepdaughter, and seven beautiful grandchildren whom I love to spend time with.

It has been a long journey from Oxford Circle in Philadelphia, one that no one—including me—ever anticipated. My successes and failures have taught me much about leadership, relationships, and living a life of purpose and impact.

Today, Blackstone is thriving in the hands of its third generation of leaders. Its culture is stronger than ever. The 10s we hired have hired other 10s, and our meritocracy has created one of the most famous and admired financial companies in the world. We have been able to turn $400,000 of start-up capital in 1985 into over $500 billion of assets under management in 2019—a growth rate of about 50 percent a year since we started. The scale of our business today is incredible—we own approximately two hundred companies, employing over 500,000 people, with combined revenues of over $100 billion, over $250 billion in real estate, as well as market-leading activities in leveraged credit, hedge funds, and other business lines. We have earned the trust and confidence of almost every major institutional investor who invests in our asset class, the reward for a powerful global brand, a duty of care, and delivering compelling and consistent investment performance for over thirty years.

But beyond our size, our growth, and even the external accolades, I see a firm that reflects the core values I have worked so hard to instill. Establishing and imparting a strong company culture is perhaps one of the greatest challenges any entrepreneur and founder is tasked with, but it is also one of the most gratifying if you get it right. I take immense pride in the firm we have built, and every day, when I see our culture of lifetime learning, excellence, and relentless innovation in action, I know that the best is yet to come.

My political and philanthropic activities equally fascinate and engage me. My willingness to get involved and create new paradigms has put me at the center of many dynamic and exciting developments, in the United States and internationally. Most recently I had the unusual opportunity to serve my country as we negotiated new trade agreements with Mexico and Canada, and worked for over two and a half years to try and achieve a major trade agreement with China. In both situations, I used my relationships of trust with the parties involved to advance understanding of the US position through countless calls and meetings. This resulted in signed agreements between the US, Mexico, and Canada, as well as a series of intense and unpredictable outcomes related to the US-China negotiations.

It seems that the larger my separate worlds become, the more they overlap. A lifetime of listening to others, forging relationships and constantly asking how I can help has compounded to the point where many of the biggest challenges and best ideas now find me. In politics and philanthropy, it has been my privilege to conceive and help bring to life many remarkable projects and create institutions that will influence generations for years to come.

———

Every summer now, I travel to Beijing to address the graduating class of Schwarzman Scholars. As I prepare my remarks, I try to recall what I would have liked to have known if I were one of the scholars sitting in the audience.

"Regardless of how you begin your careers, it is important to realize that your life will not necessarily move in a straight line. You have to recognize that the world is an unpredictable place. Sometimes even gifted people such as yourselves will get knocked back on their heels. It is inevitable that you will confront many difficulties and hardships during your lives. When you face setbacks, you have to dig down and move yourself forward. The resilience you exhibit in the face of adversity—rather than the adversity itself—will be what defines you as a person."

Failures, I want them to know, can teach us more than any success.

"Devote your time and energy to the things you enjoy. Excellence follows enthusiasm, and doing anything solely for prestige rarely leads to success. If you have passion for pursuing your dreams; if you persevere; and if you are committed to helping others, you will have a full and consequential life and always have a chance at greatness. And the benefit of your enormous gifts will accrue to yourself, the people you love, and to society at large."

Speaking at the Schwarzman Scholars graduation has become one of my favorite things to do every year. I love looking into the audience and seeing the eager faces of an extraordinary group of future leaders, their brilliant purple Schwarzman Scholars ties and scarves, and eyes radiating with promise. The room can barely contain their boundless ambition and the ear-to-ear smiles of their parents, beaming with hope and pride. I feel a deep sense of joy and satisfaction that is difficult to describe.

As I present a diploma and shake the hand of every graduate who crosses the stage, I can't help but ask myself a simple question: *What's next?*

Who knows?

25 RULES FOR
WORK AND LIFE

1. It's as easy to do something big as it is to do something small, so reach for a fantasy worthy of your pursuit, with rewards commensurate to your effort.
2. The best executives are made, not born. They never stop learning. Study the people and organizations in your life that have had enormous success. They offer a free course from the real world to help you improve.
3. Write or call the people you admire, and ask for advice or a meeting. You never know who will be willing to meet with you. You may end up learning something important or form a connection you can leverage for the rest of your life. Meeting people early in life creates an unusual bond.
4. There is nothing more interesting to people than their own problems. Think about what others are dealing with, and try to come up with ideas to help them. Almost anyone, however senior or important, is receptive to new ideas provided they are thoughtful.
5. Every business is a closed, integrated system with a set of distinct but interrelated parts. Great managers understand how each part works on its own and in relation to all the others.
6. Information is the most important asset in business. The more you know, the more perspectives you have, and the more

likely you are to spot patterns and anomalies before your competition. So always be open to new inputs, whether they are people, experiences, or knowledge.

7. When you're young, only take a job that provides you with a steep learning curve and strong training. First jobs are foundational. Don't take a job just because it seems prestigious.

8. When presenting yourself, remember that impressions matter. The whole picture has to be right. Others will be watching for all sorts of clues and cues that tell who you are. Be on time. Be authentic. Be prepared.

9. No one person, however smart, can solve every problem. But an army of smart people talking openly with one another will.

10. People in a tough spot often focus on their own problems, when the answer usually lies in fixing someone else's.

11. Believe in something greater than yourself and your personal needs. It can be your company, your country, or a duty for service. Any challenge you tackle that is inspired by your beliefs and core values will be worth it, regardless of whether you succeed or fail.

12. Never deviate from your sense of right and wrong. Your integrity must be unquestionable. It is easy to do what's right when you don't have to write a check or suffer any consequences. It's harder when you have to give something up. Always do what you say you will, and never mislead anyone for your own advantage.

13. Be bold. Successful entrepreneurs, managers, and individuals have the confidence and courage to act when the moment seems right. They accept risk when others are cautious and take action when everyone else is frozen, but they do so smartly. This trait is the mark of a leader.

14. Never get complacent. Nothing is forever. Whether it is an individual or a business, your competition will defeat you if

you are not constantly seeking ways to reinvent and improve yourself. Organizations, especially, are more fragile than you think.

15. Sales rarely get made on the first pitch. Just because you believe in something doesn't mean everyone else will. You need to be able to sell your vision with conviction over and over again. Most people don't like change, so you need to be able to convince them why they should accept it. Don't be afraid to ask for what you want.

16. If you see a huge, transformative opportunity, don't worry that no one else is pursuing it. You might be seeing something others don't. The harder the problem is, the more limited the competition, and the greater the reward for whomever can solve it.

17. Success comes down to rare moments of opportunity. Be open, alert, and ready to seize them. Gather the right people and resources; then commit. If you're not prepared to apply that kind of effort, either the opportunity isn't as compelling as you think or you are not the right person to pursue it.

18. Time wounds all deals, sometimes even fatally. Often the longer you wait, the more surprises await you. In tough negotiations especially, keep everyone at the table long enough to reach an agreement.

19. Don't lose money!!! Objectively assess the risks of every opportunity.

20. Make decisions when you are ready, not under pressure. Others will always push you to make a decision for their own purposes, internal politics, or some other external need. But you can almost always say, "I need a little more time to think about this. I'll get back to you." This tactic is very effective at defusing even the most difficult and uncomfortable situations.

21. Worrying is an active, liberating activity. If channeled appropriately, it allows you to articulate the downside in any situation and drives you to take action to avoid it.

22. Failure is the best teacher in an organization. Talk about failures openly and objectively. Analyze what went wrong. You will learn new rules for decision making and organizational behavior. If evaluated well, failures have the potential to change the course of any organization and make it more successful in the future.

23. Hire 10s whenever you can. They are proactive about sensing problems, designing solutions, and taking a business in new directions. They also attract and hire other 10s. You can always build something around a 10.

24. Be there for the people you know to be good, even when everyone else is walking away. Anyone can end up in a tough situation. A random act of kindness in someone's time of need can change the course of a life and create an unexpected friendship or loyalty.

25. Everyone has dreams. Do what you can to help others achieve theirs.

ACKNOWLEDGMENTS

This book has been in the making for over a decade since Hank Paulson suggested I write one.

I'd like to thank Matt Malone for traveling with me periodically from 2009 through 2016, taking notes and creating transcripts based on answers to questions about my background, my career at Lehman, and the founding and development of Blackstone.

In 2017, I interviewed a variety of book agents and selected Jenn Joel from ICM Partners. She was a terrific choice. Jenn advised me on interviewing publishers. We selected Simon & Schuster, which has proven to be an excellent decision. Ben Loehnen was assigned as my editor and has done a brilliant job. He has great judgment and formidable editing skills. Also, Christine Anderson, the head of public affairs at Blackstone, was instrumental in all of these interviews and helping to refine the concept for the book. She has read every draft and led the marketing plan as well. She has been involved for many years as the project has evolved.

As a group, we interviewed a few different writers to bring this book to life. Ultimately we selected Philip Delves Broughton who has written a brilliant book on Harvard Business School, my alma mater. Philip has followed me around the world and spent substantial time with me at home and in the office. He managed to take the transcripts, personal interviews, and public material and weave it into a highly readable and integrated first draft. We worked together over a period of two years to craft the book. His contribution was essential in enabling me to do my own line-by-line edits and transform his draft into a book in my own voice. I owe him an enormous debt of gratitude.

My chief of staff, Shilpa Nayyar, performed an absolutely vital role. She collaborated with Philip and me, drafting certain sections and coordinating all of the comments made on various drafts of the book by our readers. Shilpa did an incredible job both as a writer herself and project manager who brought the book to completion.

I'd like to thank my friends and colleagues who read the manuscript and provided detailed comments which resulted in many changes to the book. These readers include: Jon Gray, Tony James, John Finley, Paige Ross, Amy Stursberg, Wayne Berman, Nate Rosen, John Bernbach, Dr. Byram Karasu, my oldest friend, Jeffrey Rosen, my children Zibby Owens and Teddy Schwarzman, my wife, Christine, and our team of Jenn, Ben, Christine, and Shilpa. Their contributions helped improve the final manuscript in numerous important ways.

I'd also like to thank Amy Stursberg for her tireless work as the head of the Blackstone Foundation and executive director of both the Stephen A. Schwarzman Education Foundation and the Stephen A. Schwarzman Foundation. Amy and I work together on a daily basis. I never could have executed the charitable initiatives described in the book without her judgment and project management. She is an extraordinary person who has helped bring my numerous philanthropic ideas to life.

I want to acknowledge the unique contributions of Wayne Berman, head of government relations at Blackstone, with whom I talk daily, including weekends, given the innumerable issues Blackstone must engage in at the federal, state, and city levels in our country and around the world. Wayne has become a great friend as well as a trusted and valuable advisor.

I want to acknowledge the heads of our major business units at Blackstone, including: Joe Baratta, head of private equity; Ken Caplan and Kathleen McCarthy, co-heads of real estate—Blackstone's largest business; David Blitzer, head of tactical opportunities; Sean Klimczak, head of Blackstone Infrastructure Partners; John McCormick, head of Blackstone Alternative Asset Management (BAAM); Dwight Scott, head of GSO, our credit business; Vern Perry, head of strategic partners, our secondary investments business; Nick Galakatos, head of Blackstone Life Sciences; Jon Korngold, head of Blackstone Growth Equity; Michael Chae, chief financial officer; John Finley, general counsel; Joan Solotar, head of private wealth management; Paige Ross, head of human resources; Weston Tucker, head of shareholder relations; and Bill Murphy, head of information technology.

I also want to mention Ken Whitney, who worked at Blackstone starting in the eighties and made enormous contributions in the early days of the business. Ken helped recruit John Schreiber, who started our real estate business, and Howard Gellis, who started our credit business. Ken helped raise all of our private equity and real estate funds in the nineties and served as our head of limited partner relations.

Special thanks goes to my late founding partner, Pete Peterson, his wife, Joan Cooney, and Pete's children. Without Pete's active involvement in the early stages of the firm's business, there would be no Blackstone.

I would like to thank John Magliano and Paul White who run my family office and help keep my life in order.

I'd also like to thank my former partner, Antony Leung, and current partner, Liping Zhang, who have served as successive chairmen of Blackstone Greater China. Without Antony, we would not have attracted the government of China as an investor in Blackstone when we went public in 2007. That transaction has helped change the future of our firm's development as well as the course of my life. It enabled the founding of the Schwarzman Scholars as well as my relationships with senior leadership in China. Without Liping I would be deprived of an enormous asset in terms of understanding what is going on with contemporary

China. Together, he and I spend considerable time visiting important members of the Chinese government, our Chinese investors, and important business leaders in China. Liping provides invaluable insight and has become a very good friend.

I would like to thank the many people at Schwarzman Scholars who have made it the success it is today. The list is too long to mention everyone individually, however, I would like to especially thank the former president of Tsinghua University, Chen Jining, who is now serving as mayor of Beijing. Without former president Chen's focus to get me to make a major gift to Tsinghua, it never would have happened. He was critical in helping the program gain the acceptance of the Chinese government as well Tsinghua University. He has become a lifetime friend and also done great service to China as its minister of environmental protection.

Chen Jining's successor, President Qiu Yong, has been my partner in the development of Schwarzman Scholars. This unprecedented program could not have been implemented without his support and enthusiasm, for which I will be eternally grateful. Party Secretary Madame Chen Xu at Tsinghua has also been an essential part of the senior leadership who created the opportunity for Schwarzman Scholars to occupy a unique position at the university. She and President Qiu have helped create broad support for the program within the Chinese government. I always enjoy meeting with her and President Qiu on my frequent visits to Beijing.

We are fortunate to have Dean Xue Lan, the former dean of the School of Public Policy and Management at Tsinghua University, as the current dean of Schwarzman Scholars. Dean Xue has helped oversee continual improvements in the program and has addressed very important issues that will enable Schwarzman Scholars to continue to grow in terms of size, prestige, and excellence. I would like to thank Founding Dean David Li and Executive Dean David Pan, both of whom have worked with the program since the announcement in 2013, through the graduation of the first class in 2017. David Pan continues with the program.

ACKNOWLEDGMENTS

I'd like to thank the Schwarzman Scholars Staff in New York led by Amy Stursberg with enormous time and emotional commitments by Rob Garris, our former head of admissions; Debby Goldberg, our head of development and alumni relations working with Julia Jorgensen; Joan Kaufman, our head of academic programs; Helen Santalone, our head of finance; and Lindsey Bavaro, our chief administrative officer. In Beijing, I would like to thank Melanie Koenderman, associate dean of student life; Julia Zupko, director of career development; and June Qian, associate dean for academic affairs. Bill Stein and Tim Wang from Blackstone's real estate business helped oversee the construction of the building along with Missy DelVecchio and Jonas Goldberg at Robert A.M. Stern Architects, who designed Schwarzman College. Missy and Jonas spent a year living in Beijing off and on to help oversee the final construction. Without all of these dedicated people both in Beijing and in New York, the Schwarzman Scholars program could never have come to fruition. I also want to thank Professors Bill Kirby and Warren McFarlan from Harvard who served on the initial board of the Schwarzman Scholars and helped recruit our Academic Advisory Board who planned the curriculum, recruitment of students and faculty, and help oversee the program from an academic perspective. Their help was invaluable. I'd also like to thank Sir John Hood, former chair of the Rhodes Trust, as well as Elizabeth Kiss, warden of the Rhodes Trust, both of whom have created a strong link between the Rhodes Scholarship Program and the Schwarzman Scholars. John also helped provide interviewers who select Rhodes Scholars to help us recruit the first several classes of Schwarzman Scholars.

I have many friends and colleagues in the Chinese government whom I would like to acknowledge and thank for the courtesy of meeting with me during my numerous trips to Beijing. These include President Xi Jinping, Premier Li Keqiang, Vice President Wang Qishan, Vice Premier Liu He, People's Bank of China former governor Zhou Xiaochuan, current People's Bank of China

ACKNOWLEDGMENTS

Governor Yi Gang, People's Bank of China Deputy Governor Pan Gongsheng, former deputy managing director of IMF Min Zhu, former vice minister of finance Zhu Guangyao, Member of the Standing Committee Wang Yang, former vice premier Liu Yandong, who had direct responsibility for the Schwarzman Scholars and is a special friend, and Vice Premier Sun Chunlan who now has responsibility for the program. And of course, Lou Jiwei, the former minister of finance who also served as the first president of China Investment Corporation as well as the late Jesse Wang. In Washington, I enjoy a close relationship with Ambassador Cui Tiankai who does a masterful job representing China in the United States.

I sit on the board of the Tsinghua University School of Economics and Management International Advisory Board where I've met many fascinating individuals including Jack Ma, founder of Alibaba; Pony Ma, founder of Tencent; Robin Li, founder of Baidu; Tim Cook, CEO of Apple; and Mark Zuckerberg, founder of Facebook. These five individuals are just the members from technology companies on a board that was initially assembled by former premier Zhu Rongji and Hank Paulson, then chairman of Goldman Sachs. It comprises some of the most distinguished and brightest people in the world. The group meets with the dean of the School, currently dean Bai Chong'en and with former dean Qian Yingyi.

Of course it's impossible to thank here all one hundred and twenty-five donors to the Schwarzman Scholars Program, so I'll only mention our six largest donors, each of whom has contributed $25 million: BP (our first donor), China Fortune Land Development, China Oceanwide Holdings Group, Dalio Foundation, HNA Group, Masayoshi Son Foundation, and the Starr Foundation. Ray Dalio was our second donor and he and I have become great friends. Masa Son not only contributed to the Schwarzman Scholars, but also used this template to develop major new philanthropic programs of his own for Japan. He too is a great friend who visits me in New York and we run into each other around the world. Finally, Hank Greenberg of the Starr Foundation and former chairman of AIG is one of the most distinguished Americans dealing with China. He also was the first outside investor in Blackstone in 1998.

I've been fortunate to get to know the last five Presidents of the United States while they were in office: President Donald Trump, President Barack Obama, President George W. Bush, President Bill Clinton, and President George H.W. Bush. I was lucky to meet President Bush 41 in 1967 at Parents' Day at Yale University at Davenport College where his son, George W. Bush was an undergraduate, one year ahead of me. George W. and his wife Laura were particularly welcoming when he was president. My wife and I saw them frequently at the White House and later at his Presidential Library and at his ranch. I met President Barack Obama during his 2008 Campaign and subsequently had numerous interactions with him in my position as chairman of The John F. Kennedy Center for the Performing Arts where I had been appointed by President George W. Bush. During President Obama's term in office, I also got to know Valerie Jarrett, who was always extremely responsive to my calls and helped solve a variety of important issues. President Donald Trump, whom I've known for over thirty years from New York, appointed me as chairman of the Strategic and Policy Forum. I've been privileged to have Secretary of the Treasury Steven Mnuchin as a very good friend for decades and have met Ambassador Robert Lighthizer through my friendship with the Secretary of Commerce Wilbur Ross, whom I've known for over thirty years as well. I'd also like to thank Jared Kushner and Ivanka Trump for their public service and the close working relationship we've established on a number of issues. Secretary of Transportation Elaine Chao and Senate Majority Leader Mitch McConnell have been friends for decades as well. I've also enjoyed my friendship with Senate Minority Leader Chuck Schumer who visited me at Lehman Brothers in my office when I was only thirty-one years old and he had recently been elected to Congress. I've known Nancy Pelosi, Speaker of the US House of Representatives for the last fifteen years. Coincidentally, I learned that Nancy's daughter worked at one of our Blackstone portfolio companies. I've always enjoyed Nancy's company and having completely open discussions with her. I've also enjoyed my relationship with former Speaker John Boehner and worked frequently with former Speaker Paul Ryan and former House Majority Leader and current House Minority Leader Kevin McCarthy. I also would like to thank former House Majority Leader Eric Cantor for all of his assistance during the fiscal cliff negotiations when I was helping President Obama. I'd like to thank Senator Roy Blunt who invited me to a wonderful lunch in his office to discuss American history when he was a member of the House of Representatives. Finally I'd like to acknowledge the friendship of Senator Ted Kennedy who supported me in all of my work at the Kennedy Center. Ted visited me in New York and asked me to take on this important responsibility, and he and his wife Vicky hosted me at their home in Washington. They made it easy for me to be successful at the Kennedy Center and in Washington.

I also want to thank former secretary of state John Kerry for his support of the Schwarzman Scholars and his friendship over the years. I met John in 1965 when I was trying out for the soccer team at Yale and John was on the team as a senior. Our paths have crossed continually since then and I have enormous admiration for his service to our country and his personal energy and drive.

I'd also like to thank former secretary of state Hillary Clinton for her support over a very long time including during my term at the Kennedy Center. Similarly, former secretary of state Condoleezza Rice has become a long term friend from the Bush Administration. She has a dazzling intellect with great charm and also made a major difference at Stanford University during her service as Provost. Her predecessor, former secretary of state Colin Powell, whom I met in 1984 eating pizza at Ron Lauder's house in

Washington after an inauguration event for President Reagan, is a truly extraordinary person. His service as chairman of the Joint Chiefs in the Pentagon and contribution to Gulf War I inspired a nation. Colin, who is also from NY originally, is a great dancer and loves vintage cars, while also being a truly inspirational leader.

I've been lucky to get to know former president Enrique Peña Nieto of Mexico and his finance minister, Luis Videgaray Caso, who also became foreign minister. Also, I've been fortunate to develop a very good relationship with Prime Minister Trudeau of Canada and his senior staff comprised of Katie Telford, Gerry Butts, and Foreign Minister Chrystia Freeland. I've known Chrystia for decades from her earlier career as a journalist at the *Financial Times* and *Reuters*.

I'd like to thank the outside board members of Blackstone for their guidance, insight, and believing in the firm's future: Jim Breyer, Sir John Hood, Shelly Lazarus, Jay Light, The Right Honorable Brian Mulroney, and Bill Parrett. I'd also like to thank the board of the Stephen A. Schwarzman Education Foundation: Jane Edwards, J. Michael Evans, Nitin Nohria, Stephen A. Orlins, Joshua Ramo, Jeffrey A. Rosen, Kevin Rudd, Teddy Schwarzman, Heung-Yeung "Harry" Shum, Amy Stursberg, and Ngaire Woods.

I want to acknowledge my lifetime friendship with the late Bobby Bryant from Abington High School, who was the State Champion in the 220 yard dash and the anchor leg on our State Championship 4 x 440 yard relay team, as well as his wife, Sundie. I also want to acknowledge my friendship with another track colleague from Abington, the late Billy Wilson and his wife, Ruby.

I want to acknowledge my remarkable teachers, including Norman Schmidt, my history teacher from Abington High School who made learning a joy. During my senior year, Mr. Schmidt had two students in his American History class in the top four in the metropolitan area of Philadelphia. Also, Alistair Wood, the research assistant for my freshman year English class, rescued me from potential abject failure during my first semester in college.

He took me up as a special project, taught me to write, and then taught me to think. Without Alistair Wood's initiative I doubt my life would have evolved as it has. Lastly, the late Professor C. Roland Christensen at Harvard Business School who taught corporate strategy and was one of the few university professors at Harvard. He made learning so exciting that time flew.

I'd like to thank the late Cardinal Edward Egan and his successor Cardinal Timothy Dolan for their friendship and remarkable commitment to making the Catholic schools astonishingly successful in educating both Catholic and non-Catholic students to the highest level of excellence one could imagine. Also Susan George from the Inner City Scholarship Fund supporting the Catholic schools does a terrific job of fundraising in order to help as many families as possible send their children to these magnificent primary and secondary schools.

I'd like to thank French President Emmanuel Macron for his friendship as well as President Jacques Chirac for awarding me the Légion d'honneur from France. His successor President Nicolas Sarkozy promoted me in the Legion. More important, he became a very close friend who invited my wife and me to the Élysée Palace numerous times, and his residence in the South of France for lunches and dinners. I'd also like to thank President François Hollande and Minister Ségolène Royal for promoting me a second time in the Legion of Honor. Ségolène hosted a wonderful luncheon at Chambord in the Loire Valley at the magnificent chateau built by King Francois I. I also owe a debt of gratitude to Jean-David Levitte and François Delattre who both served as ambassadors from France to the United States and have become close friends. Additionally I'd like to thank Gérard Errera, Blackstone's chairman in France, who advises me on all things French.

I'd also like to thank former Yale president Rick Levin for his friendship and collaboration over the many years during his term at Yale. He helped put Yale on a great path for excellence. I also want to thank President Peter Salovey for his responsiveness in

the conceptualization and execution of the Schwarzman Center which will change the student experience when it's opened in September 2020.

A special thanks goes to President Rafael Reif of MIT, with whom I have become particularly close and share a common view on the importance of developing US leadership in artificial intelligence and computing technologies. Without his curiosity and persistence, the Schwarzman College of Computing at MIT would not have come into existence. He's opened my eyes to a new community focused on science at the highest level, which has led to further friendships with global experts in this field. He's changed the focus of my life for which I will be eternally grateful. MIT Provost Marty Schmidt is remarkably capable with great judgment. He's helping to make Schwarzman College a reality as well as helping to integrate it into the MIT community.

At Oxford University, I would like to thank Vice-Chancellor Louise Richardson for spearheading the idea for the Schwarzman Centre for the Humanities. Without her taking the initiative to call on me in New York and introduce the idea, I would never have become involved. She has been an excellent shepherd of the project, managing to solve the myriad issues that were raised trying to get something of this complexity done. Also at Oxford, Sir John Hood, former vice-chancellor; Ngaire Woods, dean of the Blavatnik School of Government; and Sir John Bell, Regius Chair of Medicine, provided me with advice on the Schwarzman Centre project and deserve my most sincere thanks.

I'd like to thank Bob Greifeld and Tom Jackovic from the USA Track and Field Foundation. Bob's persistence in helping develop my interest as an adult in the track and field world again resulted in my involvement sponsoring many of our nation's top athletes. It's been a great benefit to the athletes but also adds continuity to my interests in life.

I'd like to cite Michael Kaiser, former president of the Kennedy Center, for his excellence in running the best performing arts center with all its complexity, and for his input on several of my projects which include major performing arts components.

I want to acknowledge Kathy Wylde, the exceptionally able executive director of the Partnership for New York City where I was co-chairman first with James Gorman, chairman of Morgan Stanley, and then with Mike Corbat, CEO of Citigroup.

None of us can have a full and joyful life without friends who bring amusement and richness into our lives and I am lucky to be surrounded by many friends around the world. There are a few individuals I would like to thank for bringing their particular brand of joie de vivre and friendship into my life. They include my oldest friend Jeff Rosen whom I met when I was sixteen at the National Association of Student Council Presidents, Prince Pierre d'Arenberg, Dorrit Moussaieff, Doug Braff, John Bernbach, François Lafon, Rolf Sachs, André and France Desmarais, and Susan and Tim Malloy.

I'd like to thank my two mentors who themselves have had incomparable careers: Felix Rohatyn, certainly the most famous financier in the seventies and eighties, and former secretary of state Henry Kissinger. Henry is one of the most remarkable individuals I've ever met. He's writing elegant and insightful books in his nineties. He's been on the world stage as an advisor since the 1960s. He travels incessantly, freely gives his advice to me and others on matters of great consequence, and is one of the few people anywhere who has maintained his intellectual acuity into his mid-nineties. It is a privilege to spend time with Henry and I would like to thank him for serving on the International Advisory Council of the Schwarzman Scholars as well.

As I get older I appreciate the great service rendered to me by the doctors who have helped me as an adult. Thanks go to Dr. Harvey Klein, to the late Dr. Mark Brower, and Dr. Richard Cohen who all have served in sequence as my internists. They've all given me instant attention and they are masters of their craft. I'd also like to thank Dr. David Blumenthal, my gifted cardiologist. Of course

ACKNOWLEDGMENTS

I want to acknowledge my therapist Dr. Byram Karasu who gives me excellent advice on virtually any subject. In addition, I'd like to thank my trainer, Rande Bryzelak, whom I see every day and who helps keep me fit, as well as Eveline Erni, my physical therapist, who helps with periodic physical repair work. Finally, I'd like to thank Dr. Steven Corwin, the CEO of New York–Presbyterian, where I serve on the board. Steve does a remarkable job of running one of the highest rated hospitals in the United States.

No one can do the volume of activities that I do without the remarkable support staff in my office. Samantha DiCrocco and Amy Rabwin have led my staff over the last decade which has increased over time to four people to handle the endless volume of dictations, meeting schedules, and international trips. My office operates on a twenty-four hour a day basis and Samantha and Amy are exceptionally effective, but also cheerful and enthusiastic. They rise to whatever challenges are presented. I'd also like to thank my former secretary Vanessa Gates-Elston who helped review drafts of the book and gave insightful comments on potential revisions.

I'd also like to thank my driver, Richard Toro, who has worked for me for over twenty years. We start early each day and end very late after business and social events at night. Richard is extremely capable, dedicated, and always delivers for me. I appreciate all of his efforts and sacrifices to get me wherever I'm supposed to be on time, whatever the difficulties.

Without my late father and mother giving me the values, motivation, and the correct mix of genes, I never would have been able to accomplish what I have done in life nor live the type of life that I'm living. It's only as an adult one can see the profound impact and wisdom of what my parents provided for me. There's no way to adequately thank them but I tried to do so when they were alive. I'd so like to talk to both of them again about my life and tell them I love them. The cycle of life makes that impossible, of course, although I still think of both of them often.

Also I'd like to thank my twin brothers, Mark and Warren, for a lifetime of laughter, loyalty, and mutual admiration. Apparently it's unusual for families to have seamless relationships. My brothers and I are the exception. I admire them and their wonderful families, and appreciate their support, energy, and loyalty. I was very lucky to have them both as siblings.

I want to send my love to both of my children, Zibby Owens and Teddy Schwarzman, the joys and pride of my life. There is no experience like having children and watching them grow into adults. Each of them has brought me the joy of grandchildren. In Zibby's case: Owen, Phoebe, Sadie, and Graham, and in Teddy's case Lucy, William, and Mary. I truly enjoy the time I spend with all of them. It's hard to believe my children can be in their forties now and that they each are parents themselves, along with their wonderful spouses, Kyle and Ellen, respectively. Also I send my love to my stepdaughter Megan whom I first met as a feisty five-year old. I admire her passion for animals and working with them as her vocation. Megan has helped us train our three Jack Russell terriers, Bailey, Piper, and Domino, who bring much contentment and joy into our lives.

Finally, I'd like to thank my wife, Christine, for our remarkable relationship of love for over twenty-five years. I met Christine during the five years when I was single in mid-life. She has changed my life and made it much more fun and happy than I could have imagined. I had no paradigm for the type of joy Christine brought into my life. Every day is an adventure. She is endlessly inventive, enthusiastic, endearing, exciting, intelligent, and beautiful. She never seems to age. She also put up with all the travails of my writing this book with all of its drafts and graciously answered my endless questions on language and content. She served as a hostess for various writers who visited us around the world and intruded on our private time together. She has managed to be the perfect stepmother to my children and grandchildren. I am a very, very fortunate man to have her as my wife.

INDEX

369

INDEX

INDEX

INDEX